Praise for
The Clinician's Guide to Intensive Couples Therapy

"Liz is truly a master at intensive couples therapy, and now she has written the master guide. *The Clinician's Guide to Intensive Couples Therapy* offers concrete tools and session structures that therapists can immediately implement in their practice."

—Amanda White, LCSW, owner of Therapy for Women and author of *Not Drinking Tonight*

"Couples therapy can be powerful, but often, real progress gets stalled when life gets in the way of weekly sessions. The traditional model simply isn't always enough to create the change couples are longing for. *The Clinician's Guide to Intensive Couples Therapy* offers a clear and accessible roadmap for doing meaningful, focused work with couples in a condensed format. This is an essential resource for clinicians ready to expand their practice and support couples in transformative ways—beyond the limitations of the weekly model."

—Dr. Tracy Dalgleish, psychologist, couples therapist, and author of *I Didn't Sign Up for This*

"This comprehensive manual for couples intensives is an absolute must-read for any therapist interested in offering this format. It beautifully explains the benefits of intensives, instructs therapists on best practices, includes extensive guidelines for structuring the intensive and specific assessment and interventions to consider, and provides illuminating case examples to illustrate each concept. Earnshaw has created the go-to guide to couples intensives."

—Isabelle Morley, PsyD, clinical psychologist and author of *They're Not Gaslighting You*

THE CLINICIAN'S GUIDE TO

Intensive Couples Therapy

AN **ACCELERATED** APPROACH

TO **REPAIR**, **STABILIZE**, AND

STRENGTHEN COUPLES IN CRISIS

ELIZABETH EARNSHAW, LMFT

THE CLINICIAN'S GUIDE TO INTENSIVE COUPLES THERAPY
Copyright © 2025 by Elizabeth Earnshaw

Published by
PESI Publishing, Inc.
3839 White Ave
Eau Claire, WI 54703

Cover and interior design by Emily Dyer
Editing by Chelsea Thompson

ISBN 9781683738435 (print)
ISBN 9781683738442 (ePUB)
ISBN 9781683738459 (ePDF)

All rights reserved.
Printed in the United States of America.

Table of Contents

Introduction vii

1. An Introduction to Intensive Couples Therapy 1
Defining Couples Therapy 1
The History of Couples Therapy in the United States 1
Current Couples Therapy Modalities 8
The Costs and Benefits of Intensive Couples Therapy 16

2. Preparing 25
Training 25
Policies and Paperwork 26
Administrative Policies 45
Marketing 58
Initial Contact and Scheduling 64
Preparing Yourself 71

3. The Intensive, Day 1 75
Key Processes of Day 1 77
Joining 79
Assessment 101
The First 90 Minutes 104
Observation 131
Closing the Joint Session 132
Individual Sessions 135
Providing Feedback and Goal Setting 148

4. The Intensive, Day 2 153
Enactments 154
Exercises 162
Interventions 194
Concluding the Intensive 234
Special Considerations for the Final Hour 250

Conclusion 253
References 255
Acknowledgments 261
About the Author 262

Introduction

Early in my career, I met for a first session with Harry and Leona, a couple who had recently experienced a relational norm violation of sexual infidelity on Harry's part. Leona felt as if her life had crumbled in front of her eyes—everything that she had believed to be true was upended. Harry, while remorseful, had difficulty expressing emotions, showing regret, and listening. In the days following Leona's discovery of the infidelity, his reactivity and poor coping skills were only making their situation worse. They needed *a lot* of help.

When the couple arrived on their first day of couples therapy, Leona announced that she was ready for a divorce. Harry, shocked, sat still and did not respond. This prompted Leona to add, "You see? He doesn't care!"

While I didn't know Harry yet, I knew there was a possibility that he did care but was too frozen to respond. I took a deep breath, then repeated back Leona's position, empathized, and asked her if she'd like to continue with the first session or if she had already made her decision and would like to end the session instead.

"Well," she said, "I don't want to divorce him, but I can't stay in this if therapy doesn't work. It's too painful. I can't stay with someone who doesn't care the way he doesn't care."

I took this as my cue to enter back into what I usually do during the first session: provide an overview of the assessment process, then begin to ask my initial assessment questions. As I started to explain the process—"We will meet for this session, then I will meet with you both individually, and later we will come back together to discuss my feedback and the plan. We will do one session a week to complete this"—I could see Leona's face drop and slowly turn red.

"Wow." She shook her head. "That's going to take at least *four weeks* just to get started! I cannot wait that long for things to get better."

I realized she was right. Four weeks was far too long to ask this couple to wait before we could start doing the work that would help them to at least stabilize their situation. I also knew I couldn't just dive in without doing a full assessment—solutions without understanding don't stick. Looking at their downcast faces, I made an impulsive offer: "How about we meet all day on Saturday and try to really get down to it?"

Relieved, they both agreed.

I went home and searched furiously for any information on longer couples therapy sessions. At that time, there wasn't much on the topic. With little information to go on, I was forced to operate on instinct and discernment, stitching together what I would typically cover in the first four to six sessions of couples therapy into a single weekend session. To my delight, it went well, not only for them but for me. I was able to lead the couple through a genuinely transformative therapy experience, unbothered by the merciless ticking of the clock. It was a long day, but I left feeling inspired, even energized. After countless couples sessions curtailed by lack of time, this extended session felt like a breath of fresh air.

In hindsight, it seems self-evident that an individual therapy session does not provide an appropriate framework for a couples session. First, it stands to reason that two people working through issues requires more time for discussion than does one. Fifty minutes is hardly enough time for an adequate discussion even when it goes smoothly; given that dysregulation is common in couples counseling, and that reducing physiological flooding usually takes at least 20 minutes, it's easy for half the session to be occupied with restoring the clients' capacity for reflection and respectful interaction.

Many therapists have the experience of a couple coming into the therapy room with a pattern of relational dysfunction that simultaneously requires complex analysis and urgent improvement. No sooner do they start to discuss the issue that brought them in than their conflict swells, even as time ticks on closer and closer to the 50-minute mark. Instead of focusing on the help that the couple needs, the therapist must think about how to quickly transition them from their difficult conversation to the end of session. All too often, we must knowingly send them out into the world with wounds reopened and their dysfunction activated.

I have experienced this from both sides of the table, so to speak. My husband and I attended couples therapy shortly after the birth of our baby. We really needed help—our conflict had hit a fever pitch, and things felt unmanageable. During the initial session, we both had so much to say with very few tools for how to say it. By the time the 50 minutes were up, I hadn't even had a chance to talk, and my husband was left dysregulated. After the therapist ended the session, we walked out and didn't talk to each other the rest of the evening.

The first session has major implications for the success or failure of the entire therapy experience, as it influences how people end up feeling about couples therapy, whether they believe it can help them, and whether they will reach out for help in the future. This was certainly true for my husband and me. We both felt so defeated after that initial session that we never made a second appointment; moreover, the experience left a lasting negative impact on how my husband feels about couples therapy in general.

In addition, a 50-minute session significantly extends the assessment period for couples into multiple weeks. The established protocol for couples therapy calls for a couple to meet with the therapist for an initial interview, followed by two individual sessions, followed by a 50- to 90-minute feedback session during which the couple hears the therapist's assessment and treatment plan; all of this is preamble to beginning any meaningful therapeutic work. Couples in distress, like Harry and Leona, usually can't wait multiple weeks to receive tools for improving their relationship, let alone any sense of relief or hope. Add in the challenge of scheduling sessions around busy families, demanding careers, and the general unpredictability of life, and the likelihood of therapy drop-out only increases.

Without adequate time to experience effective conflict navigation, use tools to self-regulate, and either reach satisfactory resolution or, at very least, regulate and repair in a way that preserves or restores their emotional connection, the very thing intended to be a source of relief and support becomes just another burden adding to a couple's relational distress. While 50 minutes might be enough to understand the patterns, perceptions, and feelings of an individual client, when it comes to treating two people, you simply need more time.

As it happened, the week after my spontaneous all-day therapy session, I attended a training in New York City for Gottman Method Couples Therapy. In my mostly fruitless search for information on long-form couples sessions, one resource I had found came from the Gottman Institute website, referring to something they called Marathon Couples Therapy. I asked our trainer, Don Cole, to share more about it. During a break, he obliged by providing an overview on their model for all-day sessions with couples. He emphasized that what made this model effective was the time it allowed to slow down, go deeper, and truly stay present with what was unfolding.

I understood how he could believe that. I had just seen a monumental change take place for Harry and Leona the previous Saturday as they worked through their pain, learned new skills (and practiced them together in front of a therapist), and not only stabilized but also increased hope for their situation. I truly believe that if I had asked that couple to follow the traditional format, they would have dropped out of therapy and divorced. However, over 11 years later, they are still married and happily so.

Since that first improvised long-form session, I have refined my approach into a consistent format that I use for intensive couples sessions and, in recent years, to train other couples therapists. In this book, you will find this format shown in detail, learn why it works, and gain the skills and best-practice guidelines to use it yourself.

Although intensive couples sessions are becoming increasingly popular across all models of couples therapy, a consistent model has yet to be established for incorporating this extended session into existing modalities. This book offers a detailed roadmap for incorporating intensive sessions into any couples therapy practice while providing a consistent definition for what intensive couples therapy is, showing how significant changes to the established session format result in fulfilling therapeutic goals within the unique context of couples work.

I believe that as you start integrating this form of couples therapy into your practice, you will see your couples make monumental strides in overcoming their relational issues and moving forward.

CHAPTER 1

An Introduction to Intensive Couples Therapy

Defining Couples Therapy

Couples therapy is a modality of therapy that helps couples reduce relationship distress and enhance relationship quality, with the unique advantage of having both partners present and participating in the process. This conjoint feature allows the therapist to hear about an individual's perspective of the problem while also hearing their partner's perspective on the same problem. In other words, a couples therapist is given the gift of a lot more information than they would receive if they were only meeting with one person.

While couples therapists are trained to understand many of the same things that an individual therapist must understand—trauma, mental health conditions, protocols for suicidality, and so forth—couples therapists also must understand how to look at and treat a relationship in light of each individual's history, challenges, hopes, dreams, and feelings. In a sense, couples therapy involves two forms of therapy happening at once: the therapy between each individual and the therapist, but also therapy being done between the two partners with the therapist as a support.

The History of Couples Therapy in the United States

According to Alan S. Gurman and Peter Fraenkel (2002), the development of couples therapy in the United States moved through four distinct phases, starting with an atheoretical phase and moving toward the theory-heavy field of today. Through these phases, couples therapy has moved from psychoeducational work to psychoanalytic work to systems work to, finally, becoming a field of its own.

Pre-professional Origins

Throughout history and across cultures, partnerships have always been seen as important for varying reasons—alliances between nations, reproduction, economic gains, stability, spiritual fulfillment, and, as the biggest focus now, love. It follows that communities have long been invested in figuring out how individuals can best build their partnerships within their specific cultural frameworks and values. Prior to the development of professional organizations, community elders were often the primary resource for helping people navigate their committed partnerships, whether it be through spiritual ceremonies, role-driven guidance, or practical decision-making.

Phase 1: The Marriage Counselor as Advice Giver

From the 1920s to the 1960s, an atheoretical phase of marriage therapy developed in which people began to consider the importance of creating a profession that could help married couples improve their relationships and manage sexual issues.

Ernest Groves, a family sociologist and minister, developed the first college course that helped people prepare for marriage, which he taught at Boston University in 1922 and later at the University of North Carolina in 1927 (National Council on Family Relationships, 2024). Owing to his interest in marriage, Groves was sought out by students for his advice and support for premarital and marital issues. He was frank with students that he was not a psychotherapist but was willing to provide them guidance when it came to evaluating their choices, processing problems, and acting as a listening ear in a private environment. In 1933, Groves published the first university-level text on the subject, titled *Marriage*. This increased interest at the university level to better understand marriage and help people in their relationships.

At the same time, Dr. Robert Dickerson, a New York-based gynecologist, noticed that his female patients were struggling with intimacy in their relationships and began offering a sort of sex therapy and marriage therapy to his patients. He began to speak on topics of sexual and marriage issues to groups of urologists, psychiatrists, and OB-GYNs. (This group included Dr. Emily Mudd, who went on to found the Council for Relationships, the training institute I attended in Philadelphia.) The doctors who met under Dickerson's leadership were primarily focused on how they could help their patients navigate the sexual issues that were hurting their relationships.

Eventually, the Dickerson group and the Groves group began to integrate. In 1942, Ernest Groves established this combined organization as the American Association of Marriage Counselors (AAMC), which aimed to provide networking opportunities to professionals interested in developing a theory and practice of marriage counseling (Rubin & Settles, 2012).

While the name "marriage counseling" was in use by that time, the practice did not look the way marriage or couples counseling looks now. Today, we would call it psychoeducational work. It was most often conducted with an individual, rather than with both people in the room, and it focused on the couple's presenting problem. In addition, this early form of counseling was more about teaching people "best practices" rather than understanding their unique dynamic. There was a sense that all marriage problems were the same and therefore could be solved by following specific directives or values, as determined by a medical doctor, social worker, or clergyperson.

Over time, however, it became clear that distressed relationships needed more than prescriptive advice and that actual therapy might be needed to address the issues. This led to psychoanalysts beginning to implement their work in regard to relationships.

Phase 2: The Analyst Attempts to Cure the Individual's Relationship Ills

Six years after the creation of the AAMC, Bela Mittelmann, a psychoanalyst with the New York Psychoanalytic Institute, published the first account of **concurrent marital therapy**. This paper reported that after providing analytic therapy to 12 married couples, 11 of the couples showed signs of improvement (Mittelmann, 1948).

> **COUPLES THERAPY DICTIONARY**
>
> **Concurrent Therapy**
>
> Concurrent therapy involves the simultaneous treatment of partners by the same therapist. Each person meets with the therapist individually to explore relational issues and attempt to resolve them.

The underlying belief of the concurrent marital therapy approach was that treating someone individually for a stressor related to their marriage meant leaving out important information about the other partner and the relationship as a whole. Meeting with both people provides the analyst with a fuller picture of what is going on, empowering them to help everyone manage their transference in the relationship.

Mittelmann also stressed the importance of utilizing **object relations** when working with couples, rather than assuming all issues are related to individuals' intrapsychic issues. This was a departure from the field of psychoanalysis and introduced the concept that couples do not only have issues due to their individual histories, traumas, stressors, and mental health concerns; rather, it is the dynamic of these individual features that can cause challenges within the relationship.

> **COUPLES THERAPY DICTIONARY**
>
> **Object Relations**
>
> *Object relations* refers to how a child related to the people in their lives and internalized those relationships, and how that internalization plays a role in the dynamics of their adult relationships today.

Phase 3: The Emphasis of a Systems Perspective

In the 1950s, pioneering psychologist Nathan Ackerman began encouraging psychiatrists to consider the role of family systems in their work with couples and families, rather than only including intrapsychic factors. His perspective was that it wasn't only the individual with the issues; sometimes it was the interactional patterns of the family as a whole that influenced individual well-being.

During the early development of family therapy, researchers became interested in how communication patterns influenced the functioning of families and individuals. The theory of the **double bind** was formulated by Gregory Bateson, Don Jackson, Jay Haley, and John Weakland; Bateson also introduced the idea of **family homeostasis**.

> **COUPLES THERAPY DICTIONARY**
>
> ### Double Bind
> A double bind occurs when two seemingly contradictory messages exist and lead to confusion. For example, a loved one might tell you that they want to hear about your feelings, but when you cry, they tell you, "Stop crying!" Another example might be when someone asks you to take a risk but then tells you that you should be careful.
>
> ### Family Homeostasis
> Family homeostasis is the capacity and mechanisms by which equilibrium is restored in a family after change (Kim & Rose, 2014). For example, some families are able to return to a sense of stability after change through functional mechanisms like communication and support, whereas other families might only return to "stability" by protesting against change.

As the field evolved, Don Jackson continued to lead the charge on developing a systems perspective by founding the Mental Research Institute (MRI). Today, he is best known for his commitment to drive the field away from a focus on individual pathology and toward a relationally oriented concept of problems (Ray, 2000). Around the same time, Carl Whittaker began to see a use case for including spouses and family members within the individual's therapy sessions. Rather than utilizing concurrent sessions, Whittaker began using "dual therapy"—later known as **conjoint therapy**—and published his account through Emory University in 1958 (Gladding, 2014).

> **COUPLES THERAPY DICTIONARY**
>
> ### Conjoint Couples Therapy
> Conjoint couples therapy occurs when both partners are in the room at the same time for therapy.

As the ideas of double bind, homeostasis, and conjoint therapy were being explored to help relationship systems, Ivan Boszormenyi-Nagy developed contextual therapy, in which the concepts of fairness, loyalty, and reciprocity were utilized to improve trust and commitment in a relationship.

Many of these same systems thinkers remained prominent forces in developing the field into the 1960s. Jay Haley became the editor of *Family Process*, the first journal in the field of family therapy. Haley also helped in the development of the Child Guidance Clinic in Philadelphia alongside Salvador Minuchin, who developed **structural family therapy**. Minuchin took special effort to consider how cultural factors can play a role in relationships and how well a therapist can truly understand their client. Structural family therapy introduced the practice of utilizing **enactments**, an intervention that is frequently used during intensive couples therapy.

> **COUPLES THERAPY DICTIONARY**
>
> ### Structural Family Therapy
> Structural family therapy assesses subsystems within a relationship. In this theory, the therapist believes the structure of the family is developed through the way the family manages boundaries, hierarchies, and coalitions. Direct engagement between family members, also known as an *enactment*, is relied on as the primary method of change.
>
> ### Enactment
> Enactments are a therapeutic intervention in which the therapist invites the couple to interact directly with each other, with the goal of bringing the relationship in its "real-life totality" (Butler et al., 2011, p. 205) into the room. During an enactment, the therapist temporarily steps back from directly interacting with the couple to observe their dynamic in real time, offering coaching and guidance as they engage with each other.

In the early 1960s, Murray Bowen began to introduce ideas related to the **family of origin** and its influence on relationships. Bowen recognized that many families experienced emotional reactivity when they had to solve problems together. This emotional reactivity destabilized the family and made it difficult for each person to maintain their identity and consciously choose their actions. This, he found, was caused by what he called an "undifferentiated ego mass" (Lassiter, 2017).

> **COUPLES THERAPY DICTIONARY**
>
> ### Family of Origin
> A person's family of origin is the family in which they were raised. This does not need to be biological family.

Bowen began implementing interventions that helped families reduce chaos during moments of family crisis by helping them build appropriate boundaries, avoid **triangulation**, and resist scapegoating. All of these tasks are to help individuals remain a **differentiated self**. Much of the work we still do in couples therapy is related to helping couples manage reactivity, maintain healthy boundaries, and remain differentiated. During intensive sessions, you will find that these are prevalent themes.

> **COUPLES THERAPY DICTIONARY**
>
> ### Triangulation
> Triangulation is a systems-level process in which a dyadic relationship draws in a third person to distribute stress, anxiety, or power throughout the triad. This happens when people have a low level of differentiation or high levels of emotional stress. For example, a couple might triangulate during moments of distress by sharing too much information with their in-laws in order to distribute stress. Couples might also triangulate their children by telling their children about conflict between the adult partners rather than dealing with it directly within the adult hierarchy (Bowen, 1978; Kerr & Bowen, 1988; Minuchin, 1974).
>
> ### Differentiation of Self
> A person with a well-differentiated self is able to remain connected to others while also remaining connected to the self during moments of conflict. These individuals are less likely to become enmeshed or cut off from the important people in their lives because they can distinguish their thoughts from their feelings and utilize self-regulation to communicate and act in ways that align with their own needs and the needs of the group (Bowen Center, n.d.).

Psychotherapist Virginia Satir, who was working at MRI, began to move beyond focusing on "problems" with the families she worked with and toward topics like self-esteem, compassion, and expression of emotions (Gladding, 2014). She was known for her warm and nurturing spirit, as well as her optimism about people's potential for change. Couples therapists today still lean into Satir's example of showing empathy toward clients and offering hope as an integral part of creating change. In addition, Satir's 1964 book *Conjoint Family Therapy*, offering greater detail on the process that had evolved out of dual therapy, influenced more therapists to begin doing conjoint work with the families and couples they were seeing in their offices.

All these novel ideas and approaches led to a concept called systems theory, which posits that individuals are impacted by each other and, therefore, the cause of relational issues is not linear but circular. As systems theory took hold, family therapists became more confident in the distinct perspective they brought to the world of psychotherapy.

Phase 4: A Field of Its Own

As we have seen, the focus of couples therapy has shifted over time: from psychoeducation in the first phase, to experimentation related to psychoanalysis in the second, and to the development of systems family therapy approaches in the third. The current phase has focused on making conjoint relational therapy a field of its own.

In 1963, California introduced the first state licensure for family therapists. In the 1970s, the continued refinement of theories in the field rose, as did membership in the American Association of Marriage and Family Therapy (AAMFT), which began publishing its own professional periodical, *The Journal of Marital and Family Therapy*. At the same time, a group of Italian psychoanalysts gained esteem as the Milan Group, emphasizing the skills of **circular questioning** and **triadic questioning** within family and couples therapy sessions.

> COUPLES THERAPY DICTIONARY
>
> ## Circular Questioning
> Circular questioning occurs when a therapist moves back and forth between individuals in the room to highlight differences among family members. For example, the therapist might ask partner A, "What do you think about that?" and after hearing their response ask partner B, "What's your reaction to that?"
>
> ## Triadic Questioning
> Triadic questioning occurs when a therapist asks a third person to comment on how they believe two other people (typically, family members or members of a couple) relate. For example, a therapist might ask a child, "What do you think about how your mom and dad solve issues?"

In 1978, Rachel Hare-Mustin wrote an article entitled "A Feminist Approach to Family Therapy," which brought into focus the ways that family therapy techniques were promoting a status quo that can be harmful to women by not recognizing power differentials in relationships. Alongside Hare-Mustin, other women began to dominate the field of family therapy. A field mostly known for prominent male researchers and therapists now included the likes of Monica McGoldrick, Cloé Madanes, Froma Walsh, and Betty Carter, among others. The feminist family therapist movement has advocated for equality in relationships and a focus on recognizing bias. In couples therapy today, it is important to help couples have discourse regarding the ways that cultural and social factors influence their relationship.

In the 1990s, family therapy saw the influence of social constructionism, the philosophy that our experiences are a function of how we think about things rather than objective realities. Social constructionism helps couples therapists navigate diverging viewpoints on interactions between partners by helping them to understand that each person's internal role has played a part in the way they experience the relationship.

In the 2000s, focus continued to be placed on creating a distinct field of family therapy by investing in the creation of organizations, accreditation, training programs, licensure, and more.

From the early days of marital support being offered by community members through advice, guidance, and even making decisions *for* the couple, to utilizing psychoanalysis simultaneously to improve a relationship, to looking at how the internal experience of each person relates to the system of the relationship, specific forms of couples therapy emerged. Therapists and psychologists such as Sue Johnson, John and Julie Gottman, Harville Hendrix and Helen LaKelly Hunt, Stan Tatkin, and Terry Real began developing specific formulas or modalities for conducting couples therapy. These modalities utilized theories and research from earlier pioneers in the field—including the importance of boundaries, empathy, structure, and cultural awareness—while providing direction and containment for navigating the issues that a couple brings into therapy.

Current Couples Therapy Modalities

Many major models of couples therapy have been adapted for longer formats. This intensive approach provides a focused and condensed format of couples counseling over a period of two to three consecutive days, usually a weekend. In general, each day consists of the couple meeting with the therapist for five to six hours, with breaks built in for lunch, reflection, exploration, and exercises.

Below, you'll find a brief overview of the five most popular couples therapy modalities in use today. While these are not the only modalities in use, they tend to be the most sought-after by the general public. Unsurprisingly, they also lend themselves to the intensive format; in fact, many of them were developed with longer sessions in mind.

Emotionally Focused Couples Therapy

Emotionally focused therapy (EFT), developed by Sue Johnson and Les Greenberg, is an attachment-based couples therapy that focuses on de-escalating negative interaction cycles and strengthening emotional bonds (Johnson, 2004). It is defined by its founders as "the practice of therapy informed by an understanding of the role of emotion in psychotherapeutic change" (Greenberg, 2017, p. 3). Popular interventions utilized in EFT include cycle tracking, evocative responding, heightening, empathic conjecture, restructuring interactions, and reflecting underlying emotions.

> **COUPLES THERAPIST SKILL**
>
> ### Cycle Tracking
>
> Cycle tracking is the act of helping a couple track their dysfunctional interaction cycle. The therapist helps the couple identify a pattern of individual positions, thoughts, emotions, and attachment needs when they face conflict or stress. In order to cycle track, the therapist asks each partner questions like:
>
> - What do you do when things become difficult between you and your partner?
> - When this happens, how do you protect yourself?
> - What are you thinking about your partner while this is happening? What are you thinking about the relationship? About yourself?
> - What are you feeling?
> - Are there any other feelings? If we look deep inside, are there any other feelings that might feel hard to say?
> - How do you act during these difficult moments? What do you show others on the outside?
> - What do you think you're really longing for in these moments?
>
> The therapist could also ask the couple to reflect individually on the following prompts:
>
> - When we are not getting along, I feel _____.
> - When I feel that way, this is what I do: _____.

- I do this because I hope _____.
- When I do this, I notice that you _____.
- When you do this, I feel _____.

After they each write their own answers, the therapist can ask them to share what they wrote and help them to diagram their negative cycle in the form of an "infinity loop" on a whiteboard or piece of paper. This gives the couple a visual reminder of their negative cycle so that they can work toward changing it in the future by being more sensitive to each other's feelings and needs.

Here is an example:

```
Partner 1 feels hurt          Partner 2 feels abandoned
and withdraws, hoping         and frustrated and
to avoid conflict and to      pursues the issue, hoping
be comforted.                 to be understood.
```

COUPLES THERAPIST SKILL

Evocative Responding

When a clinician is utilizing evocative responding, they tentatively capture the experience of each partner by asking questions about their present experience. This includes asking questions about what is not being said but is being shown.

For example, they might ask surface questions like "What is happening for you right now as you tell me this story?" They might also ask questions related to observations: "I just noticed your body language seemed to change. Can you tell me what's happening for you right now?"

This evokes awareness of each individual's experience in the room while helping them to bring it forward to be a part of exploration, connection, and change.

COUPLES THERAPIST SKILL

Heightening

Heightening involves highlighting specific interactions and responses to make the client's experience more evident (Johnson, 2004). For example, the therapist might notice that the client is feeling a lot of pain as they consider whether they should divorce their partner. Rather than saying, "It sounds like a complicated problem to solve," the therapist might say something like, "It's been so hard to even think about this topic because it's not anything you ever wanted. Just thinking about it makes you want to run away and hide and pretend like nothing is happening. That's why it's taken so long to talk about. It's so painful that you just want to hide from it." This skill helps the couple become more vulnerable and receptive to each other.

> **COUPLES THERAPIST SKILL**
>
> ## Empathic Conjecture
>
> Through the use of empathic conjecture, the therapist helps the client understand themselves more by helping them clarify the emotional experiences (often related to attachment fears) underneath their interactions. The following are examples of empathic conjecture:
>
> - "As I hear you talk, I am getting the sense that you aren't only angry about this but perhaps you are also very confused and sad—am I right?"
> - "I hear you say that you just need help around the house. And what I also think I am understanding is that it's not just about the help, it's about feeling like you have someone who is there for you no matter what. Am I getting that?"

> **COUPLES THERAPIST SKILL**
>
> ## Restructuring Interactions
>
> *Restructuring interactions* refers to the therapist supporting the couple in changing their interactional pattern. They can utilize previous cycle tracking to ask the couple to make different "moves" in the "dance" to change how they relate. The goal is to help each client understand what is happening inside of them so they can change their interpersonal action.
>
> For example, the therapist might say, "What just happened there, Claudia? I noticed that you started to open up and really hear what Jerry was saying, but when he began sharing his feelings, you started to turn away from him. I wonder what it would be like if you turned back toward him again—can we try that?"

> **COUPLES THERAPIST SKILL**
>
> ## Reflecting Underlying Emotions
>
> The therapist utilizes this skill to highlight emotions that might not be obvious to the individual or their partner. For example, when the therapist notices that the client is saying something sad but not sharing that they feel sad, the therapist might say, "Yes, of course. What you just described is so hard. You're feeling sad about it." This skill increases vulnerability and honest discourse.

Imago Couples Therapy

Imago therapy is a type of couples therapy that helps people "achieve a conscious relationship and [. . .] facilitates the healing of childhood injuries between spouses" (Dehnavi et al., 2023). Imago therapists believe that people choose their partners based on unconscious images of people from their past from whom they seek healing. This modality uses techniques such as the Imago dialogue (Hendrix & Hunt,

2021), a conversation process that includes mirroring, validation, and empathy, to help people have difficult yet kind conversations with each other. Imago therapy also helps clients consider the positive and negative characteristics of their caregivers to better understand how their experiences with their caregivers have impacted their romantic relationships.

For example, an Imago therapist might help a client identify how they often felt emotionally neglected as a child. When they feel emotionally dismissed as an adult, not only is it painful due to that instance, but it also activates a deep yearning to receive healing from their partner for an injury from their childhood. The hope is that the client could express how painful it is to be emotionally neglected and that their partner could become attuned to addressing this need for their partner.

COUPLES THERAPIST RESOURCE

Imago Dialogue

In the Imago dialogue, there is a "sender" (speaker) and a "receiver" (listener). Before talking, they become clear on which topic they are addressing. After the sender expresses themselves, the pair goes through the following three-step process before switching roles.

Step 1: *Mirror*

After the receiver has heard everything their partner has said and there is a pause, the receiver repeats back what their partner said. It is important to repeat it back as the sender intended rather than modifying or critiquing it. The receiver might say:

- "What I heard you say is . . ."
- "I think what I got from what you just shared is . . ."

Then the receiver asks for confirmation that they understood everything.

- "Did I get that right?"
- "Is there more?"
- "Tell me more."

Step 2: *Validate*

The receiver shares with the sender why what they said makes sense.

- "It makes sense to me that you feel this way because . . ."
- "I completely understand why you thought that. If I saw it the way you saw it, I would feel that way too."
- "I see where you are coming from."

Step 3: *Empathize*

The receiver guesses what the sender was feeling or, if the sender has already stated how they felt, reflects this back. After empathizing, they check with the sender to see if they were accurate.

- "As I was listening to you share your story, I was imagining you were feeling very sad when that happened. Is that how you felt? Is there anything else you were feeling?"

- "It sounded to me like maybe you were feeling embarrassed. Is that right?"
- "I'm not completely sure, but I think you might have been really confused. Let me know if I'm wrong about that."

Switch

Once the sender has said everything they need to say and the receiver has completed these three steps, the receiver gets an opportunity to talk about what came up for them while they listened. During this time, they will switch roles and go through the three steps again.

Gottman Method Couples Therapy

Gottman Method Couples Therapy is a comprehensive modality created by Drs. John and Julie Gottman following years of research on relationships in their well-known Love Lab. The approach uses principles from various therapeutic beliefs, including systemic theory, existential perspective, and narrative therapy, to provide structure to couples therapy sessions (Mardani et al., 2023). Core to its identity is that it is research-based and skills-based.

Along with a wide range of exercises for therapists and couples to utilize during sessions, the Gottman Method relies on research that identified effective traits in marriage. Known as "the Sound Relationship House," these traits create a strong foundation and a sturdy framework for interactions that helps relationships thrive.

The Gottmans and their lab have also explored the habits that break down relationships. Their most prominent framework is known as "the Four Horsemen of the Apocalypse," a play on biblical theology referring to destructive communication habits that signal the "end times" of a relationship. These habits are criticism, defensiveness, stonewalling, and contempt.

Gottman Method therapists utilize conversational enactments with their couples that are designed to contain the couple while helping them build understanding and learn new skills. The most-used enactments are the Dreams Within Conflict Conversation, the Stress Reducing Conversation, the Regrettable Incident Conversation, and Getting to Compromise (also known as Compromise Ovals).

COUPLES THERAPIST RESOURCE

The Sound Relationship House

- **Trust:** Couples who have trust believe that their partner acts in ways that are considerate to their own well-being. In short, they believe their partner has their back. When one partner has acted in ways that did not consider the well-being of their partner, this will shake trust and therefore security.

- **Commitment:** Couples who are committed have a belief that their relationship is a lifelong journey. This belief is stabilizing in that when things get tough, the couple knows that they have time and motivation to improve the relationship. When one or both partners believes their partner has one foot out the door, it becomes more difficult to act with openness and vulnerability to solving dilemmas. When a partner lacks commitment to the relationship, their attempts to improve the relationship will be halfhearted.

- **Build Love Maps:** The first level of the relationship house is building love maps. This term means, simply, that the partners know each other. A love map is a map the client has of their partner's internal world—what they like, who they aspire to be, how they are doing, and so on. When the couple spends time being curious with each other and sharing information, they know each other's love map. When they stop spending time with each other or are no longer curious, they begin to lose the map of their partner.

- **Shared Fondness and Admiration:** Knowing your partner appreciates and likes you is core to a healthy relationship. If both people are expressing appreciation and sharing their positive feelings with each other, it's easier to assume the best when things are hard. When they are not expressing their gratitude, recognizing each other's efforts, or sharing compliments, it becomes harder for each partner to feel valued in the relationship.

- **Turn Toward Instead of Away:** Healthy relationships have a good number of positive bids for connection—attempts to connect with one's partner. Some bids might be small, like commenting to a partner how beautiful the weather is, while others might be more obvious or take more effort, like asking for a hug or requesting an important conversation. When someone in the relationship makes a bid for connection, the other person can turn toward, turn away from, or turn against the bid. The more often a partner turns away from or against their partner, the less often their partner will make bids for connection, which results in the couple becoming distanced from each other.

- **The Positive Perspective:** When couples are building love maps, sharing appreciation, and making and turning toward bids, they will have *the positive perspective*. This means that overall, they see their relationship in a good light, even when there is difficulty. For example, if they have an argument, a couple in the positive perspective will think, *That was such a bad argument, but it's not like us. I believe we can overcome it.*

    When there aren't love maps, appreciation, or bids for connection, a couple will develop what's known as *negative sentiment override*. This means that the couple begins seeing their relationship in a negative light that overrides even attempts at positive engagement. For example, the couple might have a positive week together, but when the therapist asks about the week they will say, "It was really nice, but I doubt it will last. I think it was just because the week was easier in general. Nothing will be different long term."

- **Managing Conflict:** Gottman Method couples therapists teach clients how to manage conflict by helping them learn to dialogue, self-soothe, and compromise. When couples struggle to manage conflict, it is usually because they can't do at least one of these three things.

- **Making Life Dreams Come True:** Fulfilled couples believe their relationship is helping them to meet their goals and create their dreams. These couples share their hopes and aspirations with each other and also feel as if they can live in a way that aligns with their own philosophies and values. The underlying desire is to have a relationship in which both people benefit.

- **Creating Shared Meaning:** Couples who create shared meaning have a sense of being aligned in their goals and values. They are able to compromise and come together to create a shared vision for their life together. They also have rituals or traditions that help them create a "culture" of their relationship. When a couple lacks a shared vision and meaningful traditions, their relationship often struggles because they have no unifying sense of direction.

Psychobiological Approach to Couples Therapy

The Psychobiological Approach to Couples Therapy (PACT) was designed by Dr. Stan Tatkin (2020a) after researching secure attachment within couples. At the heart of PACT are principles of neuroscience, arousal regulation, and attachment theory to help couples manage conflict in real time. Interventions like cross-tracking rely on micro-attunement to subtle facial and somatic cues. Within this model, therapists help couples learn to develop secure attachment bonds with each other by paying attention to their psychobiological needs, historical experiences, and current social needs. They are taught to create a "couple bubble" (Tatkin, 2024) that increases security within the relationship.

COUPLES THERAPIST RESOURCE

The Couple Bubble

A couple bubble helps the couple protect their relationship. It includes boundaries around the relationship that create a sense of security for each person within the relationship.

The guidelines for developing a secure couple bubble are:

1. **Creating safety and security:** People in healthy relationships focus on what will help their partner feel safe and secure in the relationship. They understand that certain actions (e.g., making decisions unilaterally, bad-mouthing their partner to their mother, neglecting their partner when they are at social gatherings) will create a sense of insecurity for their partner, so they make sure to take actions that will promote their partner's safety and security instead (involve them in the decision-making process, speak about them respectfully, check in on them throughout the gathering).

2. **Putting an equal amount of work into the relationship:** In a healthy relationship, both people are putting equal amounts of work into making the relationship thrive. Both people consider how their moods impact each other, work on their own communication skills, consider how to take time to bond, plan dates, and so on.

3. **Prioritizing the relationship:** In a committed relationship, the partners consider the "we" before they consider individual needs. They recognize when something is creating a wedge between them and work as a unit to remove the wedge. For example, if their child is getting into bed to sleep in between them every night and it's affecting their connection and intimacy, the couple works together to change the family's bedtime routine.

4. **Taking time to plan:** Protecting the couple bubble means the partners take time to plan their relationship. They check in on how things are going, consider their future goals together, and work to recognize issues ahead of time that might arise later.

Relational Life Therapy

Introduced by Dr. Terry Real in the early 2000s, Relational Life Therapy (RLT) addresses dysfunctional patterns that negatively impact a relationship and encourages partners to take responsibility for changing the patterns. Known for its emphasis on honesty, directness, and personal responsibility, RLT confronts social expectations, particularly gender norms, and the impact of trauma to help individuals master what Real calls "the art of relational living." An underlying belief is that relationships can be improved when the individuals take responsibility for their adult behavior and work toward changing their character.

COUPLES THERAPIST RESOURCE

The Steps of RLT

Relational Life Therapy works in three steps (RLI, n.d.):

- **Step 1: Waking Up:** RLT therapists use loving confrontation to help people wake up to their own negative relational behaviors. Individuals are asked to look at the ways in which they bring harm to the relationship.

- **Step 2: Healing and Transformation:** RLT therapists use trauma work and inner child work to help people understand and overcome negative relational behaviors. This work is done in the presence of the partner, which helps both people build empathy and create larger change than if done alone.

- **Step 3: Relational Skills for Life:** RLT therapists equip their clients with skills that help them maintain change over the lifetime of the relationship.

COUPLES THERAPIST RESOURCE

The Relationship Grid

One of the core tools in RLT is "the Relationship Grid" created by Real, which helps diagnose and treat couples' issues by identifying four main types of behavior manifested by partners within their relationship difficulties. The four quadrants of the relationship grid are (Hill et al., 2025):

1. **Walled off and grandiose:** When people are walled off and grandiose, they are love avoidant. They are indifferent to the relationship, use passive aggression, and have a one-up attitude, seeing their partner as not worthy. They might show contempt and dismissiveness.

2. **Walled off and shame:** Individuals who are walled off with shame are also love avoidant. They show up in the therapy room as resigned, distanced, withdrawn, and depressive. They often seem to have little energy to do anything to improve the relationship and might act as if they have no options for change.

3. **Boundaryless and grandiosity:** When someone is boundaryless and grandiose, they will try to utilize power and control to manage their "love dependence." They often express anger without limits and will do and say things that are not respectful to their partner. They take a one-up position, like the walled-off and grandiose person; however, they are often actively aggressive in their perceived superiority rather than passive-aggressive.

4. **Boundaryless and shame:** When someone does not have boundaries and they also feel shame, they will take a one-down approach, but rather than being withdrawn like the walled-off and shamed individual, they are often desperate and will use manipulation within the relationship. They might not respect their own boundaries and give too much to the relationship, thereby fostering their own resentment of their partner and the relationship.

Ultimately, RLT therapists work with their couples to get them to "health," a state of relationship that includes boundaries and strong self-esteem.

The Costs and Benefits of Intensive Couples Therapy

As I mentioned in the introduction, Harry and Leona were my first couple to participate in an intensive session, and the amount of healing and change this format brought to their relationship set me on the path toward exclusively offering intensives in my practice. That said, therapists (and their clients) considering the intensive format must be made aware that an intensive session isn't guaranteed to result in what one or both clients want. Sometimes, upsetting or shocking news is revealed, people walk out of a session and don't return, or one person decides the relationship should end while the other person is still hopeful it can continue. When any of these things happen, it might feel more abrupt than if had it happened over a series of weeks.

These occasions present an opportunity for the therapist to think creatively and use the time to support the couple, or the individuals, in figuring out next steps. For example, if shocking information is revealed during the intensive, the couple has a therapist there to help them process and move through the distress over the next several hours, rather than having to go home and sit with the shocking information until their next session. If someone announces a desire to divorce, there is an opportunity to provide adequate support to both people before they go home. Having the time to make this announcement might also act as a "rip the Band-Aid off" effect, where otherwise the partner who wanted the divorce might have kicked the can down the lane week after week.

Given the potential for surprises like these (and knowing that they will be stuck with the fallout of such surprises for quite a number of hours), therapists who conduct intensives have to be able to think on their toes and follow where the couple takes the session while still providing direction.

It's critical to discuss the costs and benefits of intensive couples therapy prior to scheduling a session with a couple. During consultation calls and in paperwork, the therapist should be clear about the many benefits of an intensive session while also being honest about the challenges the couple may face during the process.

Benefits of Intensive Couples Therapy

> **The length of time allows for more thorough assessment, complex conversations, and the ability to overcome dysregulation in session.**

During a 50-minute session, the therapist is spinning plates. They have to decide whether they should ask a question that needs answering but might take them off course, or if they should just allow a conversation to continue. When one or both partners become flooded, the therapist might need to use the rest of the session helping them regulate, only to hear the couple complain in the next session, "Last week we hardly dove into any of the issues we want to talk about. We hope we can get to them this week."

During an intensive, the therapist can use all the tools they would like to use. They can ask questions, veer off course when necessary, allow people to talk for longer periods of time, facilitate regulation, and still have time left for lunch!

On their own, couples often struggle to fully discuss their issues. They become stressed and upset with each other and, as a result, close the door on the conversation. A typical couples therapy session often repeats this pattern: An issue is opened, the couple grapples with it for 10 or 20 minutes, and then they have to sweep it under the therapist's carpet until the following week. Needless to say, relationship issues are not helped by having their at-home experience mirrored in the therapy room. In an intensive session, when the clients become distressed, they are offered skills, empathy, or a break, then they return and continue to discuss their issue. By practicing this regulation in real time, with a guide, their cycle has an opportunity to change.

> **Because they are scheduled over two days, couples can commit to fully focus on the couples therapy work without being distracted by the business of everyday life.**

"Did you have a chance to try what we discussed this week?" I would ask my weekly session couples time and time again.

"No—we meant to, but got too busy," was their almost invariable response.

Because I had to pick and choose what we focused on in session—a conversation? A repair? Skill building?—I often sent couples with "homework" that we hadn't been able to adequately practice in session. In theory, the couple was dedicated to building this new relationship skill, but amid the busyness of day-to-day life, it was difficult to find any time to practice it.

In an intensive, couples get the opportunity to not only learn about new skills but also practice them over and over again during the hours they spend with you. This helps them better internalize the skills and makes it easier to replicate them at home.

Another common hiccup in my weekly sessions were distractions to the work that arose from week to week. The couple would come in to one session determined to talk about one topic: "Liz, we really need to focus on our sex life." We would all agree on this topic as the focus for the next several weeks, only for the couple to open the next session with, "I know we said we needed to focus on sex, but this past week our daughter didn't sleep well. Maybe we should focus on parenting instead."

Having two days together, back to back, allows you and your clients to fully focus on whatever goal they came in for. The goings-on of the world stay still for a moment while the couple discusses their challenges, works through their conflicts, and has time to explore possibilities for what is next.

> **Couples can get more adequate support for crisis issues—like the discovery of an affair, the consideration of a separation or divorce, a major loss, or the aftermath of a major fight—instead of having to wait for support between typical sessions.**

When a couple is in crisis, the days between sessions are brutal. The pain, the dysregulation, and the likelihood of worsening conflict is difficult for the relationship to bear. When the couple comes in for their session, the therapist must take care to create an environment of safety before diving into anything too deep. Often, no sooner has that safety been created than the therapist must announce, "Time is up."

While all couples therapy benefits from time, it's especially important when someone is having a profound emotional experience, such as grief, shock, betrayal, or rejection. The care that these experiences require means couples therapists might have many duties:

- We provide psychoeducation so each person knows what's happening to them and can understand themselves within the experience.
- We provide a framework that helps the clients feel contained and limits the sense of chaos or impending doom.
- We give each client the opportunity to talk, cry, ask questions, express their rage and their hurt, and discuss their worries. We also provide support and guidance for the other partner hearing them out.
- In response to both clients' expression, we provide feedback and skill building, including recognition of emotional flooding in their bodies and self-soothing techniques.
- We provide lots of breaks and help our clients re-regulate so that the work can continue effectively.

It's impossible to adequately fulfill all these duties in a 50-minute session! (And at some level, the clients know that as well as the therapist.) There is an immense pressure that clinicians feel when they need to open two people up and then quickly sew them back together before the session ends. This pressure might, inadvertently, cause clinicians to sidestep important issues due to fear there won't be time to finish up. They may also avoid taking breaks or forgo enactments that need more time. They are limited in how thorough they can be in teaching skills, providing feedback, or helping a client to process their feelings and thoughts. Finally, the pressure of completing a session in such a short time frame might induce therapist anxiety, which could increase the likelihood that they become withdrawn or even overly activated, adding to the clients' distress.

> **For many couples, intensives make scheduling easier.**

Some couples choose an intensive session because they are in crisis or because they've been so unhappy for so many years that they need time to peel back the layers of a very large onion. Other couples opt for intensives simply because they can't find the time on a weekly basis to nourish their relationship the way they'd like. For some couples, it might be too difficult to find a predictable time to meet due to travel-heavy work schedules; for those with children, getting a babysitter for two days straight may be a more reasonable option than finding childcare from one week to the next.

> **Intensives help "frontload" the early work of therapy.**

Instead of waiting four to six weeks to get through the assessment phase of therapy, couples get through assessment in one day and dive into intervention within the second day. Whether the couple is experiencing a distressing situation or wants to improve relational basics, this might be preferable. Should the couple continue with weekly sessions after the intensive is complete, they will be able to see significant results sooner rather than later.

> **Couples who partake in intensive sessions tend to have higher levels of motivation and therefore better outcomes.**

Because of the resources required to schedule and partake in an intensive couples therapy session, clients tend to come ready to participate, are more open to feedback, and are more open to taking risks. As a result, even couples with mixed agendas typically experience more satisfying results from their intensive. Their commitment to making this major investment of time and emotions translates to a commitment to doing the work necessary to improve the relationship.

Costs of Intensive Couples Therapy

> **Intensives are expensive.**

Due to the time and expertise it takes to facilitate an intensive, these sessions are expensive for clients. Moreover, they are not covered by most insurance policies. (I've had a few lucky couples get their insurance to provide out-of-network reimbursement, but it's the rare exception, not the rule.) In addition, couples often need to take time off work or find childcare, which only expands the financial investment.

> **The number of hours might be challenging to commit to.**

While the duration of an intensive session allows for more thorough assessment and intervention, it can be challenging for people to dedicate 12 to 18 nearly continuous hours to attending therapy. Again, the challenge is heightened by the effort to take time away from work or find childcare during their session.

> **Unequal buy-in might create a sense of being "forced" into a major commitment.**

From time to time, I have seen couples show up for an intensive with unequal buy-in—that is, one partner is only there due to guilt, obligation, or discomfort with letting their partner know how they really feel. Needless to say, it can be a distressing experience for someone to spend 12 hours in an emotionally charged situation that they don't actually want to be in. Consultation calls and individual assessment on the first day increases the likelihood that the therapist will catch this dynamic, empowering them to intervene as necessary.

> **Intensive couples therapy can be overwhelming.**

Intensive couples therapy is, well, intense. If sessions are not conducted with great care, an individual or couple could experience more harm than good. It's not unusual for heavy, painful, and shocking topics to be raised right off the bat. People might find out information they were not prepared for, such as the disclosure of an affair or a request for divorce. On occasion, sessions can open the door to traumatization or abuse. For example, if there is an abusive dynamic and the therapist is not able to identify it and respond effectively, a client could be left at the receiving end of abuse for an entire weekend. While intensive therapy tends to be helpful overall, there are scenarios in which a person or a couple might leave feeling worse than when they came in.

> **The large investment might lead to anger or disappointment if expectations are not met.**

No therapist can promise that a relationship can be saved. Nevertheless, many couples will come to an intensive with high hopes that it will mend even the most broken of relationships. When the intensive results in an outcome that goes against the hopes and desires of at least one partner, they might feel incredibly disappointed in the process or even angry with the therapist. This is understandable and can be challenging for a therapist to navigate, especially when they know they did their best.

Of these challenges, one of the most common is the possibility of unequal buy-in. This was the case for Harry and Leona, whose goals for an intensive couples therapy session at first seemed misaligned. While Harry wanted to save the relationship, Leona just wanted to express why she was ready to leave.

Because expectation setting is important, I shared my concerns about them being on different pages and emphasized that intensive couples therapy sessions don't have a guaranteed outcome, particularly when there is a mixed agenda on goals. The couple ultimately decided that they wanted to proceed, even if it meant that most of the intensive would be exploring their mismatched goals and making a decision on what should come next.

I spent the initial 90 minutes of the session talking with the couple together. Harry, through tears, expressed how much he valued their relationship of over 25 years and how committed he was to saving it. Leona sat stone-faced, listening; when it was her time to talk, she shared that she had been invested in the relationship for many years while feeling completely alone and neglected. "I asked Harry again and again to go to couples therapy with me. I want this to work. But he never cared. Work was always more important."

Harry teared up again at this. Turning to Leona with a hopeful face, he said, "That's why we are here now. I am ready to make this right with you." Clearly, by the look on her face, Leona wasn't convinced. After I got through my initial questions for the couple, I asked Leona and Harry to take a quick bathroom break and instructed Leona to come back to my office to spend time with me for her one-on-one session.

Harry was given options for what he could do with his time—he was welcome to sit in my waiting room, take a walk, go grab some food, or do anything else that he'd like to do. I told him to plan to come back in an hour unless he heard otherwise from us.

When I met with Leona alone, she expressed that while a small part of her was curious to see if the intensive would change anything, she was overall confident that it was time to end the relationship. Most of her motivation to attend lay in giving Harry what he wanted one last time so that he wouldn't be able to say that Leona didn't try.

"So there isn't much Harry or this intensive weekend could do to change your mind?" I asked.

"Not really," she answered.

"I can't keep that from Harry," I told her.* "Let's talk together about how you can share that when we all come back together. Or, if you're not ready to share it, we will need to decide whether we can proceed with the weekend."

"I can share it," Leona said. Her shoulders dropped and she looked somewhat relieved.

At this point in the session, instead of meeting with Harry individually, I decided it was best to bring them back together. I didn't want to prompt Harry to tell me his hopes and dreams for a future with Leona while already knowing there was no chance for that future to come about.

"Harry, I know you might be wondering why I called you back in before meeting with you individually," I began. Harry looked nervous. He knew this wasn't the normal order of operations and understood he was about to hear something he had been dreading. "Leona wanted to share something with you, and I thought it was important to talk about before you and I met one on one. Go ahead, Leona."

Leona turned to Harry and, in a completely matter-of-fact manner, said, "There is no hope for us. You lost me years ago. I'm here because you wanted me to come, not because I want things to get better. There's nothing you can do."

I was glad that Leona was able to express herself clearly and, at the same time, deeply saddened for Harry. As he took in the information, his face slowly dropped, and he started to cry. He rested his head into his hands as he sobbed. Leona looked at me and shrugged.

"Leona, how about you go take a walk around the city, get some lunch or something, for about an hour?" I suggested. "I'd like to spend some time with Harry."

Leona walked out of the room and closed the door. I spent the next hour processing with Harry how he was feeling about what he just heard. Most of that hour was spent in denial—he was having a hard time accepting that Leona could be so sure about the end of their relationship. While it was possible that Leona might come around, it seemed as if Harry wasn't able to consider the significant impact on Leona after years of disconnect in their relationship and the fact that perhaps Leona had been thinking on this for much longer than he was aware.

"I don't think she means it," Harry insisted. "Sometimes she gets this way, but we have a good relationship. Things haven't been so bad. I think she just needs to see I can change."

The couples therapist's role in these scenarios is to empathize with the individual and allow some space for hope, but also help them to hear the reality. It would not have helped Harry if I had said, "You're right. I think if Leona can just see how much you'll change she will be on board." What mattered more

---

* In chapter 2, I discuss in more detail my personal policy and recommendations for managing information that one partner is not privy to (see page 40).

was responding to Harry in a way that helped him feel heard—"I hear you are really hopeful that Leona will give you another opportunity"—while also asking him to reflect on what he heard from Leona by asking questions like "Can you share with me what you've heard Leona say?" and "Do you have thoughts on what has gotten Leona to the point of expressing the desire to end the relationship?"

I reminded Harry that it wasn't my job to change Leona's mind and that if Leona was serious about wanting a separation, we would need to spend our time exploring the separation. We couldn't pretend it wasn't on the table.

Throughout the conversation there were points where Harry expressed frustration at feeling as if I was giving up on them. I empathized with this feeling. I told him that we could bring Leona back in and spend time talking about the decision further so that Leona could answer any questions Harry had. However, I made it clear we couldn't pretend as if Leona hadn't shared that information with us and that it wouldn't be helpful to work on "fixing the relationship" if Leona had already decided it was over.

I also spent time talking to Harry about his hope, of course. We explored what he believed would need to happen if there was a chance to be had. I balanced this by asking him how he would feel if the intensive did not bring him the desired outcome of getting together again.

We discussed the goals for the intensive—if Leona did want to end the relationship, how could the intensive be helpful to Harry? I shared with him that there are multiple options: ending therapy after the first day, spending the second day in mostly one-on-one sessions to help both of them cope with the change, or spending the second day talking as a group about how to navigate the end of the relationship with love and respect.

Harry said he'd leave it up to Leona.

Usually, at the end of the first day, I meet with the couple to let them know what I've observed and assessed, explain how I think I can help, and paint a picture of our work together in the next day or two of the intensive. In many ways this time was the same, but without as much hope.

When Leona joined us again, I asked Harry to share what he had shared with me. He turned to Leona and said, "I don't want to accept that I've lost you, and I also recognize that you've been distant and decisive about this for weeks. I haven't wanted to hear what you're saying, but I heard it today. I know I've lost you and it's the end." His face red and his eyes watering, he continued, "I'd like to spend tomorrow with you talking about what happened to our relationship and about next steps, if you'd be open to it."

I let Leona take in what Harry said. When it was clear she wasn't going to respond in the moment, I cut in. "If it's okay, I'd like to share with you my thoughts from today. After meeting with you as a couple and then meeting individually, what I hear is that there is a decision being made by Leona for the relationship to end. Leona, I hear this has been something you've been processing for a long time, and for you, Harry, it's very fresh. I want to share with you how I might be able to help you tomorrow, and then I'd like to hear your thoughts.

"One option is that we can meet tomorrow to process what happened to the relationship, appreciate the good times, and express any gratitude. Then, we can talk about what you both envision and need for moving forward and we can plan. Another option is that you could end our time together now. I am happy to meet with you in the future if needed. What do you both think?"

Leona looked up. "I don't want to just end our time right now. It's too abrupt. I do think we should talk tomorrow."

Harry agreed. "I need more time to sit with this and talk about it."

The second day of this intensive looked different from how they usually do. I wasn't teaching the couple new skills or helping them to reignite intimacy and connect. I was helping them to say goodbye. But even though the weekend ended in Harry's heartbreak, there were some positive outcomes for the couple. The length of the session allowed Leona to finally stand in her truth—she had enough time to talk with Harry about the relationship, followed by enough one-on-one time with me to suss out what she really felt and build the courage to say it. For Harry, while he'd hoped for a repaired relationship, the benefit was having the time to process the end of the relationship with Leona. If he became upset or dysregulated, he could take a break, come back, and finish their conversation. This is something Harry and Leona had never been able to do in the past, which led to their relationship dragging on unhappily for years.

Of course, there were downsides as well. I think that Leona felt somewhat forced to attend. While the session ultimately gave her the opportunity to communicate what she hadn't been able to before, attending couples therapy for 12 hours probably felt like a steep cost for that benefit. Meanwhile, Harry put a lot of resources into the intensive—time, money, and emotional energy—and while the experience brought truth to the light, it was also disappointing.

The "heavy lifting" required in an intensive can make an unexpected or undesired outcome that much more of a blow. For that reason, it's important for therapists to acknowledge this possibility and discuss it with couples at the outset, along with the other pros and cons of intensive couples therapy. (I suggest putting these advisories in writing in your paperwork and on your website, as well.) Just because something has downsides doesn't mean it needs to be avoided, but it's important to set expectations so that your clients understand what they're getting into.

As Harry and Leona's story shows, when there have been major losses, betrayals, and traumas, people need time to explain themselves, soothe, and feel safe with the therapist and each other. They need to know that if they raise their voice or cry or need to take a break, they can do that and there will still be time to come back and try again. They need to have an opportunity to complete the stress cycle in the session before going out into the world feeling raw and vulnerable.

However, intensives aren't only for couples in crisis. There are many other reasons people might benefit from intensive couples therapy:

- They have complicated schedules that make it difficult to schedule weekly therapy.
- They are experiencing high conflict due to life circumstances or have recently experienced a significant loss or trauma that puts stress on their relationship.
- They have a big decision that needs to be made and don't have months to figure it out.
- They have neglected their relationship for many years and realize they need to jump-start it in a big way.
- They are considering a divorce and would like to give enough time to really think it through. (Although the consideration of divorce is painful, it is not always a "crisis." The couple might want an opportunity to explore their options and "consciously uncouple," should they decide the relationship should no longer move forward.)

While short weekly sessions can have a frustrating "start and stop" rhythm, intensives allow couples to fully express their perspectives on the relational dysfunction, offer space for deeper clinical assessment, and provide time to explore complex issues.

Recognizing this has led many clinical thought leaders to not only adopt longer sessions but advocate for them. The Gottman Institute, which refers to their intensive sessions as "Marathon Couples Therapy," mentions that many of their trademark structured conversations feel rushed in the context of a shorter session. I asked Psychobiological Approach to Couples Therapy (PACT) founder Dr. Stan Tatkin in a personal communication why his modality is organized around meeting with couples for three to six hours per session. He shared three primary reasons:

1. **Safety:** The clients' work in session—to think, to investigate thoroughly, to determine who and what is in front of them—is most effective when they do not feel time pressure.

2. **Better assessments:** A longer session provides the opportunity to see the partners shift states more often, offering a better representation of how the partners operate outside the session. Shorter sessions may mask state shifts that only occur with a degree of fatigue.

3. **Lowered defenses:** In Dr. Tatkin's words, we all get a little "squishier" with familiarity—as time progresses, the couple's defenses soften. They can do more work, have deeper conversations, and create more lasting change by becoming softer with each other through having the safe container of time.

He sums it up this way: "The therapist's best friend is time."

Ellyn Bader and Dr. Peter Pearson, founders of the Couples Institute, state it more severely: "The current model of couples therapy is broken. Not only that, it's almost unethical" (Couples Institute, n.d.). Their indictment concerns the necessity of asking the couple to discuss topics together that might cause emotional flooding. We know that it takes at least 20 minutes to reduce emotional flooding, yet the flooded state might not happen until 30 to 40 minutes into session, leaving no time to help the couple navigate self-soothing. They also call out the likelihood that time pressure might lead a therapist to avoid utilizing enactments (characterized by the couple talking directly to each other with the therapist as coach) because they take longer than therapist-centered approaches (when interaction is channeled through the therapist). As a result, the therapist often becomes the person who "manages" the couple's dysregulation rather than teaching them how to manage their own dysregulation.

There has been an ongoing evolution regarding the most effective way to help couples improve their relational life with each other. The newest frontier in this evolution, I believe, is questioning the way in which those therapies are offered. Intensives help couples get to the heart of the issues that challenge their relationships. They allow therapists to truly support clients in getting over the hill of dysregulation and to the other side so they can experience effective communication in a regulated state. They invite a couple's real experience into the room and create the opportunity for real progress to be achieved—not weeks or months down the road but *now*, when the couple needs that support and hope.

CHAPTER 2

Preparing

Preparation is crucial before you begin to offer intensive couples therapy sessions. Since these sessions are distinct from weekly therapy, you should prepare by being adequately trained, having policies and procedures in place, and knowing how to get the word out about your offering. In this chapter, I will go over the importance of training, policy considerations, and marketing suggestions. We will also explore how to prepare through assessments and your consultation call.

Training

Therapists conducting intensive couples therapy should be practicing within their scope. This means that, at a baseline, you should have training specific to couples therapy. As discussed in the last chapter, there are many couples therapy modalities, and it is encouraged that prior to offering intensives, you are well versed in your chosen modality (or modalities).

On top of couples therapy training, you should consider further training in niche areas. For example, you might choose to work with clients who have experienced infidelity and therefore seek out further training specific to the treatment of affairs and betrayal. Finding your niche area takes time. Some considerations include choosing an area in which you find yourself interested, in which you've received enough training to adequately support individuals and couples experiencing the specific issue, and in which you've received your own supervision regarding how the work influences you to ensure you are aware of your own countertransference. (Often therapists are drawn to work in areas where they need healing themselves, so this is especially important to avoid causing harm.)

The following areas of expertise are commonly needed during intensive couples therapy sessions:

- Betrayal
- Discernment
- Perinatal mental health
- Trauma
- Sex and sexuality
- Substance use

When therapists attempt to provide intensive sessions without adequate training in couples therapy, it could create an experience for the couple that is unhelpful at best and dangerous at worst. Risks run the spectrum from failure to recognize dangerous interactional patterns (for example, those that indicate intimate partner violence) to forgetting to consider the systems perspective and inadvertently acting as an individual therapist. Couples therapists receive crucial training on how to intervene in activated arguments between two people, whereas those who are not trained might not know how to appropriately respond and will either intervene too abrasively or will not intervene due to feeling frozen and overwhelmed.

Policies and Paperwork

While it is rare to have negative experiences with intensive couples therapy clients (I can count on my hand the number of issues we have had in my practice while serving hundreds of couples over the last ten years), it will serve you well to determine your clinical and administrative policies prior to offering intensives. Clearly defining the boundaries of your work will ensure that you are prepared for the worst-case scenarios instead of figuring them out when they happen.

Prior to or during the intensive, you might come across information that you have to act on. Well-documented and ethically sound clinical policies will help you respond to fraught situations. This includes knowing when to pause the intensive to triage legal concerns such as duty to warn or breaches of safety.

Clinical policies should include how you will respond to:

- Suicidality
- Domestic violence
- Secrets
- Substance use/addiction

Because intensives represent a big commitment of time and money, couples tend to feel more anxiety related to them. Most couples have never done an intensive before, and they might feel apprehensive about what it even entails or worried that their major financial commitment might not result in what they had hoped for. As we know, with higher levels of anxiety, there can be a higher likelihood of misunderstandings, disappointments, or frustrations. Clear policies reduce opportunities for misunderstanding, provide guidelines for both the clients and the therapist, and offer everyone protection from potential reactions to disappointment or miscommunications. For example, clients may believe that the therapy should "guarantee" their relationship stays together and later feel disappointed or even angry if their work with you does not lead to reconciliation. This can lead to conflict over financial expectations, such as the couple asking for a refund. Clear paperwork outlining that results cannot be guaranteed—and that refunds are not provided—ensures clients know what to expect beforehand.

Administrative policies you will want to consider include:

- An outline of what to expect in a session
- Billing
- Cancellation
- "Unhappy customer" responses
- Paperwork completion

Let's look at each of these policy areas in more detail.

Policies Regarding Suicidality

A few years into offering intensives, I received an assessment back from a couple the night before their session was to begin. As I scanned the results, my eyes were drawn to a question beneath the heading "Suicide Potential." The question read, "In the past few weeks have you been thinking about killing yourself?" The client's answer: YES.

What do I do here? I wondered. It was already 9:30 p.m., and I was slated to work with this client and her husband the next morning at 8 a.m. *Do I call her now? Or do I wait until I see them in the morning?*

Because of the high level of risk shown in the assessment, I called the client then and there to conduct a suicide assessment. In response to my questions, she indicated that while she often thinks thoughts in her mind like *I want to die*, these thoughts were often related to not knowing how else to get rid of her pain. She indicated she didn't have any plan to kill herself and that she was motivated to come to therapy and work on her relationship.

COUPLES THERAPIST RESOURCE

Suicide Assessment Questions

"I saw you indicated you've been thinking about killing yourself over the past few weeks. Do you have those thoughts now?"

- If yes, "Do you have any plans to kill yourself?"
- If no, "Can you tell me a little more about what was going on for you when you filled out the assessment? What has changed or not changed?"

If the client reports still having thoughts indicating suicidality:

- "Do you have a plan?" or "If you were going to kill yourself, how would you do it?"

As I listen, I consider how detailed the plan is, how motivated they are to act out the plan, and whether they have access to means. Depending on the risk level of the suicidal ideation, I would create a safety plan, do lethal means counseling, do crisis response planning, or ask the person to get immediate medical attention.

COUPLES THERAPIST RESOURCE

Suicidal Ideation Interventions

Safety Planning

Safety planning is commonly used across therapeutic modalities when someone expresses suicidal ideation without immediate risk for harm. Frameworks include the Stanley-Brown Safety Plan and Crisis Response Planning (Stanley & Brown, 2012). Overall, safety plans are designed in collaboration with the client and include the following components:

- **Warning signs:** What does the client recognize about themselves prior to having suicidal ideation? How would they know that things have become more dangerous for them?

- **To-do list:** Write a list of what the client will do when they have distressing thoughts about self-harm. This might include people they will talk to, activities they will participate in, and mental wellness strategies like mindfulness, journaling, or exercise.
- **Removal of lethal means:** This includes a written agreement that the client will remove things from their home that could increase the likelihood of lethality.
- **Social supports:** The safety plan should always include a list of social supports—safe people in the client's life who can be there to connect with or to talk to when there is an emergency.
- **Crisis plan:** This includes what to do, who to talk to, and who to call in order to keep the client safe. The crisis plan should include how the therapist would be involved in that process, emergency room information, the suicide hotline, and anything else that seems relevant to keeping the client safe during a crisis.
- **Hope:** An integral component of the safety plan is exploring hope for the person's life. Here the client can consider what they feel hopeful about, why they want to live, and what they desire for their future. This should not only be discussed but written into the plan.
- **People who can distract:** Make a list of people the client can call to help them with distraction. These can be friends and family they can lean on for support and who would be willing to take a walk with them, for example.

Lethal Means Counseling

The goal of lethal means counseling (LMC) is to reduce the risk of suicide by removing lethal means (such as firearms, sharp instruments, or medications) from the home. It is recommended in combination with a safety plan when someone expresses they are at risk for suicidality but it is not appropriate for them to go to the emergency room. This plan focuses on removing lethal means, at least temporarily, due to the understanding that people can have rapid mood shifts that could lead to a deadly situation if means are available.

LMC includes another person in the client's life to reach the goal of removing lethal means and ensuring safety. In the case of intensives, this would most likely be the partner; however, if the relationship is the source of the distress or if the relationship does not seem safe, the therapist works with the client to explore who else could be involved as a support. For example, the client might call their mother to come and pick them up from the intensive and agree to remove lethal means from the home of the client.

LMC includes the following:

- Expressing concern for the client's safety
- Letting the person know that it's important to remove any lethal means from the home to keep the person safe
- Emphasizing that since you can't predict a crisis, it's important during moments of vulnerability to reduce access to anything that could be lethal
- Focusing especially on the intended method of the person with suicidal ideation
- Asking the support person to keep the person in "line of sight" until the person has gotten care or seems to be stabilizing

> **Crisis Intervention**
>
> At times, it will be clear the client needs immediate intervention that a safety plan, therapy appointment, or loved one may not be able to provide. In this instance, the recommendation is for the client to go to the emergency room. If they refuse and it is clear they are at risk of immediate harm, you will need to intervene as determined by your state laws and professional ethics or encourage a family member to intervene.

I could hear from this client that she had hope for the future, that she did not feel activated in that moment, and that she had no plan, means, or desire to harm herself. But because our call changed the usual course of my work—I was spending a significant amount of time with her on the phone prior to meeting with them as a unit—I wanted to ensure that we weren't disrupting the couples therapy dynamic by becoming joined in a way that felt secretive to her partner.

"Does your partner know you have these thoughts?" I asked her.

"I haven't ever shared it with him. It feels too embarrassing."

"I'd like us to find a way to let him know tomorrow how you've been feeling. How do you feel about that?"

"I think he needs to know. It's a part of the issue between us—he doesn't realize how distressed I am."

"Would you feel comfortable bringing it up when I ask you both to share what has been going on for you and in the relationship?"

"Yes, I can do that," she responded.

When we met the next morning, the client shared with her husband how depressed she had been, how she had felt so much pain that she fantasized about dying, but that she was hopeful their dynamic could change once they got the help they needed. The husband was clearly pained to see his wife's pain, but he embraced her and thanked her for sharing. After conducting the risk assessment, I documented the session and safety plan and consulted with a trusted colleague to ensure continuity of care.

From that point onward, my policy for when suicidality comes up in the assessment paperwork has remained the same. Prior to meeting the couple as a unit, I talk with the client individually on the phone and do a suicide assessment. If the person is not in imminent danger, I process with them how they can share with their partner if we talk about their distress. During our one-on-one meeting on the first day of the intensive, I do further assessment of their well-being and mental health and provide referrals and support for individual work.

Policies Regarding Domestic Violence

Many clients who attend couples therapy, and therefore intensive couples therapy sessions, might have become "physical" with each other at some point. In couples therapy training programs, there is often an oversimplification of how therapists should manage intimate partner violence (IPV)—they typically teach that couples therapy is not indicated if there is IPV present.

However, these mandates fail to recognize that there are different types of IPV and thus fail to help therapists accurately assess a couple's situation. When considering IPV and whether couples therapy is appropriate, the therapist must assess whether it is constitutes *situational couple violence* or *characterological abuse*.

Situational couple violence is when there is violence in a relationship arising from a specific argument that does not include general patterns of dominance. This is the type of violence therapists will come across most often when working with couples in the general public. A study by Neil Jacobson and John Gottman (1998) bears this out, showing that 80 percent of couple violence is situational, while another study showed that 50 percent of physically aggressive couples exhibit low levels of mutual violence that is situational in nature (Straus & Gelles, 1986). Not only is it incredibly common to witness this type of behavior in couples therapy, but research has also shown that conjoint couples therapy can be applied safely and effectively with situationally violent couples "without increasing levels of violence" (Stith et al., 2004; Simpson et al., 2008).

Several years ago, I had an intensive therapy session with Debbie and Kyree. While discussing their recent arguments, Debbie hung her head and shared, "I knew we needed this session when we got into an argument while we were out with our friends and I was so enraged that I threw my phone across the room and it hit Kyree."

If I had taken the advice of couples therapy traditionalists, I might have ended the session there. Instead, I explored what happened. Following Debbie throwing the phone, Kyree kicked a hole through the door of their bedroom. At this point, they knew they needed to disengage and Kyree left the house to stay with his friend. While this helped them avoid further physical outbursts, they continued to argue by text message, sending hurtful messages to each other.

I learned that they had both been drinking heavily at the time of this incident. When I explored the frequency of events like these, both partners shared that this was the first time their outbursts had resulted in direct physical injury, although they had previously damaged property during escalated arguments. There had been a regrettable moment in which Debbie threw a glass across the room and Kyree slammed a door so hard it broke the door frame. These behaviors, they expressed, were not acceptable to them. They wanted help to make sure it wouldn't happen again. They expressed remorse, embarrassment, and a sense of urgency to make it right.

From all of this, it was clear that both Kyree and Debbie were engaging in situational couple violence, which typically involves mutual physical aggression tied to poor conflict management, rather than a pattern of control. Debbie and Kyree's descriptions of mutual escalation, along with their remorse and commitment to change, pointed clearly to this category. According to Jacobson and Gottman (1998), these cases are the result of two things:

- A lack of social skills and communication skills that would allow the partners to express their needs and reduce conflict escalation
- Mismanaged flooding and diffuse physiological arousal (DPA)

In my experience, many of the cases are also the result of substance misuse that is believed to be "socially acceptable" by the couple. This may look like drinking wine at the end of the night while having a difficult conversation or frequenting the bar at a friend's wedding only to get into an altercation.

Instead of discontinuing the session, we spent much of the time discussing the situations that cause Kyree and Debbie to become dysregulated and to act out physically. They were able to leave the session with a safety plan, referrals for individual therapy, and an agreement that alcohol was no longer welcome in their relationship, as it had consistently been a contributing factor in their physical altercations.

Months later, Kyree and Debbie reached out thanking me for helping them to navigate their anger with each other differently. They were no longer drinking and had not had any more physical altercations. Couples therapy had helped them.

On the other hand, there is another type of violent offender that is not appropriate for couples therapy. A *characterological abuser* is someone who has an overall pattern of dominating and controlling their victim (Stith et al., 2012). This type of violence accounts for 20 percent of IPV and is what traditional advice in couples therapy—to discontinue couples sessions and encourage individual therapy—is aimed at. This is because characterological abusers are dangerous and couples therapy does not help them to stop their violent behavior. If anything, it might embolden them by creating a vulnerable space in which they gain more control or increase the likelihood that they will further abuse their partner as "retribution" for disclosures the partner makes during therapy (Holtzworth-Munroe, 2001).

Characterological abusers come in two forms: those who are vicious and violent to many different people, and those who are only vicious and violent toward their intimate partner. In either case, the behavior of characterological abusers follows any or several of the patterns listed below (Pence & Paymar, 1993):

- **Coercion and threats**
    - Making and carrying out threats to harm a person in some way (emotional, physical, financial, etc.)
    - Threats to leave the relationship in order to maintain control
    - Threats of suicide in order to maintain control
    - Threats to call the police on the person or report the person to some other institutional entity to maintain control (e.g., "I'll call the police and let them know what you told me about ___" or "I will tell the IRS what you did on your taxes last year if you don't ___")
    - Attempts to get the person to partake in illegal activities so that the abuser may hold something over their head

- **Economic abuse**
    - Stealing, spending, or using the person's money without permission or through coercion to create a sense of financial instability
    - Giving an allowance that restricts the person's ability to have autonomy
    - Restricting or withholding access to information about family income
    - Preventing the person from getting or keeping a job (e.g., making the person late so they get fired)

- **Using children**
    - Evoking the feelings of the children to maintain control over the partner (e.g., "If you do this and ruin our family, the children won't forgive you")
    - Using children to relay messages (e.g., "Tell your mom she really let our family down today")

- Threats to take the children away
- Use of legal system regarding children to cause psychological and financial distress

• **Minimization, denying, and blaming**
  - Minimizing abuse
  - Making fun of the partner's reaction to the abuse
  - Saying abusive instances did not happen
  - Shifting responsibility for abusive behavior
  - Reversing the perpetrator role and saying the other person caused it

• **Isolation**
  - Damaging relationships that are important to the person (e.g., starting fights with their friends)
  - Controlling where they go and who they talk to
  - Getting angry when the person has outside interests or obligations and gradually asking the person to remove any outside obligations from their life
  - Using jealousy to get the person to remove themselves from their important relationships

• **Emotional abuse**
  - Chronic put-downs
  - Name-calling
  - Mind games or deliberately causing confusion
  - Humiliation
  - Inducing guilt

At times, an individual or couple that is not characterologically abusive might have some of the aforementioned issues—for example, as couples therapists we come across name-calling all the time. You'll want to take into account the severity of the presentation as well as the number of items from the list that the couple is experiencing. If most or all of these things are present, then you may be dealing with characterological abuse. If only a handful of these things are present but at a high intensity, this could also indicate characterological abuse. For example, perhaps the name-calling is so contemptuous, belittling, and incessant that it indicates characterological abuse rather than unresolved anger or poor coping mechanisms.

Besides the items in the previous list, therapists can also recognize characterological abuse when there is:

- **Belligerence:** The person is argumentative, stubborn, and aggressive. Their belligerence increases with anger and is used as a way to control their partner.
- **DARVO:** If their partner points out their harmful behavior, they **d**eny any wrongdoing, then verbally **a**ttack their partner, **r**eversing the **v**ictim and **o**ffender roles by claiming it is the partner who is mistreating *them*.
- **Lack of remorse:** They show little to no remorse for their harmful behaviors.

- **Condescension:** They lecture from a one-up position, making it clear they believe their partner to be "less than." They may also express contempt toward and belittle others, especially those that seem to matter to their partner.

- **Dominating and controlling behavior:** As mentioned previously, a characterological abuser may attempt to socially isolate their partner or fully control their partner's finances. They may also attempt to control even the minutiae of day-to-day living—for example, with regard to how the children are raised or how the house is cleaned. This is different from having a strong preference; rather, their partner cannot safely have a different opinion on how things should be done.

- **Fear and intimidation:** They use threats and coercion, as mentioned earlier, or other means of inspiring fear and intimidating their partner. They might use information or lies against their partner, like "If you break up with me, I'll tell your family about the abortion you had and they'll disown you" or "I've hidden drugs in the house and I'll call the cops on you if you cause any more issues" or "I have more money than you do, so if you try to leave I will fight tooth and nail to get full custody of the kids."

- **Aggressive body language:** The abuser will often lead with their forehead or chin when domineering. They also tend to puff up, sneer, glare, and clench muscles; however, these latter behaviors can also indicate anger and not necessarily abuse.

- **Provocation:** The abuser will attempt to provoke a response from their partner by continually pushing boundaries and using psychological manipulation. When they are successful, they use their partner's reaction to "prove" that their partner is crazy.

- **Charisma:** Abusers can be charming and highly manipulative, but not always.

Characterological abuse will not always be obvious in early consultation calls or within the assessments given prior to the intensive session. Rather, it is often disclosed during the one-on-one session between the therapist and the partner who is being abused. This creates a dilemma: First, the therapist at this point understands that couples therapy will not be effective for the couple, and second, the therapist realizes that the disclosure has increased the client's risk to their own safety. Therefore, the next steps aren't always as straightforward as just canceling the session midway through.

While it has been a rare occurrence, I have seen a few cases in which characterological violence was apparent during an intensive session. On the first day of my intensive with Sara and Ivan, I noticed that Sara seemed to be nervous—not about the process necessarily, but about Ivan's reactions to the process. During our time talking together, she often looked over at Ivan. She would only answer questions briefly, and she held her arms around her body as if to protect herself.

Their assessment had been unremarkable. They both reported that they were worried about the health of their relationship, that they had some issues with conflict, and that their sex life had decreased. On the areas meant to assess for IPV, neither partner reported any hitting, kicking, or pushing. However, my gut told me something was off.

When I met with Sara alone, I allowed her to spend some time talking about her perception of the relationship. Her descriptions were brief. Instead of beating around the bush, I asked directly about intimate partner violence, then explored the possibility of characterological violence. Often, our clients need us to ask about "taboo" subjects directly.

"Something I ask during my one-on-ones," I began, "is if there is ever any violence in the relationship. Is there ever any violence?"

Sara quickly answered, "No, not at all."

Keeping my attitude neutral, I went on, "I just want to make clear that sometimes people think violence is only hitting, kicking, or shoving—however, there can be psychological violence too. For example, if you feel threatened by someone, afraid of them, or trapped by them. Do you ever feel any of those things?"

Sara looked down at her hands, taking several moments before speaking. "I guess I didn't think of those things as violent, but yes. If I tell you about it, will you tell him? He will be so mad, and honestly, I just want to get through this weekend without making things worse."

I nodded to show my understanding. "As I mentioned before, I do have a no-secrets policy, but that changes when I believe there is the possibility for danger. I won't violate your trust by sharing anything with him, and it will be up to you what you'd like to share with me. However, I'd like to use our one-on-one time to hear more about what you're experiencing so I can make sure I'm approaching our time together appropriately."

Sara bit her lip. "Okay. I do want to talk about it because I feel stuck. I don't know what to do."

I asked her to share more. Sara said that when they first started dating, she wasn't sure about him. A couple months in, he said he needed to stay with her for a few weeks due to work being done on his apartment. But then he never left.

"I told him he could not live with me," Sara continued, "but he's refused to leave. It has gotten worse, to where I notice that he will follow me to work, and I think he is tracking my car."

"It sounds as though you're being controlled by him," I told her, "and stalked?"

Sara nodded miserably. "Yes, he is stalking me. So I don't know how to get him to leave the house and I can't even figure out how to talk safely about it because I think he is tracking me. I even left my cell phone in the waiting room in case he could somehow listen in."

Having confirmed that Ivan was indeed attempting to control her, I asked Sara if she knew anything about his history.

"When he moved in I didn't. We had been dating for such a short time. However, a few weeks ago I got the guts to contact one of his exes. I asked her to tell me more about their relationship. She said she can't talk to me but for me to get out as quickly as I can."

"It sounds like there is some sort of history here with others as well." I paused, giving her a moment to steady herself amid these disclosures. It seemed she'd been waiting quite a while, consciously or not, to let all of it out. "What happens when you've pushed back? For example, when you told him he needed to move out?"

"He accused me of cheating on him." Sara threw up her hands. "He said I would only ask him to do that if I was no longer into the relationship and that I must be cheating."

"Is this common? That when you make a request, he will accuse you of something?"

"Yes. It gets so confusing. I'll express something I am unhappy with, and by the end of the conversation he has made *me* the problem."

"And what happens if he doesn't get his way?" I asked. "Has there been a time where you've put your foot down?"

"Yes, there has been. He got so angry." Sara covered her face for a moment and took a deep breath. "He started yelling at me and telling me that if I even thought about leaving, he would ruin my life. He said he has information on me that would ruin my life."

"Wow." I let the word sit for a moment before confirming to her, "This sounds like a really scary situation."

As I explored the possibility of characterological abuse with Sara, it became clear she was in a dangerous situation. What was unclear was what my next steps should be. Ivan was in the waiting room and Sara did not feel safe sharing any of these concerns with him. I agreed with her that it wouldn't be safe. He had already set a precedent that he would dominate and control her if she went against his wishes, and I was worried what would happen if he learned all that she had disclosed. While having two days together in some ways made things complicated, it also gave me time to think through our next steps.

"Sara, what would you like to do if you could?" I asked. Given the severity of the threat, I knew continuing the intensive might not be possible. But I also knew that stopping it abruptly could place Sara at further risk.

Sara did not hesitate. "I want him to move out and I want to move on with my life, but I don't think it's safe."

I nodded. "From what you've described here, there are a lot of risk factors, and I want to support you in navigating this in a way that feels safe. One option is for me to avoid rocking the boat by meeting with Ivan for our one-on-one session as planned. Then, during the time I would usually offer feedback to you both, I can share that based on what I've assessed, I'm not sure that you are good candidates for an intensive. To avoid blowback for that, I'm happy to offer a refund for tomorrow. In the meantime, I can get you set up with some referrals to help support you in your next steps. Of course, I'm open to hearing any alternatives you might be considering."

Sara hesitated. "I think that sounds like a good plan, but I don't want him to assume that it's me who made it seem inappropriate."

"I can't guarantee what he will assume," I told her, "But I can tell you that I will not say you led me to believe that it's not appropriate. I will instead use my own observations. Another option is that we continue the day as-is. When we all meet tomorrow morning, I will provide my feedback about not continuing the usual process, then I will meet with each of you individually to discuss next steps."

Sara nodded vigorously. "I like that option better. I like the idea of being able to hear it in the morning and then Ivan being able to talk to you, and me being able to talk to you again. If it can look like it's your decision to not keep going with the couples therapy, like you said, I think I can manage that. I just need to get through this safely."

With our plan in place, I ended my time with Sara and went on to meet with Ivan so I could hear his thoughts on the relationship. Although he did not disclose that he had threatened Sara, he did describe characterologically abusive behavior. It was clear he was not remorseful, that he had in fact convinced himself that his behavior was an appropriate reaction to Sara.

"She's really hard to trust," Ivan told me. "She will seem too distant and it's clear she is doing something she shouldn't be doing."

"Beyond her being distant, what else has Sara done to make her untrustworthy?" I asked.

"I'm not sure, but it's why I keep her on a short leash," Ivan answered. "I asked her to rebuild my trust, and I told her that to do it she needs to be completely transparent with me."

I nodded neutrally. "Interesting. I'm a bit confused. It sounds like Sara hasn't done anything to break your trust, but you're asking her to recover your trust?"

"She hasn't done anything I've *caught* her for." Ivan raised his eyebrows, as if to suggest something significant. "But she did ask me to move out, and I know it's because she's up to something."

I asked Ivan to tell me a little bit about how they ended up living together. He repeated the same story Sara had told me about staying with her due to work being done on his apartment and simply never leaving. In his words, "It made the most sense for me to stay."

"Have you liked living together?" I asked.

"Yes," Ivan said. "I love her and it's the best way for us to build our relationship. If I lived separately, we wouldn't have enough time together."

As we continued to talk, Ivan described to me feelings of jealousy he had over an ex of Sara's, his perspective on his own past relationships ("My ex was such a liar; at one point I even hired someone to follow her"), and his current goals for this relationship ("She just needs to stop lying to me and prove she's committed"). Throughout our conversation, he talked about Sara as if she were a child.

"I hate to say this, but Sara isn't super smart," he intimated. "She's not like you, at least—you've got a degree and run a business. But Sara isn't smart, and she can't make decisions on her own very well." This reinforced my assessment that Ivan held a position of dominance and contempt, both of which are classic markers of coercive control.

"You think Sara isn't smart?" I repeated.

"That's right." He shrugged. "It's nothing against her, but she just needs to grow up."

"If you don't trust Sara and you don't think she's smart, why are you still with her?" I asked Ivan this question because it played into his narcissism, giving him an opportunity to hint at how wonderful he was for wanting to take care of Sara despite her many flaws—while also starting to lay the path toward my feedback session that the relationship did not seem viable.

For the remainder of our conversation, I listened as Ivan continued to discount Sara. From time to time, I pointed out his disdain for her and ventured questions to learn if he saw any benefit in the relationship. He couldn't share one way in which he felt the relationship benefited him, only focusing on the ways in which he thought he benefited Sara.

Once my one-on-one meeting with Ivan was done, I let them both know that I didn't think we had enough time to do more meaningful work in the 45 minutes we had left and that I would prefer to start fresh in the morning. As soon as I went home, I called a colleague to consult on the case. I shared my observations from the oral assessment and asked for their impression. Their conclusion aligned with what I had been thinking: couples therapy wasn't appropriate.

The next day, I shared with Sara and Ivan that based on my assessment, I felt that they weren't going to benefit from couples therapy. I noted that trust and commitment are the bedrock of relational health and that it did not seem like Ivan trusted Sara. I went through the Sound Relationship House (described on page 12) using Ivan's descriptions to point out how they were struggling in each area. This helped to provide a framework for why I didn't think couples therapy would be productive. A framework helps make the recommendation less personal so the couple can hear it as something that is based on professional expertise. It also provides guidance for how to have the conversation with the couple. Most couples therapy modalities have a framework that could have been inserted within this conversation.

I showed deep empathy for both clients regarding how hard this must be to hear. Ivan responded in his typical fashion: "She's hard to be with, but I'm the type of guy who sticks through it."

"I hear that, Ivan," I said, "and it's important that I am honest about what I can and can't do here. I don't think I can help your relationship. I would like to talk with each of you separately about next steps, see how you're feeling about all of this, and give you some resources, if that would be okay. Ivan, maybe you and I can meet first?"

Ivan agreed. During the 90 minutes we spent together, I gave him honest but gentle feedback that to be in a functional relationship, he would need to work on his level of contempt and his insecurities. I did not make this about my personal opinion, but rather cited the research on contempt in relationships, jealousy, and the importance of being able to trust people. I gave Ivan referrals for an individual therapist, and he said he would consider seeing someone. We were even able to discuss him moving out to "benefit his own mental well-being." For Ivan to do anything, he needed it to be about himself and the benefits it brought to him, not doing the right thing by Sara.

I let Ivan know that he could leave and I would meet with Sara next. This provided Sara a feeling of safety, knowing she could talk freely without him listening through the door.

During our conversation, Sara expressed her fears, we created a safety plan, and she explored her options for immediately after the session. She decided she would let Ivan know she was going to go to her parents for a few days while she figured things out and would take the opportunity to go straight there after the session. We also explored how she could build a community of support around her so that she would have an easier time extricating herself from him. She needed people in her corner who understood what was going on and who could act as cheerleaders, sounding boards, and reality checkers. Finally, Sara reached out to an individual therapist while in the meeting with me and scheduled an appointment.

At the end of the session, she left and went straight to her parents, where she ended up staying for six months. I know this because I received an email from her afterward:

> *Dear Liz,*
>
> *I wanted to express my appreciation to you for navigating the situation with Ivan. After leaving, I spent six months at my parents' house. It was a really difficult time. Ivan did move out, saying that I didn't deserve him, but my neighbors told me they found cameras he'd put in the hallway and they said he often walked by the place. It felt like a trap, so I didn't go home. He also somehow got into my email and my Cash App and was tracking where I was going and what I was doing. Every now and then he would send me cryptic messages. Ultimately, I had to get the police involved when I found a GPS tracker on the bottom of my car. Since police involvement he has backed off. It's been so hard, but I am glad I got out when I did.*
>
> *Thank you.*

Between my training in couples therapy, consultation with trusted colleagues, and a handful of experiences like the ones I've described, I have developed a specific set of policies that help my clinical decision-making during an intensive where intimate partner violence is a factor. I encourage you to seek supervision, look toward your licensing and training authorities, and consider your specific modality and how it responds to IPV. My policies include the following:

- As Debbie and Kyree's case demonstrated, I do work with couples who have experienced situational violence, provided they take responsibility, express remorse, and are committed to creating a safety plan together. While there are many contributing factors, I often find these situations involve skill deficits and emotional dysregulation that intensive therapy can address.

- If characterological violence is apparent prior to the intensive session, I will not meet with the couple for the intensive couples therapy session. I will refer both to individual therapy.

- If characterological violence becomes apparent during the session, I use individual time with the person experiencing abuse to clearly name the behaviors, express concern, and explore safety options and appropriate referrals. I remain transparent and direct about safety concerns and avoid minimizing or deferring acknowledgment of abuse. I will not reinforce the goal of preserving the relationship at the expense of the abused partner's safety and well-being. However, depending on the situation, I will find a way to support both parties toward other goals that they set for themselves while helping the person being abused create a safety plan.

While each therapist and modality may approach IPV differently, it is essential that all clinicians prioritize client safety, remain aligned with legal and ethical standards, and seek supervision and consultation in complex cases.

Policies Regarding Substance Use

When I first started my practice, I wasn't sure what my role should be with couples who were struggling with substances. Much like the issue of intimate partner violence, substance abuse has historically been a topic where couples therapists respond with a hard line in the sand: "We don't see couples who are actively using substances." But what does this mean exactly? Clearly, therapists meet with many couples who drink wine here and there. But what about when nightly glasses of wine are consistently associated with conflict, emotional volatility, or impaired functioning? At what point does this rise to a level that warrants clinical attention? Do we turn those couples away?

Luckily, toward the beginning of my work with couples, I began collaborating with my colleague Ariel Stern, a brilliant therapist who is extensively trained not only as a couples therapist but also as a substance use/addiction counselor. Her opinions on the matter have helped me create my own policies for handling substance use in couples.

While Ariel won't see a couple if either partner is under the influence or displaying signs of intoxication, she does work with couples grappling with problematic substance use as part of the treatment plan. "Unless someone is doing something that is of imminent risk to themselves or others, I work with the couple to bring substance use into the room and to explore goals related to improving the negative impact," Ariel shared with me. "This might be harm reduction or containment or getting into treatment."

She points out that when therapists have policies of not working with people who are struggling with challenging issues, clients tend to be dishonest about what's happening in their lives. This, obviously, prevents real change from occurring in the therapy room. Her goal is to help the couple create guidelines that improve their relationship, including boundaries and therapeutic support, and when they struggle to maintain those boundaries, to be there and to use that struggle as a clinical data point.

I've worked with many couples who came to an intensive session due to chronic fighting or disconnection, only to find that alcohol was a major source of it. For example, Abby and Carmen shared during their consultation call that they wanted to work on their relationship because they weren't having sex anymore, were arguing frequently, and had started sleeping in different rooms. When I explored this with them more during the initial day of the intensive, it became clear that there were two major causes of their relational dysfunction.

Abby expressed frustration about Carmen's focus on work. "She never comes home on time and when she does, I am still completely alone to do everything for the house and the kids—she just hops back into her email on her phone. She's completely obsessed with work."

Carmen shared that her theory of the breakdown in their relationship was that Abby often drank a bottle or more of wine a night. "When she drinks, she becomes someone I don't like. She cries and argues and says awful things to me. Then she just never comes up to bed. She will stay in the basement all night drinking and texting me mean things." Carmen shared that Abby's drinking had escalated beyond casual use. It was affecting her safety and their emotional connection.

Over the next two days, we spent time talking about Carmen's hyperfocus on work and Abby's drinking. It became clear that both Carmen's work and Abby's drinking were being utilized as a form of avoidance for any intimacy in the relationship. In order to avoid the discomfort that awaited Carmen at home, she would find more and more to do at work. She admitted that she frequently took longer to leave the office than she needed to, hopeful it would mean Abby had already fallen asleep by the time she got home.

Abby shared that several members of her family struggle with substance use. She would watch her parents drink to excess when she was a child, yet she still saw them as responsible and successful. She described herself in the same light—"I know I drink a lot, but I am definitely what you would call a functioning alcoholic."

I expressed curiosity about what Abby believed were the underlying triggers for her drinking.

"Loneliness," she answered. "Whenever I feel lonely, I just want to drink. If I notice Carmen is at the office later than usual, I think, *Why not?* and I have a drink. But even if Carmen is home, I feel so much distance and tension that I drink to deal with that too."

Carmen was able to take accountability for the ways in which her distance impacted Abby. She expressed empathy for Abby's loneliness and remorse for being so avoidant in the relationship. "Work isn't more important than you. I need to be present for you," Carmen affirmed.

At the same time, Abby was able to admit that her drinking, while triggered by loneliness, was part of a bigger problem for her. Only a few weeks before, she had fallen down the steps and sprained her ankle due to inebriation. She acknowledged that not only was alcohol causing issues in their relationship, but it was an actual health risk for her.

During the intensive, we spent time processing and repairing past hurtful events between them. I taught them skills like speaking and listening with empathy and love, and we worked on exploring healthy boundaries with each other, the outside world, and oneself. Lastly, we explored their individual needs for counseling.

Although they both entered therapy guarded about the impact of their own actions on their partner and the work was challenging, by the end of the weekend, Carmen and Abby had agreed on a number of things to reduce harm and begin a path of well-being. First, they decided they would remove alcohol from the home and that Carmen would stop drinking alongside Abby. Although Carmen was not struggling with alcohol, we discussed the importance of creating security in the relationship by remembering "your problem is my problem," and Carmen agreed to not drink for the time being. They also promised each other that Abby would be given all the support she needs to seek out individual care with a therapist who specializes in substance use and trauma. Abby also agreed to begin attending AA sessions.

As with IPV, your clinical policy regarding substances should be rooted in your scope of practice, supervision, and ongoing assessment of safety and therapeutic benefit. When discussing substance use, I follow *DSM-5* criteria and rely on a functional understanding of how the behavior impacts safety, health, and relational dynamics rather than labels alone. While I am not providing addiction treatment in the intensive setting, I work with couples impacted by substance use as long as the session is safe and individual support is also being pursued.

Policies Regarding Secrets

As a couples therapist, your client is the relationship as a whole, not either partner individually. My strong conviction is that you cannot practice effective couples therapy if it's possible that you'd hold a secret for one partner that is psychologically or physically harmful toward the other partner. By doing that, you become an untrustworthy source; should the client ever find out that you held a secret from them, it could blemish the entire process of couples therapy that occurred before their discovery. In my view, it is a professional betrayal.

I have one caveat with this: If revealing the client's secret would cause or could cause serious harm to that client, I won't share it with their partner. However, if the client cannot share and it would cause their partner to experience a sense of betrayal should they find out that I know, then I will not continue with couples therapy. I will instead refer them to individual therapy.

I inform couples of my limited secrets policy as early as possible. As a mandated reporter, I also remind them that there are specific legal limits to confidentiality that apply in all therapeutic work, such as imminent risk of harm or disclosures of abuse. I include this information in the informed consent portion of the intake paperwork and then discuss it again during one-on-one sessions. I recommend discussing it verbally and giving couples a chance to ask questions, ensuring true informed consent is achieved.

Nevertheless, people still often tell me secrets and ask me to keep them. I find that this is most often a self-protective stance—they are afraid of the conflict that sharing the secret might bring up.

Common secrets include:

- "I've been thinking about divorce more than my partner knows."

- "I've had an affair" or "My affair isn't completely over."

- "I am in debt, and they don't know it yet."

- "I have a medical illness that I am too afraid to tell them about. I don't want them to be upset."

When someone shares a secret with me, I am incredibly gentle in reminding them of the policy. I ask them if they'd be willing to share the information with their partner with my help. Most people say yes. In reality, they have wanted to share the information but have been afraid of how it would impact themselves, their partner, and their relationship.

If they agree, we use the rest of our one-on-one to prepare for sharing this information. If I haven't yet met with the other partner for one-on-one time, I might bring them back and have their partner talk to them. With some secrets, it would be both unproductive and potentially harmful to meet with the unknowing partner as if I wasn't aware of the secret. For example, I don't want to know that one partner has already planned to get a divorce and then have a one-on-one session with the other partner who is telling me how much hope they have for the relationship. It would be a betrayal if they learned they shared their hopes with me only to find out I knew the entire time there was no hope at all.

Sharron and Jaden were a couple that had been married for a few years. They attended intensive couples therapy at Sharron's urging, hoping to reconnect, but it soon became clear that Jaden had other plans. During my one-on-one with Jaden, he revealed a secret: He had already started the divorce process.

"You've made up your mind?" I asked him.

"Yes, I've made up my mind," Jaden confirmed. "For over a year I haven't had my heart in it. Sharron is so sensitive that she can't hear that from me. I try to tell her how I feel but she breaks down."

"It must be really hard to feel that way," I said. "A part of you is ready to make the decision and to move on, and a part of you feels an obligation to protect her."

Jaden sighed deeply. "Exactly. I am so torn. It's horrible. But I just can't tell her."

"I know you signed the secrets policy and before you came in here with me, we talked about it as a group," I reminded him, keeping my voice as compassionate as possible. "I can't hold this secret for you indefinitely." Seeing the alarm on his face, I added, "I'm not going to just run out to the waiting room and blurt it out to Sharron. But for us to continue working together, transparency is really important. How would you feel about sharing with her the truth?"

Jaden shook his head. "She'll have a breakdown. I can't do it. She won't listen, and by the end I will somehow be convinced to stay." I stayed attuned to Jaden's distress, while also being mindful of how these descriptions might reflect a long-standing dynamic in their relationship.

"I hear you," I assured him. "I know that you've experienced her as really struggling to hear the truth in the past, and I hear you're worried that you won't be able to stick to your decision in front of her. You're worried the cycle will continue."

"Yes," Jaden said. "If I tell her that I've made my decision, she'll be so upset that I'll try to soothe her and end up changing my mind. But I don't want to change my mind."

"Play it out for me," I suggested. "If you don't tell her today, then what happens next?"

"I have no idea," Jaden mumbled. "Nothing will change, I guess."

"I think you'll end up in the same cycle," I told him gently. "How could I support you in sharing with her?"

Jaden thought for several minutes. "I think I'd like to be able to share this with her and then, if possible, I'd like to leave the room and come back a little later if it's appropriate to talk about it or ask any questions. But I don't want to get stuck in the cycle."

I repeated it back to him: "You would like to share with her, but if you start to feel pulled to take care of her, you'd like to trust she would be okay with me here and that you could take some space to not go back into your cycle?"

"Exactly," Jaden confirmed. "I think I just need to know someone else can support her when she's upset."

I let Jaden know that I could do that. Instead of calling Sharron in for her individual session, I asked her to come back and join Jaden and me. I told her that Jaden had something to share with her, then gave Jaden the floor.

Jaden let her know he had made his decision and that divorce was inevitable. He expressed that he understood she would feel surprised and sad. No sooner had he finished speaking than Sharron, devastated, began to scream at him. "I hate you! I hate you! How could you do this to me?!"

"Jaden, I'm going to ask you to give Sharron and me some space for a little bit," I said. Jaden left the room and I spent a few hours with Sharron processing her feelings. She was heartbroken, but by the end of our conversation she was ready to talk with Jaden again. When he came back into the room for our final hour in the day, Sharron let him know that she was hurt and shocked and did not want the relationship to end, but that she could respect it. She even thanked him for his honesty.

During the second day of our intensive, the couple spent a few hours processing the relationship and coming up with next steps. I spent the final hours with Sharron as she continued to explore her feelings and come up with a plan for herself.

If I had let Jaden maintain his secret, the therapy would have been a farce. We would have worked on goals that Jaden wasn't in agreement with, only for Sharron to be surprised later. Instead, we put the truth on the table, which allowed me to support the couple in facing the truth and planning around it.

COUPLES THERAPIST WORKSHEET

Reflection Sheet for Clinical Policies

Use this worksheet to brainstorm your own clinical policies regarding suicidality, intimate partner violence, substance use, and secrets. The prompts will help you think through how you will handle challenging cases that present these topics.

Suicidality

What is it like for me as a clinician when a client presents with suicidal thoughts or ideation?
_____
_____
_____

What is my clinical framework for managing suicidality in the couples therapy context?
_____
_____
_____

Intimate Partner Violence

What is it like for me as a clinician when a client shares that there has been intimate partner violence?
_____
_____
_____

What is my clinical framework for managing intimate partner violence in the couples therapy context?
_____
_____
_____

What are the red flags that would signal a need for referral instead of continuation?

___

Secrets

As a clinician, what is it like for me to be told a secret?

___

What is my clinical framework for managing secrets in the couples therapy context?

___

How will I document and follow up on disclosures made during an intensive?

___

Substance Use

What is it like for me as a clinician to learn about a client's substance misuse or addiction?

___

What is my clinical framework for addressing and navigating the topic of substance use in the couples therapy context?

___

Administrative Policies

Administrative policies help couples know what to expect from their work with you. They include anything outside of your clinical work, such as policies regarding fees and insurance, scheduling (times, days, cancellations, etc.), paperwork, how you deal with an unhappy client, and the scope of your practice.

Before an intensive even begins, it is important to communicate administrative expectations clearly so there is no confusion that could later negatively impact the clinical work. When you do not set clear expectations, it can lead to administrative headaches and even problems within the clinical work. (It's hard for a client to trust a clinician if they feel they've been misled with billing, for example.)

Setting Expectations

Prior to meeting with a couple for an intensive, you've likely offered them an overview of what the session will look like and what you can and cannot do for them. You should include these expectations on your website, and I also encourage you to include them in your paperwork. This ensures that everyone is on the same page and all pertinent information is in the same place.

The following callout shows an example of how to set expectations with your intensive couples therapy clients. You can modify it to suit your own practice.

SAMPLE

Description of Couples Weekend Intensives

Couples weekend intensives are for any type of couple who wants to work on their relationship without having to "start and stop." Couples who join us for an intensive tend to fall into one or more of these categories:

- Have complicated schedules that make it difficult to schedule weekly therapy
- Are in the midst of a crisis—for example, they are experiencing high conflict or recently suffered a significant loss or trauma
- Have a big decision that needs to be made and don't have months to figure it out
- Have neglected their relationship for many years and realize they need to jump-start it in a big way
- Are considering a divorce and would like to give enough time to really think it through

How Intensives Work

Couples weekend intensives are a focused, condensed form of couples counseling that occur over a period of two to three consecutive days, usually a weekend, using the Gottman Method [*or insert your modality*].

Couples weekend intensives allow couples to dive deeply into their issues without the frustration of the "start and stop" feeling of weekly sessions.

In general, we will meet for six hours each day, with breaks built in for lunch, reflection, and individualized activities.

Where Are Intensives Held?

I offer intensives in person and online. My in-person intensives are located at [*insert your practice address*]. Online intensives are done via a secure platform.

Couples therapists have found that in-person intensives are the *most* impactful, but we recognize that there are many reasons online might make more sense for you and your relationship and believe they also make a big difference in the relationship.

When Do Intensives Take Place?

Intensive couples therapy tends to be scheduled over a weekend. However, I am also able to accommodate couples who prefer to meet during the week.

Who Are You?

[*Introduce yourself, including your licensure, training, and areas of specialization within couples therapy.*]

Preparation for the Intensive Session

- **Discuss with your partner:** Prior to scheduling an intensive, discuss with your partner your desire to partake in intensive couples therapy. Talk about the pros and cons of doing an intensive together and your goals.
- **Schedule:** Once you've decided together that you're interested, schedule a consultation by emailing/calling [*insert contact information*]. We will talk for about 15 minutes to discuss your reasons for wanting to attend couples therapy and then, if it feels like a good fit, we can schedule the intensive sessions.
- **Directions:** You'll receive directions for getting to my office as well as any other instructions for our appointment.
- **Payment:** In order to hold the appointment, I will take a deposit of [*insert amount*]. This deposit must be paid prior to holding the appointment and will be applied to the total cost of your session. Your payment in full will be taken 24 hours prior to your session. The rate for the intensive is [*insert your rate*].
- **Assessment:** Prior to your intensive session, you will complete a thorough written assessment. This assessment is designed to provide me with insight into your relationship and also into each person individually. During the first day of the intensive, you will undergo a continuation of the assessment, which includes meeting as a group and meeting individually with me. This assessment is an irreplaceable tool for providing both you and me as your therapist essential insight into your strengths as well as areas of greatest need, allowing me to completely tailor the intensive therapy to your specific needs and goals.

The Intensive Process

- **Information gathering:** During the first day of the intensive, I will spend time with you as a couple and individually to better understand what you're experiencing, who you are, and your individual perspectives. This will help me guide you during our second day toward appropriate interventions that can help you to change the cycle you're currently in.

- **Feedback:** After completing the assessment, you will receive the results and feedback for your relationship during the first day. My feedback will be based on research-backed science related to healthy relationships. You will learn about your strengths and the areas in which you struggle as a couple. I will provide you with information about how these different areas are impacting your relationship and what can be done to address it. During this feedback time, you will also be learning about what makes relationships work and how to utilize the science of relationships to improve your own.

- **Intervention:** Once you've completed the assessment process and received feedback, the rest of your weekend will include intervention exercises. Intensive sessions are highly interactive. I will guide you through important conversations and teach you important skills that you can do at home when you have completed therapy. I will also offer interventions related to your specific issues—for example, if you are struggling with betrayal, you might spend the weekend learning how to restore trust.

- **After the intensive:** At the end of the intensive, we will discuss my recommendations for next steps. You might find that the intensive was sufficient for meeting your goals and not need or desire further couples therapy. You might also decide another intensive day is needed. Or you may want to continue weekly couples therapy with another therapist, in which case I will be happy to provide them with an overview of our work together. The aftercare plan is different for every client.

Risks and Benefits of Intensive Couples Therapy

Benefits

- Couples who do intensive sessions have more time to process their issues and learn new skills without the frequent stops and starts of traditional weekly couples therapy.
- Because it is designed to be "intense," you have the opportunity to explore issues more quickly than you might otherwise. It is designed to expedite progress.
- Couples have more time to go through a thorough assessment of their relationship. There is also more opportunity to practice emotional regulation, practice skill building, and create a strong relationship with your therapist.
- Many clients leave intensives feeling more equipped, better understood, and hopeful for their future. They also often leave feeling much more clear about their next steps and more decisive.

Risks

No form of therapy comes with a guarantee for improvement. There are some possible risks:

- Intensive therapy is not a "magic fix." Depending on the type of issue, the severity, and the length of time the issue has occurred, a couple may or may not need continued therapy following the appointment.
- Based on the assessment and the state of the relationship, you might hear a recommendation that is upsetting, disappointing, or frustrating.
- You might learn things about your relationship you did not know and this could be surprising.
- It is designed to be an intensive form of therapy. Feelings may get intense or overwhelming.

BILLING POLICIES

It's important to remember that intensive therapy takes a lot of work and time. To ensure that you are compensated for that time, you will want to think through billing policies that make your fees clear; allow you to collect the fees in a timely manner; specify what you will do in the case of a chargeback, declined card, or bounced check; and state how you will respond to requests to accept insurance for intensive couples therapy sessions.

My current policy is to bill couples in advance and require payment by credit card. First, I charge a $500.00 deposit to hold the two dates for the intensive. This is a nonrefundable deposit that is applied to the total cost of the intensive. Then, 24 hours prior to the intensive, I charge the remaining balance. At that point, the full amount is nonrefundable regardless of whether the couple attends the intensive. (It's worth noting that I have never had an experience where the couple does not attend.)

Other therapists might choose to bill differently, such as charging the entire amount up front to hold the dates, waiving a deposit, or setting up payment plans.

YOUR FEES

Before meeting with a couple, you will want to make sure your fees are clear. Specifying your fees on your website will ensure that couples know the investment up front. You should also discuss your fee during the consult call and then again in your confirmation email. Make sure to include your fee in any signed paperwork.

Fees for intensives are usually billed as a package amount. This package considers the amount of time you will spend doing the therapy, the amount of time you will spend preparing for the session (reading their assessment outcomes, etc.), and, sometimes, a surcharge for the time spent on a weekend, in the evenings, or otherwise outside of your usual client hours. This also might include a charge related to time that would usually be spent meeting with weekly clients if the intensive should need to be scheduled during that time.

When therapists first begin offering intensive couples therapy, they often ask what their fee should be. While much of this might depend on your region, I suggest that you consider pricing your first few intensives lower than you otherwise would, based on your weekly therapy hourly rate.

For example, let's say you usually charge $120.00 for a 50-minute session, and you determine that an intensive weekend session will involve six hours of therapy work per day plus two hours of prep work for the weekend, for a total of 14 hours. While you would normally charge $1,680.00 for 14 hours, you might consider charging only $1,440.00 (giving the clients two "free" hours) the first two or three times you conduct an intensive weekend.

As you continue to build your skills as an intensive therapist, you will raise your fee to be commensurate with your skill and training level.

The following are some questions to consider when deciding your fee:

- **Does it make sense to simply multiply my hourly rate by the number of hours I will spend with the couple?** The answer to this question depends on your personal situation. For some practitioners, their usual hourly rate feels very worthwhile when doing an intensive. For others, it does not feel worthwhile, especially if they are working extra hours or rescheduling other clients to accommodate the intensive.

- **Am I moving clients I would usually see during this time?** Some therapists do intensives exclusively during times when they don't otherwise see clients, such as weekends. However, there may be times when you choose to schedule an intensive on a day when you would usually meet with other clients. Since you won't be able to schedule your weekly clients on that day, that means losing those sessions' income for the week. Your intensive session fee should take that loss of income into consideration.

- **What is the value of the personal time I'm forgoing to instead meet with a couple over two to three days?** When it comes to charging for our services, some things can be hard to measure. When you're setting your fee (at least once you've started doing intensives more regularly), you will want to make sure that the change to your work schedule does not lead to neglecting your personal activities or time with family and friends—this will only foster resentment and burnout, which (needless to say) does not make for a good therapeutic environment. Choose a fee that leaves you feeling good about the work you're doing and not as if it's a chore.

- **Should I factor in the costs of materials like assessments, booklets, or anything else I provide to couples during their time with me?** I recommend that your intensives be "all inclusive," meaning that your fee includes the cost of your time, any assessments the clients might take, any materials you provide for them, and so on. This makes the financial aspect more clear to the couple and reduces the need to send more invoices.

- **Are there any other financial costs for me to offer intensives?** Consider whether intensives will require any additional expenditures compared to your usual therapy practice. For example, will you need to hire a babysitter for your children during weekend intensives or rent special office space to accommodate a couple for a full day of work?

- **How much are other intensive couples therapists at my skill level charging?** Take time to research other therapists who offer intensive couples therapy sessions. Specifically, compare rates among other therapists in your geographic area. Since rates vary according to region, it's important to align with what clients in your location are seeing and expecting, at least at first. With practice and skill, or when you find yourself in high demand, you might choose to raise your rates above the local standard.

- **Will I be a competent and skillful therapist given the amount I am charging?** Some therapists feel anxious and don't perform as well if they think they are overcharging. If this is your experience, I recommend slowly raising your fee over time as you gain confidence. On the other hand, some therapists don't perform as well when they undercharge; they might feel distracted, frustrated, or resentful. Knowing yourself when it comes to performance and money is important. Ultimately, your goal is for the couple to have a very good experience with you—not only for their benefit, but also because it wins you word-of-mouth referrals. Keep in mind that a consistently good performance will make you money over time, even if you charge less at first.

COUPLES THERAPIST WORKSHEET

Setting Fees

Use this worksheet to determine your fee for intensive couples therapy sessions.

Calculation

Number of hours in session per day:		_____
Number of days in session:	×	_____
Number of hours in session:	=	_____
Number of hours of prep time:	+	_____
Total number of hours:	=	_____
Current hourly rate:	×	_____
Total cost of time:	=	_____
Cost of materials:	+	_____
Intensive fee:	=	_____

Reflection Questions

When will I be offering intensives? Do these times indicate that I should add a surcharge for time spent away from family, friends, or activities that are important to me? Will I need to make up lost income from not being able to see other clients during these times?

_____

_____

_____

_____

Are there other financial costs to offering intensives that I have not accounted for yet? For example, will I need to hire a babysitter for my children or rent special office space?

_____
_____
_____
_____

What are other therapists in my geographic area and at my skill level charging for intensive couples therapy sessions?

_____
_____
_____
_____

How does money impact my performance? If I am new to something, do I tend to feel anxious if I charge a high rate? If so, what changes about my ability to provide effective couples therapy? If I charge too little, do I tend to feel resentful or frustrated? How does this affect my performance?

_____
_____
_____
_____

Final Totals

After considering the reflection questions and adjusting my initial calculation as needed, my intensive rate is: _____.

For my first few intensives, I will discount my rate by _____, for a starting rate of _____.

Collecting Payment

I encourage therapists to collect a deposit for their intensives and to collect payment in full 24 hours prior to the appointment. This is because we are allocating large portions of our calendar, often weekends, to intensive couples therapy clients. While last-minute cancellations are rare, they can cause scheduling and financial challenges.

THE DEPOSIT

During intake, let the couple know that you take a nonrefundable deposit to hold the date for the intensive, and that the deposit will be applied to their total. The easiest way to charge for this deposit is to include an invoice for it in their intake paperwork.

PAYMENT IN FULL

Collecting payment in full 24 hours prior to the appointment ensures that there are no surprises with declined credit cards following an intensive weekend. It also allows the couple to get the money matters out of the way so that they can focus on the therapy itself.

PAYMENT PLANS

Some therapists prefer to offer payment plans for their intensive couples therapy sessions. This is a way of making intensive couples therapy accessible to more people. However, because such a large amount of time in your schedule is allocated to the session, I encourage you to get as close as possible to collection in full prior to the session. This means that the client should start paying down the payment plan prior to their meeting rather than after.

PAYMENT POLICIES

Being clear is being kind—it reduces possible confusion and misunderstandings down the road. Moreover, in light of the (admittedly rare) possibility of clients being upset with the outcome of their intensive, it's important to make it clear that intensive couples therapy is a professional service with no guaranteed outcome and that payment is due regardless of outcome.

Insurance

When scheduling intensives, some clients will ask about utilizing their insurance. Right now, there is no Current Procedural Terminology (CPT) code for intensive couples therapy sessions and the cost is often higher than the "allowed amount" designated by insurance. Even if clients have out-of-network benefits, it is incredibly rare that anything would be covered. Be clear about all of this with your clients from the outset in order to avoid confusion later.

> **SAMPLE**
>
> ## Confirmation Email
>
> Dear [client names],
>
> Thank you for scheduling an intensive couples therapy session with me. I am honored to have the opportunity to work with you both. I have confirmed your appointment for [date] at [time] until [time] and [date] at [time] until [time].
>
> In order to hold the appointment, I take a nonrefundable deposit of $500.00. This amount is applied toward the total cost of the session. Payment in full is collected 24 hours prior to the session. The rate of the intensive is [rate].
>
> I sent you my office paperwork, which includes a form to complete, an assessment, and my policies, in particular intensive couples therapy policies. Please complete the assessments no sooner than one week prior and no later than 48 hours prior. This gives me enough time to review the information.
>
> As we get closer to our date, I will reach out to you with more information. Until then, please don't hesitate to let me know if you have any questions.
>
> Warmly,
> [Your name]

Cancellation Policies

Because intensives are high-commitment endeavors, cancellations are rare. By the time the couple makes an appointment, they have done research, talked to you, and, in all likelihood, prepared to invest in the session, mentally as well as financially.

Nevertheless, there are times when people will cancel or ask to reschedule their intensive sessions. The most common reason, in my experience, is because they've decided they no longer want to work on their relationship. Other reasons include lack of babysitting options for their children, changes in work schedules, unpredicted financial setbacks, and illness. While these are all understandable reasons, there is a real impact on the clinician when an intensive is canceled. The effects can include loss of income from clients you would have already seen, incurred costs if you already paid for the couple to take certain assessments, and changes to your plans (for example, you might have hired a babysitter or told someone you couldn't attend an event).

For this reason, it is important to establish your cancellation policies before you begin taking clients. Because I take a deposit, I allow couples to cancel up to 48 hours prior to the session and reschedule (if I have availability). However, they do not receive the deposit back. Since I do intensives outside of my regular therapy hours, a cancellation does not mean a loss of regular weekly income for me; as a result, I can be more flexible with these situations and not charge the entire fee. For me, retaining the $500 deposit after a cancellation feels fair and right—it covers any costs I have already incurred (paying for the Gottman Assessment, purchasing materials, etc.) and ensures that the clients are serious when booking the appointment.

With that being said, I do charge the entire fee of the intensive weekend if the clients cancel 24 hours or less before the session. Since I run the payment the morning before the intensive, the fee has already been paid at this point. Moreover, I have already prepared for the session by reading their paperwork, reviewing their assessment results, coming up with an agenda for the day, and getting materials ready, as well as planning for my own childcare, getting office space reserved, and so on. Professionally and personally, I have already relied on that income for the week. I am quite busy with intensives, and if people cancel with 24 hours' or less notice I am not able to fill their spot with people from the waitlist. For all of these reasons, I stand firm on this policy with couples.

In the last decade of offering intensive sessions, I have only had to enforce this policy once, when a partner decided at the last minute that they no longer wanted to come to the session. There was one other instance of a couple canceling within the 24-hour period; however, in that case it was clear they were canceling out of necessity, as they'd had to take their child to the emergency room the evening before the session. While I had already charged the full fee and did not reimburse it, I offered to apply that payment toward any of my open dates in the future. Luckily, they were able to reschedule their session for several weeks later.

Having clear cancellation policies written in your paperwork ensures that standards and expectations are clear, but it doesn't prevent you from offering flexibility when the situation warrants.

COUPLES THERAPIST WORKSHEET

Cancellation Policy

Utilize your answers to the following questions to write your cancellation policy in your intensive agreement paperwork.

Will I take a deposit? **Yes / No**

For how much? _____

Is it nonrefundable? **Yes / No**

If refundable, when does the refund period end? _____

When will I charge for the full amount? _____

Is any of that refundable after it is charged? _____

If so, when does the refund period end? _____

How many days in advance should an intensive be canceled? _____

Is there a tiered cancellation policy? (For example, do they receive a full refund 20 days in advance but a partial refund 10 days in advance?)

_____
_____
_____

Will I allow them to reschedule for no additional fee? Do I want to include this in my paperwork or decide on a case-by-case basis?

_____
_____
_____

Unhappy Client Policies

From time to time, you might have a client who is unhappy with their experience in an intensive session. This most often occurs with clients who do not get their desired outcome. Unhappy clients are rare, but they are possible due to the large sums people are spending on intensive sessions. In my entire practice of thirty-plus clinicians who have offered intensives for over a decade, we have only experienced four complaints with requests for refunds. All four were related to the couple breaking up and one partner blaming the intensive for the outcome.

Maintaining a no-refunds policy is a way for therapists to feel confident in giving honest feedback during sessions. In couples therapy, we sometimes need to provide observations or insights that make a client uncomfortable, at least at first. When there is the possibility a client could ask for a refund, the clinician may worry about potentially upsetting the client with their feedback. Holding back in this way ultimately hurts the clients, who are trusting the therapist to provide vital insights that can help them solve issues in their relationship.

It is certainly a possibility that couples will break up or learn something upsetting during or after the intensive sessions. In the wake of such events, it's not uncommon (and perhaps even understandable) for one or both partners to point the finger at the intensive session, to say that it "didn't work" or that it raised new issues rather than solving the one they came in for.

Intensives are not a magic wand or cure-all for a relationship. No therapist can guarantee a particular outcome; rather, our commitment is to offer an objective assessment and to use all available tools to support the couple. To make good on that, therapists need freedom to make our observations frankly, without fear of risking our income.

In short, couples therapy is a professional service, not a product to be returned. My practice is clear about this up front, including our no-refunds policy in our intake paperwork. (You can see it in the sample intensive agreement provided on page 57).

Paperwork Completion Policies

Your paperwork completion policies lay out your expectations for clients to complete intake paperwork and assessments prior to the session. To uphold ethical and legal standards, I require that all informed consent and confidentiality documents be signed at least one week prior to the intensive. This ensures clients are aware of their rights and responsibilities and allows time for questions. I send these documents digitally. I require that clients complete their assessments no earlier than a week before their session and no later than two days before. This ensures the relationship data is current while also giving me enough time to review the information.

The following callout shows an example of an intensive agreement. You'll notice that it includes many of the same points as the description provided earlier—this is by design. Please use it as a jumping-off point, making any changes that relate to the work you are doing in your own practice.

SAMPLE

Intensive Couples Therapy Agreement

Intensive therapy is designed for couples who do not want to or cannot do regular weekly therapy or who are struggling with an issue that requires extra time and consideration. Intensive therapy is designed to support couples through exploring their issues at a deeper level, having conversations, and developing tools for improving their relationship.

What to Expect

Prior to your intensive, you will be asked to complete the [*insert title of written client assessment(s) you will use*]. Most likely this will be sent to you within seven days of coming into your appointment so that you can complete it and give enough time for your therapist to read it.

On the first day of the session, you will be taken through:

- A couples assessment
- Individual assessments
- Feedback about your relationship

This is the general outline of the first day. However, if an issue arises that calls for another clinical response, the first day's agenda might differ depending on your therapist's professional opinion.

On the second day, your therapist will generally utilize the assessment from the previous day to guide you through structured conversations and skill-building exercises. However, it is possible this could look different depending on what needs to be tailored to you and your partner.

If you schedule a third day, your therapist will utilize their professional opinion to design a day best suited to your needs.

Intensives are not a form of ongoing therapy. In most cases, at the end of your intensive, your therapist will provide you with recommendations for moving forward. Sometimes they might suggest more therapy, either with the therapist themselves or a referral. The therapist may also offer individual referrals based on clinical assessment.

Benefits

- Couples who do intensive sessions have more time to process their issues and learn new skills without the frequent stops and starts of traditional weekly couples therapy.

- Because it is designed to be "intense," you have the opportunity to explore issues more quickly than you might otherwise. It is designed to expedite progress.

- Couples have more time to go through a thorough assessment of their relationship. There is also more opportunity to practice emotional regulation, practice skill building, and create a strong relationship with your therapist.

- Many clients leave intensives feeling more equipped, better understood, and hopeful for their future. They also often leave feeling much more clear about their next steps and more decisive.

Risks

No form of therapy comes with a guarantee for improvement. There are some possible risks:

- Intensive therapy is not a "magic fix." Depending on the type of issue, the severity, and the length of time the issue has occurred, a couple may or may not need continued therapy following the appointment.
- Based on the assessment and the state of the relationship, you might hear a recommendation that is upsetting, disappointing, or frustrating.
- You might learn things about your relationship you did not know and this could be surprising.
- It is designed to be an intensive form of therapy. Feelings may get intense or overwhelming.

Fees

Prior to your intensive, you will be told the rate for the entire intensive. A $500 nonrefundable deposit is required to hold the spot. If you cancel, that money cannot be refunded.

Twenty-four hours prior to the intensive, you will be charged the remainder of the fee. There are no refunds for intensives, as you are paying for a professional service and opinion.

Insurance does not cover intensives, as insurance companies do not find them to be medically required. We do not work directly with insurance companies and would only be able to provide you with your receipt from the intensive weekend.

We understand the above information and agree.

Names: _____   _____

Signatures: _____   _____

Marketing

Once you have your policies firmly established, the next step is finding clients who want to book intensive sessions with you. If you already have a busy couples therapy practice, this might be as simple as adding information on this new offering to your website. You can also begin to suggest the option of intensive sessions to prospective clients who come to you with interest in weekly couples therapy sessions.

Before launching any marketing efforts, consider how you will position yourself as an expert who specializes not only in couples therapy but also intensive couples therapy. In a personal communication with me, Michael Fulwiler, the former chief marketing officer of the Gottman Institute, who has over a decade of professional marketing experience in mental health, suggested that therapists consider a few things to help communicate their expertise:

- **Consider your qualifications.** Reflect on why couples should trust you with this major investment and consider how you can communicate that.
- **Gather testimonials from other therapists.** While ethics preclude you from requesting testimonials from clients, you can ask colleagues for endorsements. I recommend starting with therapists who have referred clients to you in the past for couples therapy or relationship-focused work.

- **Be clear with prospective clients about the benefits of intensive couples therapy.** Explain the unique advantages of an intensive format compared to weekly sessions, and highlight the particular relationship issues or situations that this format can be most helpful for.
- **Brainstorm areas of thought leadership to which you can contribute.** This might include writing for blogs, being a guest on podcasts, sending newsletters, hosting webinars, and speaking at conferences. These efforts can propel you into a position where you are seen as a leader in the specific field.
- **Network with other therapists.** When other professionals think that you are the leader for a specific service, their clients will trust you, too.

Communicating Your Expertise

Many therapists do a disservice to themselves by not clearly expressing who they can help and why they can help them. Take time to reflect on your own expertise and how it positions you as someone clients can trust with such a major investment of time, finances, and emotion. For example, if you are a couples therapist who also has experience with perinatal mental health, you will want to lean into how you can support couples who are going through the transition of parenthood, who have experienced the grief of pregnancy loss, and who are struggling with infertility.

You can communicate your expertise on your website and also through blogs, email, webinars, networking, and anywhere else you can publicly share information about relationship health while also talking about the specific services you offer. We will explore each of these areas in more detail in the following paragraphs.

COUPLES THERAPIST WORKSHEET

Communicating Your Expertise

Every couples therapist is different. Use this worksheet to gain clarity on the specific gifts you bring into the therapy room. Circle your unique strengths when working with couples:

- Direct
- Empathic
- Gentle
- Honest
- Solution oriented
- Process oriented
- A synthesizer
- A teacher
- Compassionate
- Expects accountability
- Fair
- Experienced
- Personal experience
- Curious
- Problem solver
- Good listener
- Structured
- Multicultural competence
- Directive
- Warm
- Funny
- Sensitive
- Serious
- Calm
- Hopeful
- Realistic
- Active
- Engaging
- Other: _____

List the trainings you have taken during your career.

_____
_____
_____
_____
_____

Looking at your trainings, do you see any common themes of expertise? Write those themes here. Be as specific as possible.

_____
_____
_____
_____
_____

Think about the cases you've been most proud of. Describe in detail how you believe your training and specific gifts helped to shape the outcome of those cases.

_____
_____
_____
_____
_____
_____
_____

Thinking about your special gifts, your training, and the cases in which you've succeeded the most, reflect on which types of issues you tend to be most prepared to help couples solve.

_____
_____
_____
_____
_____
_____
_____

Using everything you've written thus far, write a statement about whom you can help, why you can help them, and how you help them.

_____
_____
_____
_____
_____
_____
_____

You can utilize the above statement whenever you are writing about intensive couples therapy (such as on your blog or website) or discussing it with potential clients.

Crafting Your Website

Therapists should have a website with clear information about the services they provide. Adding a specific page to your website about intensive couples therapy and linking to it throughout your site will help couples learn more about your new offering. It will also help people find you through online searches when they look for therapists offering intensive couples sessions in your area.

LANDING PAGE

It's advised to create a specific page dedicated to intensive couples therapy on your website. This landing page, as it's known, should include:

- A description of intensive couples therapy
- A description of who intensive couples therapy is for (couples in crisis, couples struggling with infidelity, couples with tight schedules, etc.)
- An overview of what to expect before, during, and after the intensive couples therapy experience
- Your specific approach to couples therapy (which therapeutic model you follow, your traits and strengths as a practitioner, etc.)
- Instructions on how to schedule an intensive session
- Your fee for intensives

You might also consider including these bits of information throughout your website, whether it's in a summary on your services page or your therapist profile, or a more in-depth description in a blog post. Along with familiarizing page viewers with the intensive format and its benefits, frequent mentions distributed throughout your site helps drive your site up in online search rankings, making it more likely that prospective clients will find you.

TESTIMONIALS

Many couples will ask a therapist whether they can provide testimonials from past clients about their work. It makes sense from a consumer point of view—we'd likely ask the same questions of a car mechanic or a babysitter. Unless a client is a therapist themselves, they are unlikely to know that ethical guidelines don't allow a practitioner to ask for testimonials. What we can offer are testimonials from colleagues who understand our work and its effectiveness.

It's worthwhile to reach out to colleagues to collect these endorsements, particularly to those who have referred clients to you in the past. For example, they might write something like the following: "I trust the work [*your name*] does so greatly that I often refer couples to them. I have seen their effectiveness in breaking through difficult patterns and helping couples rebuild connection." Along with creating a section for these endorsements on your landing page, it's helpful to sprinkle them throughout your website to increase visibility within your site as well as in search engine results.

Take a moment to identify the specific colleagues you can reach out to, collect their contact information, and request an endorsement. I've provided a template for making this request.

> **SAMPLE**
>
> ## *Testimonial Request*
>
> Dear [*colleague name*],
>
> I wanted to reach out to you because I appreciate our collaboration over the years. I am very grateful for the clients we've been able to support together. I am currently collecting testimonials for my website to help clients get a sense of what it's like to work with me. I was wondering if you would be open to providing a short testimonial about the work I do and why you refer to me as a colleague. You can use this link to quickly jot down your thoughts: [*insert URL, or otherwise specify how to submit their testimonial*].
>
> If I use your testimonial on my website, I will also link back to your website so that anyone looking at my services can easily find you.
>
> Thank you so much for your consideration of this request. And, please, let me know if there is anything I can do for you in turn!
>
> Wishing you a gentle day,
> [*Your name*]

Networking

About 50 percent of the referrals to my practice come from individual and couples therapists who hear about the issues a couple is facing and recognize that the couple needs a more intensive form of therapy. Taking time to reach out to your local clinician community and letting them know you offer intensive sessions can be a powerful tool for finding clients.

When networking, it's important to build a relationship. Simply asking for referrals feels self-interested; instead, learn how you can help other clinicians in turn, and make sure you are referring to them wherever appropriate. The following are some ideas for building these types of relationships in your professional community:

- **"No strings attached" contact:** Email a clinician whom you recently learned about and let them know something you admire about their work and that you will be referring to them. Don't ask them to do anything for you.

- **Ask someone to coffee:** This is an oldie but a goodie. Whether virtual or in person, meeting people in "real life" creates a good impression and a stronger connection.

- **Give something of value to your community:** Create a community consult group, plan a lunch meet-up for therapists, or provide a free workshop for therapists who need more information on your area of expertise.

- **Collaborate:** When you are working with couples, try to collaborate with their individual therapists. Not only is this good for the couple's work, but it is also good for you in terms of building strong connections. Make sure to take into consideration the experience of the individual therapist by taking time to understand their own observations and thoughts about the presentation of the individual and the couple.

- **Open house:** Host an event where other members of the therapist community can meet and network with each other.
- **Attend other therapist's events:** When other therapists in your area host workshops, meetups, and open houses, they appreciate and remember their colleagues who show up.
- **Connect with mental health professionals who don't do what you do:** Whether it's getting in contact with a social worker at the hospital or offering a college counselor support with their students, these professionals will remember you when someone they come across needs your skills.

Thought Leadership

Thought leadership is exactly what it sounds like: the experience of being seen as a leader due to your knowledge and ideas about a specific topic within your industry. To put it more simply, thought leaders are seen as "go-to" experts. Thought leaders in mental health tend to have a specific skill set and perspective that others respect, want to learn more about, and share widely.

When someone becomes a thought leader, they may be interviewed in news publications, asked to speak at conferences, given opportunities to write, and sought out in various other ways for their expertise. This platform trickles down to the everyday person who is looking for insight or advice on that topic. Seeing you as a thought leader makes it all the more likely that they will reach out to you for a session.

Being a thought leader doesn't happen overnight, but you can begin to show thought leadership anytime by talking about your subject matter in any channel that is available to you. For many, this begins with their own blog. Over time, it might evolve into reaching out to publications and asking if you can write for them, being a guest on podcasts, or marketing yourself as a speaker.

The most effective way of positioning yourself as a thought leader is having a specific point of view on your profession or area of expertise. For example, I tend to specifically work with couples who are in their 30s to 40s and are experiencing a lot of stress. I spend a lot of time writing for publications, appearing on podcasts, and talking to other media outlets about how I think young families and young couples are impacted by stress. Because of this, many dual-income couples with young children from all over the world reach out to me for help.

If you're interested in thought leadership, start by reflecting on your specific point of view and expertise, then spend time writing about it, talking about it, and honing it as much as you can.

Initial Contact and Scheduling

When Harit and Dhwani emailed my office about the possibility of an intensive therapy session, Harit explained that he was on board, but that Dhwani wasn't quite sure if an intensive would be right for them. While she was interested in couples therapy, she was hesitant about spending so much time discussing their issues over the course of two days. The process seemed overwhelming to her, and she wanted to hear more about it before committing. Harit asked if I could set up a call with Dhwani to ease her fears.

"I would be happy to have a consultation call with you both to explain the process," I emailed back. "I prefer that we all be on the phone together to start off on the same page. The call is 15 minutes long and I will take time to learn more about what's going on for you, then give you an overview of the process and answer any questions you might have. Would any of the following times work?"

The initial contact with a prospective client serves many purposes, not the least of which is establishing boundaries right from the beginning. As you see, my response to Harit first addressed my boundary of always talking with both partners simultaneously during the consultation process. I have found that when I do it any other way, the result creates in imbalance in the couple-therapist relationship before therapy has even started.

Second, I set a boundary regarding time by letting the couple know that I will talk with them for 15 minutes. It's common for people to enter a consultation call and feel so relieved at the opportunity to talk that they end up taking up more time than intended. It's important this doesn't happen in the consult call for an intensive, as it will disrupt the flow of the overall process. Getting the story in drips and drabs creates a bumpy start to the assessment by interrupting the questions you might have wanted to ask in particular order and creating a sense that the process is not contained and structured.

Lastly, as shown in my response to Harit, I include the agenda for the consultation call. For couples who might feel anxiety about talking with a stranger about one of the biggest challenges they are facing in their lives, this helps them prepare by knowing ahead of time what we will be doing in the consultation call. For example, some couples might believe the consultation call will be more like a therapy session and will look forward to the call hoping for some therapy to be provided. If they do not receive this, they are likely to feel disappointed. Providing clarity also builds trust with the therapist—having an agenda shows that the practitioner knows what they are doing, that they are following a process rather than flying by the seat of their pants.

Consultation Call

Many therapists worry that they will not be able to keep the consult call to 15 minutes or less. This can take practice; however, it is similar to what you need to be able to do in therapy sessions—contain the experience through instructions, guidance, and boundaries. When you are clear up front regarding the agenda, most couples can stay within these bounds. From time to time, you will have someone who wants to dive into sharing the entire history of the problem or who starts pushing for advice. It's important in these moments to avoid any premature advice or assessment, as once you say something it's hard to take it back if you learn later your assessment was off or your advice was misused.

If a couple goes off track, you can gently remind them of the agenda and paint a picture of how you will help them if they choose to book the intensive. For example, if one partner says, "Before we go, can you please just tell us if what I am saying is right? I think I am right, but she doesn't agree," you can respond with what you would do in therapy regarding that question rather than actually answering the question. For example, you might say something like "I can hear that you're really frustrated with the current argument. If you decide to come in for an intensive, I will be helping the two of you navigate how you get gridlocked in these arguments so that it's not so much about right and wrong rather moving forward together."

If you have a couple who is particularly verbose and you're nearing the end of your time, gently redirect them by reminding them of the time and what else you'd like to achieve in the call, letting them know you look forward to learning more during the intensive. For example, if a client is still describing what they hope to gain from the intensive 10 minutes into the call, it's time to switch gears so that you're able to describe how you work and what the intensive process is like. You can gently say something like "Let me just pause you for a moment. Since we only have 15 minutes and we are nearing the end of that, I do want to make sure I talk a little bit about what I've heard you both share and how I do my work in an intensive. First, I want to reflect what I heard, and then I'm going to share with you how I might work with a couple who is struggling with this particular issue."

When I got on the phone with Harit and Dhwani for a consultation, I started by briefly introducing myself. "Hi, this is Liz. I'm really glad we could find time to get on the phone today to talk more about the intensive." Next, I reiterated the agenda for the call. "During our call today, I am first going to spend a little bit of time hearing more about what is going on for you and what you're looking for. Then I will share with you my thoughts about how an intensive might benefit your relationship and how intensives work. Then you can ask any questions. Does that sound good to you?"

Beginning this way offers the couple a sense of containment. Their issues might feel big and unruly, but our phone call won't. This is especially important for a client like Dhwani, who had already expressed that she feels worried about spending so much time talking about their issues.

The couple agreed that the process would work for them, so I asked them to go ahead and tell me a little bit more about themselves.

Harit began. "We've been married for 15 years. We had a really good relationship for the first 12 years, but the last three have been really hard."

"I'm so sorry to hear that," I responded. "What would you both say has happened over the last three years that has made things feel difficult?"

Dhwani answered, "Harit lost his job and I started focusing more on my work. There was just a lot of stress and tension. But it's gotten really bad now, and our kids are getting older and they see us fight all the time. It's not acceptable. I don't even know if therapy can help because I think we'll just spend the entire session fighting."

My response was to demonstrate understanding and validation of her feelings. "I hear you're on the fence with the intensive, Dhwani, because you're worried you'll end up fighting too much—is that right?"

"Exactly," Dhwani said. "Do people really come for 12 hours of therapy over two days? That just seems like a lot."

"You're not alone in that concern, Dhwani," I assured her. "Harit, tell me why you're interested in the intensive."

"I've been doing a lot of research, because I know if we don't change something our relationship is going to get worse," Harit told me. "I'm really worried about losing my marriage and breaking up our family. I found an article that talked about intensive couples therapy sessions and how effective they are. It made sense to me. I think Dhwani and I are just so busy with the kids and life that we never really get to have time to talk, and when we do, we don't know how to do it anymore. I just want us to really commit some time to this."

"Yes, that is one reason why an intensive session can be really helpful," I said, validating his perspective as well. "If you're okay with it, I'd like to take a moment to talk about what I am hearing from you both and then share how I think an intensive could help. Is that okay?"

With Harit and Dhwani both agreeing, I went on.

"Great. So, I hear that right now the main concern is that over the last few years your fighting has gotten worse and that at this point neither of you know how to improve it. Am I right about that?"

"Yes," Dhwani confirmed, "I think you've got that."

"And that is really common with a lot of the couples I work with in intensives," I continued. "Many of them come in because they used to have a really strong relationship, and then life got difficult and things started to change, and now they just feel lost with what to do. Sometimes, weekly therapy can really help with that, but if a couple is busy, it might be hard to maintain the cadence of weekly sessions. And I think that is one of your concerns, Harit. It also sounds like you have so much to talk about and maybe need help building some skills.

"I do think an intensive could be helpful to you, but I completely understand your concerns, Dhwani. I can tell you that in my experience, the intensive ends up going much more quickly than most people expect. I am there to help you both navigate conversations. We also take breaks. At the same time, it can be intense, so I want you to make the decision that's best for you." I offered a pause to let them both digest what I'd said. "Do either of you have any thoughts on what I've shared so far?"

Dhwani answered, "That all makes sense to me. And I do agree with Harit. We need more time to talk, and we need to figure out how to talk about it. When you said it goes by faster than expected, that is what I was wondering. And it's a good thing to remember it won't just be the two of us in a room for six hours."

"Exactly," I said. "I will be there to maintain some structure, while still being flexible, so you feel a sense of direction. I think now is a good time to share with you an overview of the process, if that's okay with you?"

Again, they agreed.

"If you decide to schedule," I said, "I will send you an assessment that you'll complete prior to our time together. This will give me more information about your relationship and each of you individually before we even meet. During our first day, I will spend about 90 minutes meeting with you both together. This will help me get to know your relationship, better understand what things have been like for you, and hear what you hope for. Then I'll spend about an hour with each of you to learn more about you as individuals. Afterward, we'll meet as a group again and I'll give you feedback about your relationship based on all that information. I'll let you know my professional opinion on what's going on in the relationship and where I think we need to focus.

"During the second day," I went on, "we will jump into having the important conversations based on what we uncover the first day. I will be offering you a lot of direction and feedback. During both days we'll take time for lunch and other breaks whenever you need them. How does this sound to you?"

Dhwani took a deep breath. "I feel much better about it. I think it would be good for us. What do you think, Harit?"

Harit laughed. "You already know that I think so too. I'd like to go ahead and schedule if it's okay."

"Okay!" I said. "I'm happy to schedule with you now and answer any questions. Or, if you'd like to talk together first, you can send me an email afterward to schedule."

On every consultation call, I follow a predetermined structure: a personal introduction, an overview of what we'll discuss during our 15 minutes, a brief discussion about the clients' relationship, an overview of the intensive session process, some time for me to answer the clients' questions, and an offer to schedule right then or later. I'm also careful to include a few key conversational "moves":

- **Seeking consent:** Whenever I am ready to move to the next portion of the call agenda, I ask the clients for consent to ensure they are part of the process.
- **Understanding and empathy:** I summarize their thoughts and show empathy throughout the call.
- **Containment:** Even as I ask questions and seek understanding, I do not allow the couple to get into the weeds. I want them to know and feel that I have the situation under control, right from the beginning. Many clients worry that their couples therapist will not help them contain the overwhelm they feel at home. If the conversation goes off the rails in the consultation call or if you do not follow your own process, you're communicating to the couple that they cannot be certain you'll also have control over what happens in the intensive therapy session.

SAMPLE

Intensive Therapy Consultation Call

Prior to the intensive consultation call, make a decision on how long the call will be. I recommend between 15 and 30 minutes.

1. Introduce yourself.
2. Provide an overview of the call process.
3. Ask the couple to tell you about themselves and why they are interested in intensive couples therapy. As you listen to the couple:
    a. Summarize.
    b. Ask questions.
    c. Show understanding.
    d. Offer empathy.
4. Summarize the main points you heard from the couple.
5. Summarize the intensive therapy process:
    a. Explain what they will need to complete before the intensive and what will occur on each day of the intensive.
    b. Provide some context as to how you work (e.g., "I am direct"; "I tend to be very gentle and slow").
6. Ask them if they have any questions.
7. Provide information on next steps: Let the couple know that they can schedule now if they would like, but give them permission to discuss with each other and reach back out to you to schedule.

Assessments

I suggest all clinicians send the clients some sort of assessment prior to the intensive. The assessment clarifies the state of the relationship prior to meeting the couple; it will help guide you to the places where you need to dig deeper or explore further in the session. It also provides an opportunity to uncover complex issues prior to meeting. While not everyone might answer the assessment questions honestly, they still provide us with information regarding issues of suicidality, domestic violence, and substance use. By getting this information up front, we can create a game plan to address more complicated cases before entering the therapy room with the couple.

As a Gottman Certified Therapist, I use the Gottman Relationship Checkup. This assessment is sent to the couple digitally, then is scored automatically. (It does not require manual scoring.) The assessment contains 337 questions that provide the therapist with information regarding the couple's levels of commitment, their conflict styles, their friendship, and their experience of intimacy with each other. It also gathers information regarding common areas of conflict like parenting, finances, and in-laws. Lastly, it assesses individual mental states by asking questions related to issues like depression, anxiety, suicidality, and substance use.

The core assessments utilized in the Gottman Relationship Checkup are as follows:

- **The Locke-Wallace Marital Adjustment Test** (Locke & Wallace, 1959)
    - This test measures relationship satisfaction and has been in use for decades. It asks each partner to state, on a spectrum, their level of agreement about varying factors like sex, recreation, and finances. It also asks multiple-choice questions about the relationship.

- **The Weiss-Cerreto Marital Status Inventory** (MSI; Weiss & Cerreto, 1980)
    - This inventory is designed to assess the likelihood of divorce. A score of 4 or more indicates a risk that the relationship will end.

- **The Sound Relationship House Assessment Questionnaire**
    - This questionnaire, designed by the Gottman Institute, measures each area of the Sound Relationship House (trust, commitment, love maps, fondness and admiration, turning toward instead of away, positive perspective, conflict management, shared meaning, and life goals) by asking true-or-false questions. There are brief and long versions of the assessment.

- **The Gottman 19 Areas Checklist for Solvable and Perpetual Problems**
    - This checklist asks couples to identify areas that are a problem or not a problem for them. The categories of potential problems include emotional connection, stress management and coping, how disagreements are handled, passion in the relationship, sex, important/life-changing events, children, in-laws, jealousy, betrayals, values and goals, finances, fun, spirituality, and community.

- **The Three Detour Scales**
    - These scales measure for levels of chaos, meta-emotion differences, and family history. They are called the detour scales because when there are difficulties in these areas it becomes challenging for a couple to have productive conversations without intervention.

- **Gottman Emotional Abuse Questionnaire** (EAQ)
    - This scale asks each member of the couple to answer questions related to potential emotional abuse. Their responses can help the clinician begin to assess for characterological abuse.
- **Control, Fear, Suicide Potential, and Acts of Physical Aggression Questionnaire**
    - This questionnaire, which is given to each partner, involves a series of yes-or-no questions regarding abuse and suicide potential. This assessment is incredibly important prior to an intensive, as it can flag the potential for a client to harm themselves or their partner. This allows the therapist to properly respond ahead of time if needed.
- **The Symptom Checklist-90** (SCL-90; Derogatis et al., 1973)
    - This 90-item questionnaire assesses for somatization, obsessive-compulsive behavior, interpersonal sensibility, depression, anxiety, hostility, phobic anxiety, paranoid ideation, and psychoticism. Utilizing this assessment prior to the intensive gives the therapist a better understanding of any potential comorbidities. It makes the individual sessions easier, as the therapist will have more direction in regard to exploring the mental health of each client.
- **CAGE-AID Questionnaire** (Brown & Rounds, 1995)
    - This questionnaire utilizes the mnemonic CAGE-AID to assess for drug and alcohol use. In particular, it assesses whether the client has felt the need to **c**ut down on their substance use, whether other people feel **a**nnoyed by their use, whether the client feels **g**uilt about their use, and whether the client ever has an "**e**ye opener" (drinking or using drugs first thing in the morning).
- **Michigan Alcoholism Screening Test** (Selzer, 1971)
    - Also known as the MAST or the B-MAST (brief version), this is one of the oldest alcohol screening tests. This assessment helps the clinician better understand the client's relationship with alcohol and assesses for potential dependency.

Other general assessments that can be utilized by couples therapists include:

- **Personal Assessment of Intimacy in Relationships** (PAIR; Schaefer & Olson, 1981)
    - This assessment provides therapists with information about a couple related to five types of intimacy: emotional, social, sexual, intellectual, and recreational.
- **The Dyadic Adjustment Scale** (Spanier, 1976)
    - This 32-item assessment measures each partner's perception of the relationship. It seeks to measure satisfaction, cohesion, consensus, and affection.

Whether you use an assessment process provided by your modality or create your own "packet" of assessments for couples to complete prior to attending their session, you'll find great benefit in having information ahead of time. This information gives you a picture of the couple before you meet them and helps you prepare for any issues that might need special response.

Preparing Yourself

Before offering couples intensives, take time to reflect on what practicing this form of therapy will require of you—mentally, emotionally, and somatically—during sessions. While you will of course bring your own special characteristics to the process, the following traits are particularly beneficial for intensive couples therapists:

- **Patience:** Intensive couples therapy provides enough time for you to be slow and patient. You should allow the couple to take time to express themselves.
- **Authoritativeness:** You must show confidence and competence in guiding the couple through difficult conversations and intense emotions. You should feel comfortable giving direction and making decisions throughout the intensive.
- **Bravery:** Clients in intensive couples therapy want to hear the truth. To hold a productive intensive, you must be brave enough to give direct feedback, share concerns, and model healthy behavior.
- **Empathy:** While we all know it's important for a therapist to be empathic, it's especially important during an intensive. Be prepared to model empathy to the couple through changes in tone of voice, facial expressions, and embodiment.

"Person of the Therapist" Work

In traditional couples therapy, the therapist meets with the couple for one to two hours and then has time between sessions to reflect on the couple and their issues and to seek out supervision. Intensive couples sessions require the therapist to be with the couple for several hours at a time (with some breaks). Therefore, the therapist must be able to think on their feet. They also must have a strong ability to recognize their own countertransference or physiological flooding.

During an intensive session, the therapist is challenged to sustain presence, awareness, and engagement for much longer periods of time than they are used to. The therapist also will have fewer moments to reflect on their own countertransference, physiological discomfort, and biases. Because of this, I recommend that therapists offering intensives be in active supervision, continually seeking out continuing education, and involved in their own self work—this includes working on self-soothing techniques, understanding their own triggers, and fostering differentiation.

It is my recommendation that therapists consider using the Person of the Therapist training model developed by structural family therapist Harry Aponte (2016). This training helps therapists develop a conscious, purposeful, and disciplined approach to accessing their own humanity. Its emphasis on the profound role of the therapist's self-awareness, personal development, and emotional presence is particularly relevant in an intensive session, as the extended format can often lead to the therapist experiencing fatigue, boredom, confusion, triggers, and so on.

Aponte believes that a therapist's own experiences, emotions, and vulnerabilities—collectively referred to as the "self"—are central to how they relate to and work with clients. His training model asserts that the therapist's self should not be hidden or distanced from the therapeutic relationship, but rather, the therapist should be fully present in an authentic and reflective manner, using their own personality and emotional responses to enhance the therapeutic process. At the same time, the therapist must have differentiation enough that they can identify with the client while retaining freedom to relate, assess, and intervene with the clients as needed.

To strike this delicate balance, Aponte (2016) believes that the therapist must work toward:

- **Knowledge of the self:** The therapist must continually study and examine how their past and their present impact who they are today. Gaining insight into their psychology, worldviews, values, morality, and social location, as well as their own beliefs about change in therapy, is crucial to properly assess a couple and their situation.
    - For example, a therapist might know that they struggle to believe that a person who has cheated on a partner can change. With knowledge of self, they can better question themselves when responding to a couple who has had an affair, so that they do not limit the therapeutic process through their own beliefs.

- **Access to self:** A therapist who has strong access to their self can be present with their own memories, feelings, thoughts, and beliefs about the therapeutic process. The ability to truly be in touch with the self requires us to live in the moment in the therapeutic encounter, a necessary aspect of building a relationship with the client, as well as assessing and intervening.
    - For example, most therapists have had the experience of becoming irritated with a client. If the therapist does not have access to their self in that moment, they may become aggressive toward the client, which could harm the relationship. A self-aware therapist, however, can use self-soothing or even discuss their feelings with the client if it seems to be clinically appropriate: "I'm having a really hard time empathizing with you right now—I very much want to, but I find myself closing off to what you're saying. I'm trying to figure out why that might be, and I think it might be that I'm reacting to your tone of voice. Have you heard that from anyone else before?" You can see how this is not only helps clear the air for the relationship, but also brings something to the surface that might be an interactional issue for the client elsewhere.

- **Management of self:** Aponte says therapists need discernment and discipline to open themselves to clients when appropriate and to utilize the self when it is toward the purpose of intervention. A therapist might notice themselves relating to a client and wanting to connect by sharing their own experience. However, the therapist must be disciplined enough to take the time to discern whether this information will be helpful toward the clients' clinical goals. Sometimes self-disclosure can make the therapist seem overly aligned with one specific partner and therefore cause them to lose their connection to the other partner. There are additional potential drawbacks to self-disclosure that can occur in both individual and couples therapy.
    - For example, perhaps the therapist is exploring infertility with a couple and is considering sharing their own experience with infertility to create an alliance with them. The disciplined therapist looks beyond the initial alliance to consider other impacts of sharing. If the therapist became pregnant with the help of in vitro fertilization (IVF), for instance, the couple might feel frustrated with the therapist's ability to become pregnant or they might

become hopeful using the therapist's story as a guide only to find later that their own IVF attempts were unsuccessful.

Common Feelings

During an intensive, the therapist will likely experience varying emotions of their own: self-doubt, confusion, irritation, frustration, hopelessness, overwhelm, and sadness.

It is very common for the therapist to feel self-doubt during the first day of the intensive. The sheer volume of information intake is reason enough for the therapist to leave the session feeling overwhelmed and unsure of what to do next. (It's my experience that the second day brings about clarity and energy.) Even I still frequently face my own self-doubt during the first day. And I frequently receive phone calls from therapists I am training or supervising who, at the end of a first intensive day, tell me, "I don't know if I can help these people."

Other feelings may arise based on countertransference in response to the challenges that the clients are facing. The therapist should be aware of their countertransference and utilize the emotions they feel as a guide toward understanding the couple. For example, if the therapist feels irritation, they should reflect on why that might be—is it related to their own personal experiences, or are they feeling something "for" one of the partners? How can they use the irritation to build the relationship or to help intervene in a dynamic? Perhaps the therapist feels irritated because the client has been speaking for too long. The therapist can utilize this information by asking the partner who has been listening, "How are you feeling right now as you listen?"

In short, it's normal for therapists to experience many feelings during the intensive. Self-awareness is key, and the therapist should use their feelings as information that can guide them toward better clinical treatment of their clients.

As I've outlined in this chapter, adding intensive couples therapy to your practice will require a fair amount of preparation: training, creating your intensives policies and paperwork, marketing your new services, preparing clients for this unique form of therapy, and deepening your self-awareness as a therapist. However, I have personally found the effort to be more than worthwhile, as it allows me to offer couples a truly transformative experience. In the remaining chapters of this book, I offer detailed guidance for each day of the intensive session, including case examples and specific tools you can use with your own clients.

CHAPTER 3

The Intensive, Day 1

As I describe the process of an intensive couples therapy weekend, I am going to take you through the stories of four couples:

- Ebony and Karl, who were working to overcome betrayal
- Kimmie and Selah, who felt lonely and disengaged from their marriage
- John and Amy, working parents who felt overwhelmed and stressed out
- Ron and Andrew, who didn't agree on the future of their relationship

Each of these couples came to their intensive session looking to be understood, learn new skills, and forge a path forward. Some of them felt confident about their commitment to each other, while others looked to the intensive to help them decide whether they should stay together. Through the stories of these couples, we will first explore the flow of day 1 of an intensive; then, in the next chapter, I will describe the interventions and exercises that I commonly use on day 2.

Ebony and Karl: Affair Recovery

Karl and Ebony had been together for five years and married for four. They had two small children—a four-year-old girl and a two-year-old boy—and Ebony was pregnant. She was due in eight weeks and had just discovered that Karl had been having an affair. Ebony contacted my office asking for more information about an intensive with hopes that she and Karl could recover their relationship for the sake of their family. During the consultation call, Ebony expressed shock at finding that Karl had been having sex with one of his colleagues in their shared home. Karl expressed remorse and stated that he felt committed to working through the relationship together.

They were both on the same page about doing the intensive, as it was difficult for them to find the time for weekly sessions with two small children at home and the due date for their third quickly approaching. Ebony expressed high levels of distress and shared that if she wasn't able to express her pain to Karl in the safety of a therapist's office, she was worried what the stress would do to her and the pregnancy. "I can't wait weeks and weeks to get this all out. We need to talk now. I'm in so much pain," she shared.

Kimmie and Selah: Lonely and Disengaged

Selah and Kimmie, both in their 60s, had been together for 15 years and known each other for twice as long. They met as work colleagues and became "office friends," but life took them in different directions for many years. Kimmie got married in her mid-30s and had a child. Selah had several long-term relationships but none of them ever seemed to work out. When their jobs caused them to cross paths again in their 40s, Kimmie was newly divorced, Selah was single, and they recognized a connection they hadn't noticed before. In the years since reuniting, they moved in together, coparented together, and got married.

During their consultation call, they described the first 10 years of their marriage as a breath of fresh air. "I've never felt so loved and safe in a relationship," Kimmie expressed, while Selah shared, "I finally have the family I've always wanted. It's been such a gift to have Kimmie and her daughter, *our* daughter, Maisie."

When I asked them to explain what had been going on that brought them to therapy, they said they had noticed themselves arguing more over the past two years. Within that time, Selah's mother had died suddenly of cancer, leaving Selah's aging and sick father and disabled brother alone in their home. Kimmie and Selah were also facing new challenges with parenting. Maisie, a young teenager, was having a hard time making friends at school and was lashing out at home. Throughout this, the couple was coming to terms with their own aging and a curiosity about what really matters in life.

All these challenges, and more, were leading them to more and more arguments with each other and an overall tense environment in their home. These disagreements weren't resulting in yelling or screaming, but rather loneliness and disengagement. Both Kimmie and Selah recognized that something was wrong and valued their relationship enough to work on it. They wanted to use intensive couples therapy as a symbol of their commitment to making it right.

John and Amy: Overwhelmed and Overworked Parents

Amy and John had been together since college. They married shortly after graduation and had a son, who was one year old at the time they contacted me. John was an attorney and Amy was a pediatrician. Their families lived far away, and they had little to no support from their relatives or community. Prior to getting married, Amy and John had what they described as a "healthy" relationship; however, they did argue about housework from time to time. Lately, they were arguing daily.

In the consultation call, Amy shared that she often noticed herself feeling angry, depressed, and anxious. She felt as if all the responsibility of the family fell on her shoulders and that her job was being impacted negatively. Amy also admitted that she had been drinking more than she used to and often felt hungover the next morning. John expressed that he did not understand why Amy was so frustrated. He believed they had a good life overall and stated that he wasn't sure how an intensive could help because he didn't think they had big enough issues. Amy disagreed and shared that the issues were so bad for her that she had fantasized about leaving. This came as a big shock to John— the consultation call was the first time he'd learned about the depth of her unhappiness.

After hearing this admission, John said he now felt very motivated to come in for a weekend. He did not understand what could be so bad that Amy would want to leave the relationship, but he wanted to figure it out. They also both expressed that it was impossible for them to do weekly sessions due to their child and the intensity of their jobs.

Ron and Andrew: Uncertain About the Future

Ron and Andrew had been together for four years and married for two. Since the beginning, their relationship had been tumultuous. In their consultation call, they described a pattern in which they often argued by yelling and threatening the relationship. On many occasions, Ron had moved out for weeks at a time. Recently, the couple went on a vacation together where they both drank too much alcohol and got into the biggest fight they'd ever had, saying many hurtful things they had not yet recovered from. Ron passed out after drinking, and Andrew felt completely abandoned and afraid. They said many hurtful things they had not yet recovered from.

Andrew shared that he had been feeling tired, unheard, and discouraged for a long time and was now seriously considering ending the relationship. He did not believe they could reconcile or learn how to navigate fighting in a healthier manner. Ron disagreed. He expressed that he was fully committed to Andrew and urgently wanted them to continue to work on their relationship.

In light of their different goals, Andrew and Ron wanted to come in for an intensive session to discern whether they should stay together. They believed they needed to have important conversations with a third party to make the decision in the most rational way possible.

We will follow Ebony and Karl, Kimmie and Selah, John and Amy, and Ron and Andrew as we explore how to navigate an intensive therapy session utilizing different exercises, skills, and interventions.

Key Processes of Day 1

During the first day of an intensive, the therapist is doing much of what they would usually do over the first several weeks of weekly couples therapy: working to build trust with the couple while also deeply observing their interactions, assessing the couple's history, and gaining understanding of their goals. Much of this process will feel familiar to you if you have been working with couples in a more traditional sense. The major difference is that you will be able to do the full assessment without the interruptions from the end of each 50-minute session or surprise developments from the week in between that might disrupt what you have been trying to understand.

In my experience, it also tends to be easier to join with a couple because they already know they will be spending a great deal of time with you and have committed to doing something high stakes—this makes them want to dive in and take full advantage of the opportunity to meet their relational goals.

Although you may experience many "aha" moments during the first day of an intensive, the role of the therapist is *not to intervene* during this first session. Such interventions are often premature and tend to interrupt full understanding of the issue and full buy-in of the couple. There are, of course, caveats to this rule, such as those related to the clinical policies you set in chapter 2 regarding substance use, abuse, suicidality, and secret-keeping.

Your role during the first day of the intensive is to join, observe interactions and dynamics, learn more about the couple by showing curiosity and assessing for pivotal areas in the relationship, and better understand each individual. Throughout this, you will also be conceptualizing what is causing the relationship issues and how you believe you can help. At the end of the first day, you will take all of the information from the couple's assessment and provide feedback to them about why they are facing challenges, as well as your thoughts about what can be done to improve their situation.

Let's walk through those steps in more detail.

The Role of the Therapist on the First Day of the Intensive

JOINING

Joining is the process by which you become a trusted part of the system. Christophe Panichelli (2013) notes that it involves "the therapist's ability to see the world through the clients' eyes, momentarily adopting their frame of reference" (p. 438), while Salvador Minuchin (1974) describes it as the "therapist's understanding, support, and confirmation of the family members' experiences and felt needs" (p. 113). In couples therapy, a therapist joins by creating a connection with each partner within the couple individually and by also relating to the couple as a unit.

OBSERVATION AND ASSESSMENT

During the first day of the intensive you will be observing the clients' interactions, asking questions, showing curiosity, and using an enactment to better understand the couple. Doing this helps you to assess the couple in regard to what brings them into therapy, what might be causing their issues, and what might help them to improve. Observing and assessing allows you to see "what is" before you begin to attempt to make changes. If a therapist intervenes prior to really understanding what is going on with the couple and what they'd like to see change, the interventions will not work.

PROVIDING FEEDBACK AND GOAL SETTING

At the end of the first day, you will provide feedback that integrates any assessments and questionnaires with your findings from the individual and couple oral interviews. Let the couple know what you've heard in terms of the problems the couple is facing. Then share what you believe has led to this breakdown—describing the history, events, and habits that might have created the conflict or disconnect between the partners. Describe how these issues tend to improve and suggest what the couple can do specifically. Collaborate with the couple throughout this process to get their feedback on your assessment. Lastly, help the couple to set goals for the second day of the intensive.

Over the next several sections, you will learn more about these three areas while getting a peek into therapy sessions with Ebony and Karl, Kimmie and Selah, John and Amy, and Ron and Andrew. We will start with the use of joining during the first day of the intensive.

Joining

Joining is one of the first techniques a therapist utilizes when meeting a new couple. Even asking something as simple as "How was your drive to the office?" is an attempt at connecting with the couple in a way that helps them to feel safe. You can also join by sharing (appropriately) small aspects of your life—for example, the couple might say, "There was so much traffic getting here" and you might share, "Yes, I experienced that too. I wonder what was going on."

> **COUPLES THERAPIST RESOURCE**
>
> ## Effective Joining
>
> The following actions support effective joining with clients:
>
> - Show genuine curiosity about the client's interests, occupation, and loved ones. For example, you might ask, "I see the locket around your neck—is there a photo inside?" If they answer, "Yes, it's my grandmother," you could say, "Oh wow, tell me about her!"
>
> - Share information about mutual interests or experiences: "I see your Phillies hat—are you a fan? So am I."
>
> - Share information about your professional background and the way in which you work as a therapist. This is often done during the consultation but should be done again during the first session.
>
> - Notice and aim for empathic success with the individual and the relationship. For example, if you're summarizing what you've heard a couple say and how you think they must be feeling and they nod their heads, then you have likely had empathic success with them—this means they feel understood.
>
> - Use appropriate humor. This breaks the ice and helps couples recognize that they can relax with you. (Just be cautious that the jokes you use aren't dismissive or harmful.)
>
> - Express hope through sharing with the couple your belief that things can change.
>
> - Show confidence by redirecting, providing feedback, and asking difficult questions.
>
> - Use the client's words and echoing. For example, if the client shares, "I spent the night puking," then uses their word to summarize: "Puking, ugh—that must have felt bad." If the client says, "When my mom died, it was so hard," do not replace "died" with a euphemism such as "passed away," but instead join by saying, "It's a very hard thing when a mom dies."
>
> - Use relatable metaphors. For example, if one partner is a baseball player, you might use metaphors related to striking out, hitting the bases, and working on a team to discuss what is happening in the relationship.
>
> - Use accurate prosody. This is the use of voice inflection to show understanding, and it affects how clients perceive you—whether they see you as kind, helpful, safe, and so on.

Remember, joining is done by developing a connection with each client as well as building a connection with the couple as a whole. It is integral to join with the clients prior to assessment and intervention. Joining builds the clients' trust in you; without it, you are less likely to get honest and vulnerable answers to your questions and will find it more difficult to begin intervening. Joining is also something that happens over time and should never stop during the intensive process.

Ebony and Karl: Joining

When Ebony and Karl arrived at the office, it was clear they were both highly distressed. Ebony was tearful as I approached them in the waiting room, and Karl looked agitated as he paced back and forth. After I invited them to come back to my office and take a seat, I engaged in brief small talk, though their evident anxiety led me to do less of this than I'd normally begin with.

"Do either of you need to use the bathroom before we get started? Or need any water?" I asked.

"I'm okay," Ebony murmured. "I just went, and I have some water with me."

"I'm okay too," Karl echoed.

"Okay, well, if you need anything at all, please let me know," I said. "We can take breaks for the bathroom, and I have water bottles sitting on the side table for you."

At this point, I could see in their faces that they were not only anxious, but potentially flooded. While I always want to make sure the clients' basic needs, like water and bathroom use, are tended to, any more small talk would have been unhelpful for Karl and Ebony. Wanting to provide a sense of safety and containment for them, I moved quickly to my next step.

"If it's okay with both of you," I said, "I'd like to get started by sharing with you how our day will look from here." They both nodded in agreement.

> [Part of me wanted to express that I could see Ebony and Karl's anxiety. However, I made the judgment call to wait until later. Although expressing this might have led to joining by helping them feel seen and understood, it also would have increased the likelihood of conflict before the assessment process even began. For example, if I had acknowledged that I could see how overwhelmed they were both feeling, Karl might have said something like, "She's like this every day. It never stops," prompting Ebony to defend herself. Because I knew that I had much more time to join with the couple and because I wanted us to stay on track, I held on to my observation regarding their discomfort and made a note in my mind to share it later.]

"Today is our first day together," I began. "We are going to spend the next six hours together. I know that sounds like a long time, but I've done many of these and most people say the time really flies by. Today is just for me to get to understand you and your relationship better and to start to plan what we are going to do tomorrow."

> [Here, I let them know that other couples have expressed that the session "flies by." I often share this at the start of the intensive to relieve the couple of any anxiety they might have about the amount of time they are going to spend with me.]

"First, I'm going to meet with you both together for about 90 minutes. Then I'll meet with you both separately for about an hour each. While I do that, whoever I am not meeting with can go grab a snack, take a walk, or just hang out in the waiting area.

"After those individual meetings, we'll take a break for lunch and I will prepare feedback for you. After you come back from lunch, we'll finish out our day all together again. During that time, I am going to share with you my observations of your relationship, my assessment about what I believe is causing your relationship distress, and my thoughts on what I think needs to be done next to work toward your goals.

"There are four things I like to let everyone know up front on day 1. First, I am going to be asking you a lot of questions and you'll be talking to me most of the day. On day 2, you'll be talking to each other most of the time, but today is to help me understand who you are. Second, I am not going to be having you do exercises together and I won't intervene, unless I really have to, in whatever patterns you have. I want to be able to observe the relationship fully. Third, if you have any need for a break at all, please let me know. We can stop at any time and use the bathroom, get water, get food, calm down—whatever you need. Finally, I know that six hours seems like a *lot* of time, but it goes fairly quickly. I think you'll be surprised."

I sat back, giving them both a moment to process all that I'd said. "How does that sound?"

"It sounds good," said Ebony, her voice breaking. "We are completely lost, so we're thankful for any guidance. I don't think I can live like this anymore." She began to cry.

I nodded. "It sounds like it's been an incredibly painful time for you, Ebony. I'm looking forward to hearing more and thinking through what can be done."

[*Here, I used empathy to join with Ebony. The small moments in which a therapist shows understanding of a client's experience helps to build the connection between client and therapist.*]

With Ebony still collecting herself, Karl spoke. "It's been exhausting. I just hope this weekend does something to change how Ebony is feeling because I've said I'm sorry a million times and it's not working." His tight tone of voice revealed a counterpoint to Ebony's tears—a different expression of the same grief and hopelessness.

"I can hear you're frustrated that you've tried to improve things and it's not working," I affirmed. "I am hopeful I can give you some other things you can try, Karl."

[*It is important that the therapist equally joins with the person who committed the wrong early in the session in order to remove the sense that the therapist will be biased against them or on the side of their partner. Here, I made sure to respond to Karl with empathy just as I had to Ebony. I did not remove his responsibility for his transgressions, but I did let him know I understood how frustrating it could be to feel so stuck.*]

Taking a breath to reset the stage for our conversation, I began with an opening question. "I'd really like to start by hearing more about what things have been like in general in the relationship since the discovery of the infidelity. Ebony, can you start and share with me what things have been like?"

Joining might feel harder or easier for you during intensive couples therapy sessions compared to traditional weekly sessions. On one hand, the couple is coming to you in an already anxious state. They are investing a lot of their resources—time, money, energy—on you with the hope that you will help them through something painful. Because of this, couples might come in with heightened expectations and might be harder to "win over." In turn, you might feel anxious to jump past the joining process and "prove yourself" rather than slowing down and really getting to know and build trust with the clients. This internal pressure to perform can reduce the likelihood that you will really be present and connect.

On the other hand, with intensives comes the gift I have mentioned many times—the gift of time, which provides you and the couple more space to get to know each other in your roles and to build trust. When you are able to accept that you do not need to rush through the session and instead can take your time getting to know the couple, showing empathy, and asking the questions you really want to know, you can relax, be more present, and therefore become easier to connect with.

There is also more opportunity to repair ruptures in the therapeutic relationship. If you get it wrong, it's okay because you usually have several more hours to get it right. This reduces pressure you might feel to get everything right on the first try and also allows you to "fix" the relationship with the couple during the same session rather than having to wait a week between sessions to repair empathic failures or moments in which you misunderstood or inadvertently dismissed a partner.

For joining to occur, three things must take place for the couple in the therapy room. They must:

- Feel heard and understood
- Have confidence in the therapist
- Have hope

Let's look at a few examples of how to provide these experiences during the first day of an intensive couples therapy session.

Feeling Heard and Understood

It might sound obvious, but clients need to feel heard and understood before they will be open to taking feedback from the therapist. Just as we ask our couples to understand first and provide each other feedback and advice later, therapists must also learn to develop understanding before giving feedback in order to understand what's really going on and build trust with their couple. When I am training intern level therapists, one of the biggest mistakes I see them make with couples is attempting to provide solutions or advice prior to taking time to join with the couple through building an understanding of their story and perspective.

The therapist can do a number of things to help a couple feel heard and understood, such as showing genuine curiosity about their lives outside of the relationship, summarizing what the clients say, offering validation, and helping them come up with the words to say during moments when they are flooded.

> When I finished talking with Ebony and Karl about the agenda for day 1, Ebony shared that she needed some relief from the constant pain she had been feeling, while Karl expressed a sense of powerlessness and frustration. I didn't need to spend much time with either of them to begin helping them feel heard and understood. I empathized with them both, while resisting making any sort of assessment or giving any major feedback—for example, I refrained from responding to Karl with something like, "Well, it's not going to be helpful if you try to rush the process." If I had done that, Karl would not have felt heard and understood and we would have struggled to join with each other, making feedback harder to give in the future.

On the other hand, I wanted to ensure that Ebony, who already felt so raw and tender around the betrayal, did not see my validation of Karl as an invalidation of her or as condoning his behavior. This is why I chose to quickly move forward after offering empathy. I wasn't trying to shut Karl down; rather, I wanted to ensure that, in those early moments, Ebony didn't feel that the therapy space was being co-opted by his voice before she had a chance to feel seen.

When I invited them to tell me more about what had been going on between them, I directly asked Ebony to go first.

> [Why did I ask Ebony to go first? From the moment we met in the waiting room, I could see that Ebony's emotions were overwhelming. It was clear from what she had shared and from her nonverbal signals—red face, wide eyes, quivering lip—that she was in a very flooded and activated state. While I could see that Karl was frustrated and also slightly flooded, it seemed as if he was calmer than Ebony.
>
> On top of this, Ebony was the partner who had been hurt by Karl's transgression. Of course, Karl was potentially hurting too (I wasn't quite sure at that point how he was processing the affair); however, his actions were a direct betrayal of their relationship and therefore had warped Ebony's sense of security.
>
> If I had chosen to have Karl speak first, Ebony would likely have had a difficult time listening to him. She may have struggled to stay regulated or felt the urge to interrupt. And more importantly, she might have begun to feel betrayed by the therapy process itself, thinking something like *How could the therapist make me sit here and listen to his side when I am the one who is so hurt?*
>
> Based on my experience, I tend to ask the person who seems the most activated—or, if there has been a betrayal, the person who has been betrayed—to share first. Otherwise, they will struggle to allow their partner to speak, often interrupting and potentially even having an outburst that completely sidetracks the assessment.
>
> To be clear, as we move into interventions, I work with the couple to navigate their activation so that the activation isn't "calling the shots" of who gets to speak at any given moment. Later in Ebony and Karl's intensive, I helped Ebony to self-soothe so that she could hear Karl. But during a couple's assessment process, since I am not yet intervening, I avoid activation except, potentially, during the enactment phase.]

As Ebony spoke, Karl looked down at the ground. Ebony cried and occasionally glared at Karl, raising her voice. "I'm just so hurt!" she expressed. "I don't know how someone I love so much could do this to me. How could he fucking do this to our family? How *could* you, Karl?" She turned to him with wide, accusing eyes.

"Ebony, I can see you're so angry," I said. "It's like there's so much anger in there, you don't even know what to do with it. It must be so hard to carry that with you all of the time."

Ebony nodded as she continued to cry.

> [Here, I was using the heightening technique (see page 9) to help Ebony know I understood her, even beneath her words. When Ebony nodded, I knew I was on the right track, so I continued to speak with her in this way, guided by **the nod factor**. Although it sounds counterintuitive, heightening often acts as a counterbalance. The person feels deeply understood and this, in turn, begins to help them feel soothed and more regulated.]

> **COUPLES THERAPY DICTIONARY**
>
> **The Nod Factor**
> The Duquesne Psychology Clinic (Danna, 2011) surveyed client experiences related to collaborative assessment in therapy. In this survey, they found something they called "the nod factor," named so because seeing a client nod their head is an affirmation that what the therapist is saying relates to their own life experience. You can increase the nod factor by using context from the client's life, metaphors, and themes that relate to the client's lived experience.

I shifted my eyes to Karl and saw that he was clasping his hands together and looking at the ground. "Karl, thank you for letting me take time to explore how things have been for Ebony. I know it might be hard to listen to, and I appreciate that you've been working to do that right now. It's helpful to me to get the opportunity to hear from Ebony."

Karl took a deep breath, sat up straighter, looked at me, and said, "No problem." I gave him a gentle smile and returned my focus to Ebony as I continued to ask her to share more about her experience.

> [While listening to Ebony speak, I continually shifted my eyes from her to Karl. I wanted to make sure that Karl wasn't becoming flooded. If he did, it could potentially rupture any connection we had started to make during the beginning of the session. As he listened, I decided to give brief, periodic compliments—this was an attempt to let him know that he was safe in my office, that he was seen and appreciated for his effort. My hope was that these small gestures would help him stay grounded as he continued the self-soothing work he was doing while Ebony spoke.]

As Ebony, Karl, and I continued with their first day, much of my effort at joining with them was related to helping them feel safe. I did this by remaining calm and warm, and by showing that I understood how hard the situation was for both of them. Empathy and validation are some of the most powerful tools when it comes to joining in couples therapy.

Kimmie and Selah: Joining

When Selah and Kimmie came in for their first session, they were in much different spirits than Ebony and Karl. When I walked into the waiting room to meet them, they were sitting close together, with one woman's head on the other's shoulder, laughing together about something on one of their phones.

"Hi, are you here to see me?" I approached them and reached out my hand. "I'm Liz."

"Hi, Liz," one of the women said, standing up. "I'm Kimmie. Sorry, I hope the video wasn't playing too loud! Sometimes we don't know how to behave ourselves in public." She smirked playfully.

I laughed and responded, "Me neither," then turned to the other woman. "You must be Selah?"

"Yes, that's me. It's nice to meet you," she said.

"Before we go back, I have to know—what were you watching that was making you laugh so hard? I need some good new videos to watch."

Selah, who had put her phone away, took it back out and opened the TikTok app. "Oh my gosh, we have to show you this video. Our daughter sent it to us and it's just so funny."

We took a moment to appreciate the silly cat video that had kept them laughing.

"Do you have cats?" I asked.

Kimmie replied, "Yes! Two. We love cats. They drive our daughter Maisie nuts, though . . . but I think she secretly loves them."

> [*I was genuinely curious about the video, but I was also struck by how connected Kimmie and Selah seemed despite reporting disconnection as their core issue. I filed this away in my brain and decided to continue to connect with them over the information they were sharing with me.*]

"How old is your daughter?" I asked as we began to walk down the hall to my office.

"She's 15, and it really shows," said Kimmie, smiling.

I laughed. "Oh, really? In what way?"

"She has all of the wonderful attributes of a teenager and also all of the . . ." Kimmie searched for the right word, ". . . challenging aspects, too. We are in serious teenager territory. Some days are light and funny, but it's also been a really tough time for her and for us."

> [*Because I could see that Selah and Kimmie were feeling relaxed and connected, I made the decision to begin joining with them by addressing them more casually and asking them about their personal lives (outside of the relationship). Since both partners were presenting in a calm and jovial manner, I did not need to tend to any dysregulation in the moment.*]

Asking about the video and their daughter had already created a sense of joining with Kimmie and Selah before even digging into the day that lay ahead. Once Selah and Kimmie got situated on the couch, I gave them an overview of the agenda and then asked them to share more about what brought them into therapy.

They described the events of the last few years of their life together—not only an increasingly difficult teenage daughter, but also the death of Selah's mother and her new role of caretaker to her father and brother. I wanted to take a moment to summarize to make sure I understood their perspectives on what was causing issues in their relationship.

"Selah," I began, "it sounds like you're hoping that Kimmie can be a little more patient and understanding with the changes going on in your family. I hear you saying you understand how hard this has been on the family—taking care of your dad and brother—but you just need her to be patient and understanding. Is that right?"

COUPLES THERAPIST SKILL

Summarizing

Summarizing to the couple accomplishes a few things in the process of joining. It slows down the conversation and gives the therapist a chance to ensure that they accurately understand each partner's point of view. The repetition also helps the partners to better hear each other. Finally, it builds their confidence in the therapist's ability to understand and support them.

Selah nodded. "Exactly." Unexpectedly, she started to cry. "I know it's a big ask, Kimmie. But just like Liz said, I think I'm looking for you to show me some support and to offer me some empathy while we go through this. And some patience."

"And Kimmie," I turned to her, "what I hear you saying is that there have been so many transitions, it's hard for you to keep up. And that you're really struggling with that."

Kimmie frowned. "I don't think that's quite it."

This time, I nodded. "Fix it," I invited. "Help me get it right."

> [*While you will often receive affirmation from your client that your summary was correct, there will be times when your summary is wrong. A normal part of collaboration is allowing correction when that happens. When you don't receive an obvious affirmation of your summary, you can ask one of the following questions to check in on your accuracy and invite correction:*
>
> - *"Is there anything you'd like to add or correct with that?"*
> - *"Fix it for me."*
> - *"What else did I miss?"*
>
> *By being humble enough to let my clients tell me that I've been inaccurate without becoming defensive, I create a sense of safety for them to tell me the truth.*
>
> *Therapists might wonder what they should do if they believe their assessment was accurate and their client's dismissal is more about avoidance or resistance than about the therapist's level of understanding. Even here, I encourage the therapist to ask the above questions to allow the client to express themselves more clearly and to better understand whatever it is the client thinks you are missing from your summary.*
>
> *If the client still resists, this might be a sign that there needs to be an emphasis on joining with that particular client.*]

Kimmie drew a deep breath. "It's not just about the changes. Yes, those are exhausting and it's hard to keep up. I know it's hard for Selah to keep up with the changes Maisie is facing, too. But I think where I feel the most frustrated is with the lack of boundaries. It's like Selah thinks it's okay to put me to the side—she worries about her dad's or her brother's feelings and needs more than mine. I think what I'm looking for is to feel like a priority and to see some better boundaries in the way we deal with her family."

> "Ah, I see what I missed," I said. "Tell me if I am getting it right now: You agree that the changes have been hard and sometimes it's difficult to keep up. I think what I'm hearing between the lines, though, is that you can be patient with Selah about the changes and that you're also grateful for the way Selah has been responding to Maisie. You know it's hard for both of you."
>
> Kimmie nodded, and I continued, "You're saying that's not exactly the issue. For you the issue is that you feel deprioritized and as if the boundaries you have as a family are violated in order for Selah to avoid conflict or upset within her own family. It's almost like it's easier to upset you than it is to upset her dad or brother. That's the part that really bothers you."
>
> Kimmie nodded even more vigorously. "Exactly."

While Ebony and Karl and Selah and Kimmie attended therapy for different reasons and with different emotional states, both couples expressed a sense of being "bought into" the idea of therapy. Sometimes, despite both people having agreed to come to therapy, you will have a tough customer—as we will see with John in the next anecdote. These clients often enter therapy skeptical about whether it's necessary or helpful, and they may not yet trust the process.

When joining with clients who aren't quite sure if they buy into the promise of therapy, it's crucial to avoid becoming defensive about your profession. Instead, lean into creating safety by deeply validating and accurately summarizing the client's perspective, helping them feel genuinely heard and understood.

John and Amy: Joining

When John and Amy arrived for their intensive session, it was clear that John was doubtful of the process again. I met them both in the waiting room, shook their hands, and led them back to the office. On the way there, John lagged behind, scanning the office with a wary gaze as if sizing up whether this place would be worth his time.

When we got to the room, I checked in, as I usually do, on their basic comforts. Did they need to use the bathroom? Were they hydrated? Could I hang up their coats on the back of the door?

Most clients respond to these initial questions by relaxing—a deep breath, a softened posture. They begin to feel cared for and seen. They either take me up on my offers or take the opportunity to tell me something about themselves like "Oh, no! I always come prepared with water."

This time was different. I noticed that John hardly responded to my solicitous questions. He gave brief nods but mostly avoided eye contact, keeping his distance. He was seemingly disinterested in making any connection with me at all. I wondered: Was he shutting down from feeling overwhelmed and flooded? Was it disdain for me or the process? Or simply a habit of withdrawing in social situations?

It seemed like Amy noticed the distance too. She tried to pull John in. "Honey, isn't that nice? She got us bottled water," she said, glancing at the coffee table. When John hardly responded, she looked uncomfortable.

In light of all this, I decided to change my usual approach. John had something on his mind, and I didn't want to ignore the clear signs he was giving me.

"If it's okay with you both, I'd like to start by giving an overview of the day." I paused. "But before I do, I'd like to check in—how are you both feeling right now?"

As I'd anticipated, Amy was the first to answer. "I'm really looking forward to this! Things have been impossible at home. I've been reading about this process and I'm just really excited for us to get some tools." She looked at John with a slightly forced smile. "We are excited, right, honey?"

John took a measured breath. "Honestly, I still don't get it. I'm wondering why we are here. It seems like we're spending a lot of money on something we could just talk about at home."

"John, you're definitely not alone in feeling that way," I said warmly. "Many people with otherwise good relationships wonder why therapy is necessary."

> [*At this point, I could have tried to convince John that my services were worthy of the time and the cost or even gotten defensive. Instead, I took the opportunity to show him that it was safe for him to express his doubt with me. My smile and warm voice expressed that I wasn't upset by his thought. Sharing that other clients felt similarly let him know it wasn't the first time I had heard this.*]

John gave me a tolerant grimace. "Well, we aren't like most people you probably see here. We are fine. That's why this whole thing is confusing. I think Amy is just exaggerating the issues and now here we are, spending a ton of time and money."

I nodded. "I can imagine it's frustrating to be here when you think that the relationship is good. This is such a huge investment to make in so many ways. And I'm a stranger to you and you're having to dive in headfirst. It's a big ask."

> [*If we had been in the intervention stage of the intensive, I might have asked Amy to share her reaction to what John said. Instead, I wanted to take another opportunity to join with John by validating his feelings and summarizing his position. I completely understood that it was a big ask for him to come to therapy when he didn't know if he truly believed in it.*
>
> *At this moment, I was taking some risk in losing my connection with Amy. Focusing on John risked making Amy feel unheard or unsupported in her belief that therapy could help. But given her investment, I judged this was a safe risk to take in order to build connection with John.*]

Amy broke in. "I guess this is what I'm not understanding, John. We argue all the time—how are you not seeing the writing on the wall?"

I turned to her. "You're feeling confused, too, Amy, because you are noticing problems that seem very obvious to you."

"Yes, it makes no sense." Amy opened her hands. "He says we have no problems but clearly we do."

"Okay, so we've got some common ground," I pointed out. "You're both confused. I want to help you understand each other better today. John, I know this is a big ask, but since you're here now, do you think it's possible for you to trust this process and see what it can do?"

> [*Rather than pushing back on John's protests related to the session or agreeing with Amy that John was wrong, I joined with both of them as individuals by summarizing their positions and then joined with them both by showing that I understood their joint predicament.*]

"Well," John grunted, "I'm here, aren't I?"

"You both are," I agreed. "Let me give you a rundown of the day, and then I want to hear more about the relationship and what's going on. Is that okay?"

> John crossed his arms. "Yep, I'm just going to let you guide us because I don't get it."
>
> Although John wasn't fully bought in before I continued with the session, I could see his defenses begin to soften. We weren't fully joined, but the process had started.

While John avoided discussing the issues that brought him and Amy to therapy because he didn't fully believe in the process, even clients who are fully bought in can struggle to dive into the work. Often, this hesitation comes from feeling overwhelmed by the prospect of confronting difficult topics. This was the case for Andrew and Ron, who came to me seeking guidance as they considered whether to end their relationship.

> ## Ron and Andrew: Joining
>
> On the first day of Ron and Andrew's intensive, I found them sitting on different sides of the waiting room. They both seemed exhausted.
>
> "Hi, Ron. Hi, Andrew. I'm Liz. Nice to put faces to the names," I said as I approached them. "Do either of you need to use the bathroom or get water before we head to the office?"
>
> They both shook their heads, got up from their seats, and indicated they were following me to the office. As we settled in there, Andrew began to make some small talk with me. "Your office is really nice. How long have you been here?"
>
> "We've been in this office for a few years. I love it here. Do you live in the area?"
>
> Ron responded by explaining that they used to live down the street from the office but now live about an hour away. Andrew chimed in again by asking, "Have you ever been to Davini's before?"
>
> "I haven't," I replied.
>
> "Oh, wow. You need to go. Best Italian restaurant in the area! It's two minutes from here. We used to go all the time when we lived here."
>
> Ron and Andrew continued to prolong the small talk, asking me what I thought about the weather that day and how traffic was for my drive in. They even noticed some curtains I had not yet put up in the office and shared ideas they had for how I could hang them up.
>
> While they talked, I could see that they weren't totally at ease. It wasn't similar to Selah and Kimmie, who were playful and laughing as we spent time looking at the cat TikTok video. Rather, they seemed anxious and nervous. Ron's hands were shaking and Andrew kept taking deep inhales to regulate himself. It was clear they weren't ready to dive in yet and needed some sort of soft entry into the day's therapeutic process. Noticing that Andrew was wearing a Mets hat, I saw a potential opening for a more personal connection.
>
> "Are you a Mets fan?" I asked him.
>
> Andrew's face lit up. "Oh yeah, born and raised in New York. Wearing this here in Philly definitely singles me out."
>
> "I was wondering about that—that's a bold move." I smiled.
>
> "Are you a sports fan?" Andrew asked me.
>
> I laughed. "Not really, but I appreciate hometown pride. How about you, Ron? Are you a Mets fan too?"
>
> "No way!" Ron gave a mock scowl. "I'm a big Phillies fan. Born and raised here."

"Interesting—how does that work out between the two of you?" I asked playfully.

> [While I often begin by setting structure to help couples manage dysregulation, here I judged it best to first focus on connection and easing their nerves through casual conversation. The couple did not seem at risk for starting an argument with each other, like Ebony and Karl, so I did not feel any urgency with creating structure and containment for them. Rather, I wanted to give them time to regulate their nerves before getting started and I decided to do so by joining with them through showing interest. Therapists can show interest by asking questions, using relatable metaphors, or remembering names and places that clients mention.]

After talking this way for a few moments, I could see that Andrew and Ron were feeling more comfortable. So, after getting their consent, I spent a little time setting the scene for what was to come next and then asked them if they were ready to discuss what had brought them to therapy. They began sharing with me their concerns about the relationship and what was preventing them from moving forward together. Their biggest problem seemed to be that they were on opposing sides of almost every issue (including whether they should continue the relationship) and could never come together. It was a perfect opportunity for a metaphor that would speak to both of them.

"From what you've said," I mused, "it sounds like your relationship feels a lot like a Mets versus Phillies rivalry—you're opposing teams on almost every issue."

They looked at me in surprise, then at each other, and then broke out into relieved laughter.

"Exactly!" Ron agreed. "It's ridiculous. But I do feel like we could be on the same team, and I'm hopeful we can start that process in here."

> [To continue the joining process, I utilized the Mets versus Phillies metaphor throughout their work with me. This created a sense that they were seen and understood outside of their issues.]

By taking time to connect with Ron and Andrew beyond their relationship struggles, I built early rapport that helped ease tension. Using their shared Mets-Phillies rivalry metaphor throughout therapy gave them a fresh lens, one that encouraged them to start thinking of themselves as part of the same team.

With Ebony and Karl, Selah and Kimmie, Amy and John, and Ron and Andrew—four very different couples and presenting issues—I was able to join with them by working to show I heard and understood their positions and feelings. Doing this doesn't just help the couple feel safe and connected; it can also build a sense of confidence in the therapist, another important aspect of joining with the couple in therapy.

Confidence in the Therapist

It might surprise you to learn that clients don't actually come to see you because of their problem. When studying depressed clients, psychiatrist Dr. Jerome Frank (1974) realized that people come to therapy not because they have a problem but because they've become demoralized about solving their own problem and they want another person to help them. Hearing this perspective helped me to recognize that the couple is looking to me personally for guidance. While many couples have problems, those who come to therapy are saying, "We need *you* to help us with our problems because we haven't been able to help ourselves." This is an important reminder of our role to build confidence in our clients that we are more than just someone who sits in a chair, listens to them, and then sends them back into the world with no road map.

Because the couple coming for an intensive has already decided they have some confidence in you (they've booked several hours of working with you, sight unseen!), you are entering into a relationship in which the couple already believes in the knowledge and tools you can offer.

However, throughout the first day, you'll continue to add to this perception by providing nuggets of psychoeducation, aha moments, and containment:

- **Psychoeducation** is the process of providing the couple with information that helps them process and understand their issue more deeply. It is an evidence-based therapeutic intervention that helps couples cope and instills confidence in their therapist's expertise.

- **Aha moments** are the moments when a therapist summarizes, connects information, or asks a question in a way that helps the client understand something new about themselves. Usually, these moments have to do with connecting dots between their past and present, hearing a new explanation for an old topic that never made sense before, or experiencing an emotion they hadn't let themselves experience before.

- **Creating a container** is the process of building a sense of safety for the clients by providing direction, guidance, and boundaries.

All of these increase the clients' confidence in you as a professional.

Ebony and Karl: Psychoeducation, Creating a Container, and an Aha Moment

After Ebony finished describing the discovery of Karl's infidelity and its reverberations on her life, it was time for Karl to provide his perception of the issues in their relationship. As Ebony listened, her face became tense, her brow furrowing and her lips turning into a tight frown. She shook her head as Karl spoke and made audible sighs to indicate her discomfort and anger regarding Karl's words. I observed her attempts to self-soothe as she looked out the window and bounced her knee, but no matter what she did, it was clear she was having an emotionally and physiologically difficult time listening to Karl talk about the discovery of the affair. Ebony was experiencing **diffuse physiological arousal**.

> **COUPLES THERAPY DICTIONARY**
>
> ### Diffuse Physiological Arousal
> Diffuse physiological arousal (DPA), also known as "flooding," refers to stress hormones like cortisol and adrenaline being released in the body in response to a real or perceived threat. The result is a fight or flight response. It can cause a person to become withdrawn or activated, which makes communication between the partners ineffective.
>
> When people are in DPA, they tend to experience the following:
>
> - Heart racing
> - Increased blood pressure
> - Breathing changes
> - Increased amygdala activation
> - Decreased frontal lobe activity
> - Body temperature becomes hot and flushed
> - Dry mouth
> - Muscle tension
> - Tunnel vision/defensive perspective

As soon as Karl came to a natural break in what he was saying, I stepped in. "Karl, let me ask you to pause for just a moment."

> [When I saw the signs that Ebony was physiologically flooded, I knew that I needed to initiate a pause. Physiological flooding occurs when distress overwhelms a person's capacity to cope, triggering the body's protective response. Any requests of them to communicate well—in this case, asking Ebony to listen while Karl gave his side of the story—would be misguided, as they would only result in causing severe distress to the person who is flooded. Without appropriate intervention, flooded states also result in negative communication outcomes; the flooded person is likely to either become completely withdrawn and frozen or become activated and yell or attack. On top of this, once one person is flooded, it is more likely that their partner will also become flooded in response.
>
> The signs I saw that Ebony was physiologically flooded were:
>
> - Muscles tensing in her face
> - Audible sighs that indicated changes in her breathing, difficulty catching her breath, and attempts to soothe herself
> - Bouncing her leg to navigate the surge of stress hormones causing activation in her body
> - Looking out the window to "remove" herself from the threat
> - When she spoke, her mouth suddenly sounded dry
> - Eyes very wide open, as if looking for the threat

If I had let Karl continue speaking, Ebony would have remained stuck in a distressed state and her distress would have likely increased to the point of complete shutdown or reactivity, causing her to yell or walk out of the room.

*I recognized that Ebony was experiencing pain and distress that were moving beyond her **window of tolerance**, making it unadvisable to continue my assessment right then. The experience felt out of control for Ebony, and as the therapist, it fell to me to bring it under control. In calling for a pause, I was offering containment. I could provide direction and space for her to take a moment for self-soothing.]*

COUPLES THERAPY DICTIONARY

Window of Tolerance

The window of tolerance, a concept developed by Dr. Dan Siegel (1999), is the range of emotional arousal in which we can best function in everyday life. When we are aroused outside of that window, it becomes more difficult to function mentally, relationally, and physically.

I turned my body toward Ebony and gently said, "Ebony, I notice you're in a lot of pain right now."

Ebony bit her lip, nodded, and continued to cry.

[When Ebony nodded, it was a sign I was on the right path for helping her to feel safe and understood in that moment (the nod factor). When Ebony began to cry, it was my observation that she felt a release, as her shoulders dropped and the muscle tension in her face loosened.]

"This is really painful stuff to talk about," I affirmed gently, "and you're already in so much pain. If this is too much right now, we can take a break."

Ebony stared at the ceiling and continued to bite her lip, attempting to hold back her tears. I took this as a signal that we needed a break, even if Ebony couldn't articulate it.

"Karl, how about you take a bathroom break?" I suggested. "And Ebony, I want to get you some water. I will be right back."

COUPLES THERAPIST RESOURCE

Taking a Break

Breaks are frequently used during intensive couples therapy. When the therapist notices that flooding or escalation is getting in the way of the couple creating productive change, taking a break can help reset the conversation while also modeling to the couple how they can intervene in their negative cycle at home.

> [When someone is flooded, the therapist's role is to direct them toward feeling safe again and completing their stress cycle.
>
> Asking Karl to take a bathroom break served two purposes:
> - It provided Ebony space from Karl without asking her to do much in the moment.
> - If Karl was also becoming flooded, it provided him an opportunity for space and movement to complete his own stress cycle.
>
> Offering to get Ebony some water also had several purposes:
> - It gave her space to release some of the emotion that was overwhelming her.
> - It provided an opportunity for mindfulness and grounding (by drinking the water).
> - It served a coregulatory function as I was able to offer her water in a calm manner.]

Karl exited the room and I retrieved a bottle of water, which I handed to Ebony. I sat quietly as she sipped from the bottle, softly crying and staring out the window. After several moments, she finally looked at me.

"Thank you for that," she whispered, wiping her eyes. "I couldn't even hear what Karl was saying—my heart was pounding in my ears. I'm just so upset. I don't know how to get through this."

"It's so hard," I reflected to her. "We can take breaks whenever you need to. You don't need to just push through; that won't always be helpful. Would it be okay if I get Karl from the waiting room now?"

Ebony drew a deep breath. "Yes, I'm okay now. Though I might run to the bathroom and get some more water before we start again, if that's okay?"

"Of course, please let me know at any point when you need to do something for yourself."

"I'm not usually very good at that. I usually just push through. But I'll try."

> [Here, I noticed Ebony had recognition that she needed a little more time for herself, and I also noticed she was able to advocate for her needs. I chose to reflect this to her, as I wanted to observe her response to my reflection as part of my assessment: Was she usually able to advocate for herself? Was this new for her? How would she take positive feedback?]

Once we were all back in the office, I checked in with the couple. "Thanks for letting us take a moment, Karl. I appreciate it. Ebony, how are you feeling now?"

"I feel much better," she responded, "and I think I'm ready for us to continue to talk."

"Karl, how are you doing?" I asked.

"I'm okay. I'll admit I'm a little worried about the sessions if we aren't able to talk without it upsetting Ebony so much."

I looked over at Ebony to see how this comment impacted her and saw her nod in agreement with Karl.

"I hear you're worried, Karl," I said. "I want to let you know that taking breaks during an intensive is common and it might be something we experience again during our time together. Sometimes when we hear about painful events, our bodies can have a strong reaction. Anytime you feel that, it can be helpful to take a break. It can actually be counterproductive to just push through."

> [While I try not to provide much psychoeducation during the assessment process because I don't want to provide feedback on issues I haven't taken a full assessment for, I did decide it was necessary to give some context here. In my clinical opinion, it was important to

> *"close the loop" on the break we just took by normalizing what had happened through providing the "why." Doing this creates a sense of a container and increases the clients' confidence in the therapist's expertise.*
>
> *With that being said, I did not provide the entire overview of physiological flooding then—it would have sidetracked our assessment. (I gave Ebony and Karl more information on flooding later that day, during the feedback portion.)]*
>
> Ebony took a deep breath and looked at me. "Earlier, you told me to let you know if I needed a break and I think I said something like 'I'll try, but I usually just push through.'"
>
> I nodded as I listened.
>
> "I just made a connection," Ebony continued, "You said sometimes it's counterproductive to push through. I never thought of it that way. I always thought that pushing through meant I was being resilient and a good partner, even if I felt like I was exploding inside. But looking back, I can see it probably made things worse for me, and definitely for our conversations, to just sit through it. I don't even think I ever connected before how bad my body feels in those moments. And seeing how much better I feel now that I took that break—it makes sense."
>
> Providing some basic psychoeducation on the importance of taking breaks when we are in extreme distress had led to an aha moment for Ebony. Moments like this do more than offer insight, though—they build the therapeutic alliance. By helping Ebony connect the dots between her emotional overwhelm and her coping strategies, I was not only offering information but also letting her know that I truly saw and understood her, laying a foundation for our continued work together.

When Confidence Breaks Down

Sometimes, even when we try our best to create safety and trust for our clients, we may disrupt their confidence in us. Known as *the negative impressions factor* (Goicoechea et al., 2009), this occurs when one or both members of the couple do not believe assessment is going well and the therapist doesn't repair and rejoin during the assessment phase. This can occur if the therapist provides the written assessment results too quickly without taking time to talk to the couple or if the therapist gives feedback about their observations too early in the session. It can also occur if the couple does not believe the therapist can help them—often because they perceive that the therapist "just doesn't get it" when they try to explain their situation, because the therapist doesn't provide enough structure and containment, or because they don't learn anything new from the therapist.

When an individual or couple has a negative impression of the therapist during the assessment phase, they will become or stay guarded; therefore, the therapist will not hear some of the most pivotal aspects of their experiences and perceptions. A client who has a negative impression of the therapist is also more likely to respond defensively to them. They might argue with the therapist's feedback or even become combative.

When I've met with clients who have had disruptions in confidence in their primary therapy experiences, I've heard comments like these:

- "My therapist rushed to judgment and told us they couldn't work with us because of something we wrote in our assessment. If they'd have spoken to us, we would have been able to explain our issues more clearly."

- "My therapist never gave us any feedback" or "They gave us feedback, but it wasn't right. It always seemed like they were just reading from some checklist."
- "I didn't know what we were paying them for. I thought they would tell us something to help our relationship, but really, we just went in and talked week after week without any direction."
- "They were rigid in their beliefs and not open to thinking about our issues in another way."
- "They didn't seem confident in themselves, which made us think they were new to the job."

When couples are working with a therapist, they want to be asked difficult questions, given honest feedback, and provided with direction. Not receiving these things creates a sense that the therapist is not providing the service they are looking for. At the same time, the couple will also be looking for a therapist who offers empathy, validation of their subjective experience, understanding, and expressions of care and concern for both partners.

All therapists, at some point, will respond to clients in a way that disrupts confidence. During the assessment with Kimmie and Selah, I inadvertently disrupted Kimmie's confidence in me when I shared a hypothesis about their conflict that she did not agree with.

Kimmie and Selah: Disrupted Confidence

Earlier in my assessment with Kimmie and Selah, we'd established that they were having a difficult time with the transitions they were facing together. While I'd initially focused on the transitions themselves, Kimmie had corrected my summary, explaining that the biggest source of frustration for her was the lack of boundaries that Selah had with her family when it came to managing these changes.

We began to explore each partner's family of origin. Selah shared that she grew up in a close-knit family where she felt loved and supported.

"Selah, it sounds like you had a really warm upbringing and that you felt really secure with your family?" I asked.

Selah nodded and smiled. "I was lucky. I really had a good childhood. It's why I feel so responsible for my dad and brother now. We take care of each other in my family, and I don't take that responsibility lightly."

Selah paused and I waited quietly—I could see she wanted to say more.

"Kimmie had a very different upbringing. Sometimes, I think that plays a role in our current conflict. But I won't speak for her. Kimmie, do you want to share more about your family now?" Selah asked gently as she turned to Kimmie and held her hand.

"Yeah, I can share more now. My family couldn't have been more opposite to Selah's. I was alone as a child. When I had any issue—like I was sad, or I was being bullied at school—no one was there for me. My mom had to work a lot of jobs to keep our heads above water, so she wasn't around. And my dad was never in the picture."

As Kimmie spoke, I remembered that she had written in her intake paperwork how safe and loved she felt by Selah, and how she'd never felt so secure before—not in her previous marriage nor in her family of origin. My mind jumped to the possibility that Selah needing to spend so much time with her father and brother in recent months felt like abandonment to Kimmie and brought up some childhood wounds. While this hypothesis was good, I should have kept it to myself during the assessment phase. Instead, I shared it.

"Kimmie, it sounds like you had a really lonely childhood and always hoped that you could create a close, loving family, both for yourself and then for your daughter too. You found that with Selah. Now that Selah is spending so much time with her dad and brother, I wonder if you're beginning to feel as if you've been left behind or abandoned."

For some people, this hypothesis might have built their confidence in me. They might have thought, *Wow, she really gets it! And so quickly, too!*

It did not go that way for Kimmie. After I finished speaking, she gave an exasperated sigh. "No, like I said earlier, I'm frustrated with the lack of boundaries. That's all. I don't want this blamed on my childhood."

[*It was clear that Kimmie was frustrated with me. In her perception, we had only been together for a brief time and she had already had to correct me twice. While her defensive response did align with my theory, I knew that holding too tightly to my opinion in that moment would have caused more rupture than repair. The hypothesis itself had clinical merit, but I shared it too early in the assessment process, before trust had been fully established. Kimmie wasn't ready to hear it, and it made her feel misunderstood.*

In that moment, I had three paths available to move forward. I could double down by explaining why I thought what I thought, move on quickly from Kimmie's response, or take responsibility and attempt to repair. Luckily, I chose repair.]

"I got it wrong," I stated.

"Yes, I really don't want to be seen as the one with the issue here just because of my family."

"I really appreciate when you correct me, Kimmie," I told her. "It's important that if I get it wrong you feel confident enough to tell me."

Kimmie sighed again, but this time it sounded like relief rather than exasperation.

"Thanks for saying that. After I corrected you, I started feeling like a jerk. I don't want to come across that way. It's just important to me that Selah doesn't discount my perspective about the lack of boundaries. Anyone would be upset about this. It's not just because of my messed-up childhood."

"Let me try to get it right again—you had a difficult childhood and you felt lonely. And that doesn't mean that the way you're feeling now is caused by your childhood. It's important for Selah to know that your concerns about boundaries are very important." I spoke in a measured, calm, and empathetic voice to ensure Kimmie knew I was open to correction and was not feeling defensive. "Am I closer to understanding?"

Kimmie nodded. "It's mostly right. Except . . . I guess there's a possibility that it does hurt a little bit more because of what I grew up with. So maybe you're right on that, but I don't want it to overshadow my complaint."

"I hear that. I understand how important it is to you that you and Selah discuss setting better boundaries, and you don't want that to be overshadowed by your childhood."

As I responded to Kimmie with curiosity rather than doubling down or defensiveness, Kimmie was able to respond to me with honesty rather than losing trust and withdrawing further. Later, we could talk more about how the current situation, while frustrating on its own, was likely even more painful due to the enduring pain points from Kimmie's younger years—not to dismiss the current concern, but rather to increase the level of empathy Selah could feel toward Kimmie regarding her experience.

Finding Hope

Well-known researchers and practitioners such as Irvin Yalom (1995) have long emphasized the necessity of incorporating hope into therapy. When people come to therapy, they are often worried that perhaps their situation cannot improve. Instilling hope supports their well-being and increases their motivation to participate in the therapeutic process.

In most cases, it is appropriate to encourage discussions of hope for an improved relationship between the two partners. However, in situations where you've assessed that the relationship is not safe for one or both people or where they have decided to part ways, it may not be appropriate to support the clients' hope for the relationship. In these situations, you can still incorporate hope into your work with each individual.

You can help your couples develop hope in their relationship through a number of ways:

- **Ask the "miracle question":** Say something like "Let's say that after our weekend, you go home and go to bed. When you wake up in the morning, you discover there was a miracle and suddenly you feel exactly as you hoped you would in the relationship. How do you know there was a miracle? What is different?" This exploration not only fosters hope but also supports agency and pathways thinking by helping clients identify what they want and imagine that change is possible.

- **Use pathways thinking:** C. R. Snyder (1994) states that clients need to see one or more workable routes to their goal and to believe in their ability to bring about continued movement on the selected pathway. When a therapist encourages pathways thinking, the couple might feel less limited in their ability to change by seeing alternate routes to change that they had not previously tried or discussed.

COUPLES THERAPIST SKILL

Pathways Thinking

According to C. R. Snyder and colleagues (2002), "pathways thinking in any given instantiation involves thoughts of being able to generate at least one, and often more, usable route to a desired goal" (p. 258).

The therapist can provide pathways toward change by asking the couple about alternate solutions to their issues, by describing paths that others have taken, and by planting a seed about what will happen next.

The therapist can also provide pathways of change in the way they describe what will happen next during the intensive. For example, when a topic comes up that the couple feels overwhelmed discussing, the therapist might say, "I know this is really difficult to discuss today. Tomorrow, we are going to do some interventions regarding this topic and I am hopeful it will improve the discussion," or "Tomorrow, we will have an opportunity to work on this more."

- **Encourage agency:** You can help clients feel more confident in their own agency by being curious about current and past barriers to treatment and by exploring with them what would help them remove those barriers. You can also encourage agency thinking by helping the clients consider unique outcomes in their lives—in other words, helping them reflect on other times in their lives when they've been better able to handle the challenges they are seeking to address now in therapy.

> ## John and Amy: Pathways Thinking
>
> As Amy and John discussed the history of their relationship, they started to notice a pattern to the ups and downs they had experienced in their relationship. Anytime life became stressful, they began to argue more and became dissatisfied with each other. Several times during college, they decided to temporarily break up because it was too hard to be together. After getting engaged, they argued repeatedly about who to invite to the wedding. Their relationship struggled yet again once their baby was born, and Amy admitted that she still hadn't forgiven John for his behavior during that time.
>
> "If this is how we always are, maybe there isn't any hope for us." Amy looked down at her hands. "I don't know. Now that we're talking about it, I'm starting to wonder if we just don't handle life together very well."
>
> "You're starting to see a pattern and you're worried it can't change?" I asked.
>
> Amy gave a heavy shrug. "I always thought of us as a happy couple, but maybe we're not. Maybe we just can't do it."
>
> "I can hear that's a concern of yours," I said. "I think today and tomorrow will be about figuring out what's going on during those moments of transition that make it particularly difficult to get along. A lot of couples really struggle in those moments—it's not just the two of you. I think we will need to better understand why you struggle. Is it because of how you manage stress? How you make decisions? I need to learn more about your relationship, but we might focus on those two areas tomorrow. Depending on the issue, we have options for how we talk about it and navigate it."
>
> John spoke up. "I think it definitely has to do with how we navigate stress, so I'm interested in talking more about that."
>
> Rather than becoming directive or pulling Amy back in, I wanted to support John's emerging insight and encourage pathways thinking. I responded with gentle curiosity: "Tell me more."

It's important to be cautious in how we offer hope, especially during the beginning of a session. Going overboard with positivity risks sounding dismissive of the clients' concerns. It can also come across as playing Pollyanna in a way that won't resonate with a distressed couple. Instead of leaning heavily on positive platitudes when Amy began to express doubts about the relationship, I normalized her perspective by letting her know that other people struggle in the same way and provided some potential pathways to improvement. Hearing that they were not unique in their struggles and that the therapist already had thoughts about what might help provided a sense of hope for both John and Amy.

How we instill hope becomes even more complicated when couples come into session with different levels of commitment or conflicting goals. It's easy to unintentionally lean toward one partner's story, which can inadvertently crush the hope that motivates therapy. With these mixed-agenda couples, it can be tempting to lean into extremes by either offering too much hope toward an unlikely outcome or undermining hope toward realistic positive outcomes. Undermining hope can happen when therapists make statements like the following (Doherty et al., 2024):

- That they cannot help the clients
- That the clients are incompatible
- That the relationship is beyond repair

- That divorce is the only realistic option
- That a partner has a personality problem
- That they should do individual therapy instead

Research shows that undermining statements are linked to worse outcomes for couples therapy (Doherty et al., 2024). After all, if the couples therapist is saying (or inadvertently implying) that there is no hope for the relationship to improve, why should the clients bother trying to work on their relationship under the guidance of that therapist, or even at all? Therefore, I try to avoid undermining the possibility for healthy relational outcomes, even when the end of the relationship seems near.

Ron and Andrew: Building Hope by Avoiding Undermining Statements

"I know that the possibility of a separation is on the table—can you tell me more about that?" I asked Ron and Andrew as we began discussing levels of commitment in the relationship.

Ron responded by sharing that he was 100 percent in. "I know I've done things in the past that have created doubt in Andrew about my commitment, but I want Andrew to know I am fully committed."

Andrew looked straight ahead while Ron spoke. As soon as Ron paused, he broke in by sharing that he was fairly certain the relationship was over. "It's really hard to say this, but I just can't see things improving. Too much damage has already been done."

I paused for a moment.

> [When I was a novice therapist, I might have responded to Andrew by encouraging him to maintain hope that the relationship could improve. Or, perhaps, due to my own discomfort, I would have wanted to shut it all down by letting them know that if Andrew was already out the door there was nothing else I could do. Instead, I responded by offering hope in a grounding and realistic manner.]

"Right now, you are both on different pages. Ron, you're 100 percent in and you are ready to work on improving the relationship. You want to fix this. Andrew, you seem to be 85 percent out—maybe a small part of you is leaning into the relationship, but mostly you're feeling as if the relationship cannot improve. Did I get that right?"

"You did, for me at least," said Andrew. "I would say that I'm almost all the way out of the door in this relationship, but like you said, there's a small part of me having trouble letting go."

"I can't tell either of you what exactly will happen next for your relationship," I told them. "What I can tell you is that I have worked with other people in the same situation—where one partner is committed to making things work and the other partner is considering the end of the relationship. Some of those couples decide to stay together, others decide to separate. Either way, I can support you in navigating how you both go about that decision with respect and I can support you in improving the way that you communicate about it, if you'd both like to do that."

> [Here, I did not make any promises about whether they would stay together or part ways. I did not force Andrew to imagine a world where they were together. That would only be cruel to Ron when Andrew was mostly certain he would want to separate. But I also did

> *not make an abrupt choice to end the therapy—who was I to know whether Andrew was really done or whether Ron might decide to let go? Instead, I let them know I have seen other mixed-agenda couples and described ways in which the situation could be made better through our work together, regardless of whether they stayed together or not.]*

Joining with the couple is a continual, active process throughout day 1 of an intensive session. As the therapist, you'll consistently seek opportunities to help both partners feel genuinely heard and understood, build their trust and confidence in you, and foster hope for their relationship's healing. All this happens alongside the specific clinical agenda you'll work on throughout the first day.

Assessment

The first day of the intensive is highly focused on assessment of the couple and their dynamics, and most of the day is utilized for this process. The initial (approximately) 90 minutes of the intensive session is used to assess the couple together, followed by meeting with each partner for 45 minutes to an hour. These times are guidelines rather than rigid rules. Adapt session length based on the couple's needs, engagement, and presenting issues. The remaining time will be used for the feedback portion of the day.

SAMPLE

Day 1 Agenda

- Relationship Assessment: Meet as a unit for 90 minutes
- Individual Assessment: Meet with partner 1 for 45 minutes
- Individual Assessment: Meet with partner 2 for 45 minutes
- Break
- Feedback: Meet as a unit for 90 minutes

While we will look at many granular areas of focus throughout this section, I suggest therapists utilize a Bowenian Therapy lens (Davis & Butler, 2004) to consider three primary areas for assessment:

- **Neutrality versus reactivity:** Is the couple able to see the bigger picture beyond immediate conflict? Do they recognize that many of their issues are with the system (either the relational system or the greater world system), or are they reactive and focused on blame and deflection? Are they able to self-soothe when they become overwhelmed? The therapist's goal is to help them approach their issues with more neutrality over time.

- **Relational processes:** Here you are looking to understand the capacities of each partner's relational processes. Are they able to maintain awareness of themselves, their partner, and the relationship during their interactions? For example, a partner who struggles with relational processes might be highly aware of their partner's needs and have a strong regard for protecting and honoring their relationship, but they might not advocate for themselves, set boundaries, or understand their own feelings.

- **Responsibility:** Does each member of the couple take responsibility for self-change and own their role in relational dynamics? Is there an ability to recognize and take accountability for the ways in which the individual negatively affects the relational system? Is the couple, jointly, able to have a problem-solving focus when they face challenges together? Do they believe in their shared ability to overcome difficulties, talk about possibilities, and act? The therapist will also want to observe whether there is an imbalance in responsibility taking.

As you get to know the couple, you'll begin to see their issues within these three categories and begin to explore how the presenting issues arose within the historical context of their lives as a whole and their relationship.

Ebony and Karl: Assessment Areas When Someone Has Been Betrayed

As we have observed thus far in Ebony and Karl's interactions, the couple was not able to navigate their challenges through a lens of grounded neutrality. This makes sense, as often people who have been betrayed show symptoms of posttraumatic stress disorder (PTSD). Ebony's trust had recently been violated by Karl's affair and her reactive state was one of self-protection. Asking Ebony to lean into a neutral stance without first asking Karl to rebuild trust would not feel safe to Ebony—you cannot ask someone to go against what their instinct is accurately leading them to do. At this point, Karl had proven himself to be untrustworthy and unable to make choices that would protect Ebony's emotional and physical health.

Second, we've seen that when it comes to relational processes, Karl had not been able to regard himself and his partner during his relational decision-making. By choosing to step outside of their relational contract (they both agreed to be in a monogamous relationship), Karl chose to disregard Ebony's well-being. On the other hand, I observed during our assessment process that Ebony often regarded Karl while not regarding herself. Besides the affair, both Karl and Ebony described a relationship in which Karl was often focused on obligations and interests outside of the marriage, leading Ebony to feel alone and discarded. Historically, Ebony would often suppress her needs and feelings, biting her tongue and muddling through even though she was upset. There was not a strong history of Ebony setting boundaries with Karl. Therefore, both Karl and Ebony showed difficulty creating a "we" throughout their relationship, the affair being the most recent evidence of this.

Lastly, as I assessed the couple, I had to look at the level of responsibility being taken by each partner. Even during her distressed state, Ebony generally seemed to take responsibility for herself. She expressed ways in which she could have done things differently in the past and described her own process in individual therapy. Karl also took some, but not full, responsibility for his actions. He showed remorse for the affair and a willingness to address the situation. However, he struggled to fully take responsibility when Ebony would become visibly distressed, saying things like "I don't understand how long this is supposed to take" or "How many times do you want me to say I'm sorry?"

The deeply fractured trust between Ebony and Karl created a conundrum: Where was the best place to start? If we immediately attempted to take an "equal responsibility" approach, asking Ebony to listen to Karl's complaints on their relationship just as we encouraged Karl to listen to her, Ebony would be asked to do something that her body recognized as unsafe, as evidenced by her trauma symptoms. (It's not safe to hand over trust and vulnerability to a person who has demonstrated they will harm you and has not yet demonstrated they will not do it again.) Making this request of Ebony would likely put her in a flooded state. At the same time, the relationship would not improve if Ebony continued to respond from a reactive place each time she attempted to express her needs or responded to Karl's attempts to rebuild trust. This would only degrade the relationship further.

As I continued to learn about Ebony and Karl during the first 90 minutes, I recognized that the priority was fostering emotional regulation and neutrality in their shared space—not neutrality about the harm itself. In my one-on-one with Karl, I planned to address his role in promoting neutrality by increasing his attunement to Ebony's feelings, enhancing relational awareness, and taking fuller responsibility for his actions. With Ebony, I aimed to support her in setting boundaries, cultivating self-regard, and voicing her needs—all critical for building a stronger relational stance.

COUPLES THERAPIST SKILL

Atone, Attune, Attach

When I work with couples recovering from an affair, I utilize Gottman Affair Recovery, which includes three steps:

1. **Atone:** During the initial stages of affair recovery, the therapist acts toward each partner with respect and kindness. The therapist also recognizes that the betrayed partner is in a state of distress due to their partner's trust-breaking actions. Because of this, the therapist coaches the betrayer toward being patiently empathetic, showing remorse, answering their partner's questions as honestly as possible, and speaking toward how they will rebuild trust. During this stage, the betrayed partner must have space to be angry, sad, and mistrusting. Also important in this phase is the therapist guiding the betrayed partner through conversations related to their belief of whether or not they can forgive their partner.

2. **Attune:** Once some sense of safety has been regained through the atonement phase (the betraying partner has been able to demonstrate remorse, patience, empathy, and responsibility taking), the couple will move toward exploring how to improve communication between each other and work toward a better understanding of each other. During this phase, both partners work together to increase neutrality (lessening the pointing of fingers and blame), improve relational processes (learning to care for the other person while also caring for themselves), and take responsibility for their own actions.

3. **Attach:** Finally, the couple agrees together that they will build a new relationship. There is an understanding that their relationship cannot "go back" to what it was. Rather, they will rebuild a secure attachment with each other through discussing their expectations of commitment, by using their new communication skills to discuss their needs, and by rebuilding emotional and physical connection.

Throughout the entire assessment (with the couple together and then individual meetings), you will be looking at the couple's ability to remain grounded during conversations (neutrality), see themselves and see the other person (relational processes), and take responsibility for their part.

Let's now explore how you will assess these three areas utilizing a structured assessment process that explores the problem, the history of the relationship, current levels of commitment, problem-solving, communication skills, boundaries, family history, buy-in, and goals during the first 90 minutes of the session with both partners present.

The First 90 Minutes

During the first 90 minutes of the intensive couples therapy session, you will meet with both partners at the same time to assess the relationship through direct inquiry and observation. Over the next several pages, we'll explore the areas of direct inquiry as well as areas in which you should be observing and reading between the lines.

Direct Inquiry

After spending a brief time joining with the couple, you will begin a structured process of getting to know the relationship through the following questions:

- What is each partner's view of the problem?
- What have they done thus far to solve the problem?
- What is the history of the relationship?
- What are the couple's interactional patterns (how do they communicate about problems, challenges, and decisions)?
- How has each partner's family of origin influenced them?
- What is each partner's level of commitment to the relationship?
- What are their goals for therapy and the relationship?

We'll go through each of these questions in detail below, using our four case study couples to see the different directions each question can lead.

EACH PARTNER'S VIEW OF THE PROBLEM

First you will ask the couple to describe their views of the problem that brings them in. Emphasize that differing perspectives on the problem are normal and that you want to hear from both partners. I accompany this with a reassuring smile and a nod to encourage them to start. Unless the couple is particularly hesitant, I typically let them choose who speaks first. This helps me observe who is more comfortable speaking, who is open to sharing, and who tends to take a leading role in discussions.

As each person shares their perception of the problem, listen and watch for the following:

- **Consensus:** Is this couple on the same page about the issue? If not fully, where is the consensus?

- **Body language:** When one partner shares, what is the body language of the other partner? Are they engaged, open, and respectful or distanced and aloof? Do they become combative during moments where they lack consensus on a topic?
- **Ability to listen:** On a basic level, you want to learn how capable the couple is when it comes to listening. Do they tend to interrupt each other (even though they know they will have their own turn soon)? Do they sit quietly and listen attentively? Do they pretend to listen but give off body signals that they are not (eye rolling, shaking their leg, etc.)? Can they listen to differing opinions?

Observing these aspects will help you begin to build the picture of the couple's pattern. Listen for the actual problem and within your mind work to combine their individual concerns so that you can clearly synthesize what they both are thinking and feeling about the relationship.

Ron and Andrew: Exploring Each Partner's View of the Problem

When I invited Andrew and Ron to share what brought them in that day, Andrew took the lead.

"I guess I'll answer first. I think the main issue is that we are at a crossroads. We recently had a huge argument on a vacation and it kind of woke me up a little bit. I started to wonder if this relationship is really what I want for the rest of my life. Do I really want to face the constant uncertainty or arguments? I do know I love Ron; I just don't know if I can continue to be in this relationship."

"Ron," I asked, "what's your reaction to what Andrew said?"

"I think we're on the same page about what brings us in," Ron said. "We disagree on almost everything, but we both agree that we fight too much. I think for a long time I didn't realize how much it was affecting Andrew. But I see it now. We don't want to be in a relationship where we're fighting constantly. But that doesn't mean we have to end it—I'm 100 percent committed to being in this relationship and making it right."

Andrew gave him a meaningful look. "Actions speak louder than words."

Ron's face tightened, a flicker of hurt crossing his expression as he nodded slowly. "I know my actions haven't always matched my words, but I really am trying to stay committed."

"Tell me more about what you meant when you said 'actions speak louder than words,' Andrew," I prompted.

He sighed. "Ron *says* he wants to stay together, but last night we got into an argument and he threatened to cancel our session today. Ron has a pattern of leaving me whenever things get tough, and it hasn't changed."

At this point, I offered my understanding of what they had told me. "It sounds like you're on the same page that there is an issue, but you differ on your levels of confidence on whether it could change."

Andrew answered, "Exactly. I just don't feel confident Ron can change." At this, Ron looked up to the ceiling, took a deep breath, then looked down at his lap.

I pointed out this nonverbal communication: "Andrew, what did you just notice about Ron?"

Andrew pursed his lips. "He sighed. He's annoyed with me. He gets this way whenever we're in an argument. He'll probably walk out if I keep talking about it."

Ron murmured, "You said the relationship is over. How do you want me to respond?"

"Is that what you heard, Ron?" I pursued. "That the relationship is over?"

> [*I was starting to get a picture of the pattern between them. Right now, they agree on the problem, but don't agree on the solution. When they don't agree on what should be done, Andrew expresses hopelessness, Ron gets frustrated and begins to withdraw, perhaps hearing a narrative in Andrew's words that isn't necessarily what he meant or even said. I make a note to continue to watch for this pattern.*
>
> *For quite some time, the couple has not had a relational process—when they become upset they become self-focused in an attempt to get their own needs met. They blame each other and then Ron withdraws from the situation. They aren't sure how to have dialogue that represents both of their needs and has an outcome that would work for both. The couple seems to be stuck in a cycle of reactivity in their lives with each other, however they do seem to be able to show more neutrality and groundedness during the session. It seems that both Andrew and Ron have a sense of their own responsibility for their relationship issues, however, Andrew seems to believe he has less responsibility than Ron. It is unclear how either of them has taken responsibility in the past for creating change.*]

As a couple shares with me their perception of the problem, I am not only watching for their conflict pattern. I am also:

- Digging for more
- Showing empathy and understanding
- Staying focused on observation rather than intervention

To the first point, the therapist should not take clients' answers at face value because they often withhold information or do not know how to articulate their problems clearly. They are living with the problem, so it can be difficult to explain to an outsider something that seems so clear to them.

I am adamant about not letting clients off the hook by accepting short answers to my questions. With some clients, I need to dig for more right out of the gate—I ask "What brings you to therapy today?" and they offer a brief, vague answer like "We just have terrible communication skills" or "Our relationship has lost its spark." Both of these responses answer the question, but they offer me little to no understanding of what the client actually means.

When I am given these types of answers, I prompt the clients to say more. Sometimes it is as simple as saying "Tell me more" or "Can you give me some examples of what that means?" At other times, you might have to find more creative ways to get more information. For example, you might ask the other partner to reflect on the brief answer they heard, saying something like "You just heard your partner share that they think communication is terrible between you two—tell me what you think that means."

> At one point, Andrew said, "I think our biggest issue is somewhat related to my upbringing."
>
> I waited a moment to see if he would share more; when he didn't, I prompted him directly: "Tell me more."
>
> He shifted in his seat. "Oh, you know, divorced parents and stuff."
>
> "I *don't* know," I told him, with a smile. "Help me know."

Andrew took a deep breath. "I grew up in a divorced home. My parents split up when I was young, and my dad was never around. So, when Ron threatens to leave, it brings all of that up again. It's an awful feeling. But sometimes I also jump to conclusions because of it and become incredibly anxious in an unhelpful way."

I turned to Ron. "How do you feel when you hear that?"

Ron met my gaze stoically. "He knows how I feel."

I prompted Ron to share more. "He might know how you feel, Ron, but I don't," I reminded him. "Can you share with me?"

> *[Whenever I receive an answer like "They already know how I feel" or "I already know how they feel," I take it as a signal to dig deeper. These are often protective responses against vulnerability. There are many reasons someone might take a more self-protective position—perhaps they've tried to show vulnerability in the past only to be rejected, or maybe discussing emotions creates discomfort in them due to their own life history. As the therapist, I am learning about why a person might seem more withdrawn and less curious throughout the assessment process. In the case of Ron and Andrew, Ron felt shut down due to his fears that the relationship was over. He was afraid that if he shared his feelings they wouldn't be received.]*

Beyond asking the client to tell you more or offering prompts to get their partner to further engage, some other helpful questions to get more information include:

- When did you first notice this becoming an issue?
- What have you done to try to solve the issue before?
- Have you gotten help for this issue from another professional? What was or wasn't helpful?
- Have there been periods of time when this wasn't an issue?
- How do you usually tend to solve issues together? Is your approach with this issue different from other issues you've tried to solve, or does it follow a similar pattern?

Second, showing empathy and understanding is also crucial as the couple shares their perceptions of the problem. It's important to keep both partners engaged by giving them a smile, eye contact, or a nod as they wait for their turn to speak. As discussed earlier, showing empathy and understanding helps the couple to join with you, which increases the likelihood that they will continue to share more with you rather than shutting down. Also, the more you attempt to show empathy and understanding, the more opportunity there is for the couple to clarify when you might have gotten it wrong.

And third, as couples reveal their patterns of interaction, it's not uncommon for them to enter into their negative conflict cycle. It's important to allow some of this to play out rather than jumping to use interventions or provide feedback. If the couple becomes critical or defensive, interrupts each other, or shows unhelpful body language, observe these interactions and begin to hypothesize how they play out in the relationship as a whole. When couples therapists provide interventions or feedback too quickly (before they have enough information), they increase the likelihood that they will get it wrong, which can shut down the couple's trust in the process and will limit information-gathering opportunities.

At times, therapists might find it challenging to avoid intervention for various reasons, such as a desire to show their value, countertransference regarding the conflict being witnessed, or a desire to "protect" their client. The therapist might also be used to shorter sessions in which they need to respond and intervene quickly so that the couple will not be dysregulated right before leaving the room.

Part of the work of a couples therapist during an intensive session is learning how to withstand observing uncomfortable interactions during the first day. Not only does this model to the couple that the therapist can "stick with it," but it also allows the therapist to see the evolution of the conflict as the couple might experience it outside of the room. Therapists can learn to withstand these interactions by using grounding techniques, by being clear with themselves on the ultimate goal of day 1 (to collect information), and through practice and repetition—it becomes easier to do this over time when you see that it works.

With this being said, it does not mean that the therapist provides no containment at all. There is a difference between beginning to utilize interventions or providing feedback and redirecting or requesting certain types of behavior within the room as ground rules. The goal during the day 1 assessment is to use containment to maintain safety and direction.

Let's look at an example from the first day of Andrew and Ron's intensive to demonstrate this. When I asked Ron to share how he felt hearing Andrew express that at times he felt abandoned by Ron the way he felt abandoned by his father, Ron shared that he felt incredibly sad hearing that. Andrew responded, "It's never made you sad enough to make any changes. You always say you get it, but you never do anything to change."

In this moment, Andrew was becoming critical of Ron. If we had been in the second day of the intensive, I would have asked Andrew to pause and then said something like "Andrew, right now, the way you're expressing yourself is critical and it's not going to be productive to the conversation. Can I try to help you express how you're feeling in a way that might be better received?" I would have gone on to coach Andrew to use "I statements" or a "soft start-up" approach (which we will explore on page 195).

However, since it was the first day of their intensive, I didn't coach Andrew to do any of that. Instead, I waited a moment to see how Ron would respond to Andrew's statement because I wanted to get more information on their conflict and communication patterns. As it turned out, Ron responded defensively to Andrew: "You always assume the worst of me!" This showed me that the couple tended to get caught in critical and defensive loops.

I'd seen enough at that point—allowing the couple to continue uninterrupted would not give me any further information that would be helpful to the assessment process. So I stopped them by saying, "Okay, I can see this is difficult to talk about. Is this what it usually looks like when you talk about this topic at home?"

You'll notice I did not teach them anything new at this point or ask them to try something different. I simply stopped the interaction once I could no longer learn anything else from it, summarized my observations, and redirected the couple toward what I needed next in the assessment.

There is an important exception to the rule of staying focused on observation rather than intervention during the assessment. When I can see that a lack of action on my part will create a sense for either or both clients that they are not safe in the therapy room, or when the process is pushing them outside of their window of tolerance, it might be necessary to provide intervention by beginning to introduce a concept or skill. As you might remember, I did so when Ebony became flooded as Karl described the events that had unfolded after her discovery of his affair. Had I not intervened then, Ebony would have been left in a state of distress, which would have decreased her feelings of safety and trust in the process. Because a person who is physiologically flooded is not able to communicate well, I also would not have been able to fully understand Ebony's expectations, feelings, needs, and wants. There are no hard and fast rules for when it is appropriate to intervene rather than simply observe—you'll need to use your clinical discernment.

HOW THE COUPLE HAS TRIED TO SOLVE THE PROBLEM THUS FAR

Once the couple has described the issue that brings them into therapy, you should explore with them what they've tried so far. During this time, you'll learn more about when they first noticed there was an issue and each individual's perspective about how they've tried to solve the issue. You'll also learn whether the couple has previously sought professional help and whether they believe anything improved due to the help. If the couple has previously been in therapy, you will want to understand precisely what the couple found helpful or unhelpful in order to tailor your own approach toward their needs.

Here, you are also looking for **unique outcomes**. Were there times when the couple tried to solve the problem and they noticed that there was improvement? Sometimes, the couple will say something like "We've had this issue off and on, but when we first moved to our new home, things seemed to improve." This gives you an opportunity to better understand what about that specific time period made improvement possible.

> **COUPLES THERAPY DICTIONARY**
>
> ## Unique Outcomes
>
> According to Gene Combs and Jill Freedman (2004), "our entryway for inviting people to tell and live new stories is through 'unique outcomes'" (p. 144). This term refers to outcomes that are different from how the couple usually describes themselves or the problem. For example, the couple might describe themselves as always having issues with their in-laws, but they might also share a story in which their in-laws were very helpful after the birth of a child.
>
> Sometimes these examples are offered freely; however, when couples feel inundated with their problems, the therapist will need to seek out stories of unique outcomes. A client might say something like, "Every once in a while my partner will [*insert positive behavior here*], but usually they just [*insert problem story here*]." Here, you will want to inquire further about the "every once in a while" to better understand when the partner is able to show that positive behavior, what it feels like when that happens, and what both people are thinking when it happens.
>
> Exploring unique outcomes serves the purpose of developing hope, creating a more accurate narrative, and encouraging neutrality regarding the problem. Rather than only seeing their problem story, the couple can begin to see that sometimes they are able to manage the issue through relational skills.

Kimmie and Selah: How the Couple Has Tried to Solve the Problem

"I'm wondering if you can remember when you first noticed that the two of you were becoming more withdrawn from each other," I asked Selah and Kimmie as we discussed the issues that had brought them to therapy.

Selah spoke first. "I don't know if it struck me then, but thinking back, there was a moment after my mom's funeral where I felt really unsupported by Kimmie. I know Kimmie would never want to hurt me, so I didn't bring it up, but I was hurting and I started to withdraw because of that."

Kimmie looked surprised. "I didn't know this. What do you mean? What did I do at the funeral?"

"I can't totally remember," Selah admitted, "but it had something to do with the amount of time I was spending with my dad and brother after the funeral. I think you made a passive-aggressive comment about having to eat with Maisie and me ignoring you both. I remember thinking to myself that it was really insensitive of you. So I just retreated and kept my feelings to myself."

Kimmie put a hand to her heart. "Wow, I'm really sorry. I truly don't remember that. It was a really stressful day—but that's not an excuse. So you remember this going back pretty far?"

Selah nodded. "I do. At least to my mom's funeral."

I turned to Kimmie. "When did you notice there was an issue?"

Kimmie thought for a moment. "It was a few months after the funeral. I started to notice Selah wouldn't tell me anything about her family. I'd ask what was going on and she'd just brush the question off. I started to feel frustrated because even though she wouldn't discuss it with me, caretaking her family members has a very real impact on us as a couple—our joint finances, how much time we're able to spend together, our parenting obligations."

"So you started to notice she was keeping to herself?" I repeated.

"Yes," Kimmie agreed, "keeping to herself and excluding me from information."

"What have the two of you tried before to deal with this?" I asked.

"We went to a therapist for a handful of sessions," Selah said. "They weren't very helpful. Every time we went in, it took some time to get to the point and by the time we really got into the conversation, the session would end."

"Okay, so you went to therapy. What else?"

"We've tried talking about it," Kimmie answered, "but like we said, it goes nowhere. We just don't want to get into conflict so we avoid it."

"I know you described really positive experiences with each other in your early years together," I reminded them. "Have you faced any issues like this before?"

Selah shook her head vigorously. "No, not at all. That's what I don't understand. And we've been together long enough to have faced challenges together before. So I don't get what's going on this time."

"If this isn't the usual way you solve issues, can you share more about how you usually face challenges?" I prompted them.

"We usually work as a team!" Kimmie said, with a half-smile of pride. "We've faced health challenges, financial challenges, parenting challenges . . . We've never acted *this* way. We're usually always there for each other."

"What's your theory on why this is different?" I asked.

After a moment of quiet reflection, Kimmie answered, "I think we're in a period of our lives where I expected to have fewer responsibilities and more time to connect with Selah. But all of a sudden, the exact opposite is happening, and I don't even get a say."

Selah added, "I think for me, I'm just grieving a lot. I'm grieving my own life—I feel like I've gotten old quick—and I'm grieving my mom. I'm starting to grieve the fact that my dad isn't really my dad anymore. I'm his caretaker now. I'm just having such a hard time." Her eyes began to tear up as she spoke.

I nodded. "There are a lot of transitions for both of you and this isn't what either of you expected at this stage in your life."

They both nodded in agreement. Selah wiped her eyes and turned to smile at Kimmie, who wrapped her in a hug.

> [Kimmie and Selah showed empathy toward each other as they discussed the problem. It was clear they were collaborators and had a desire to support each other, which meant that as a couple they likely had more capacity to enter into vulnerable conversations with each other. They already had a baseline of the ability to be relational with each other and show neutrality rather than reactivity.]

THE HISTORY OF THE RELATIONSHIP

Once you learn more about each person's view of the issue, you will explore the history of their relationship. First, inquire on how they met and what they thought of each other at the time. This offers insight into not only how the relationship began but also, on a meta level, how the couple thinks about those beginning moments. This helps you learn two things:

- Were the beginning moments of the relationship positive and healthy or were they chaotic, negative experiences for both people?
- Do the clients use their early days as a memory that helps them stay connected or as something that fuels their disdain toward each other?

Next, explore with the couple how they navigated each level of commitment in their relationship. For example: How did they decide to commit to each other? When did they move in together? How did they get engaged? What was the wedding like? This provides insight into their decision-making processes and buy-in throughout the relationship.

Some couples will say they decided to commit because they both "just knew" it was right; perhaps it felt easy to make this decision together. Other couples will say they deliberated about it, and some clients will say something like "We got married because I knew I had to. My partner told me they would end the relationship if we didn't get married soon." This information will help you begin to theorize about how the couple makes decisions—Is one person always in charge and the other goes with the flow? Do they use threats to get their way? Do they just "go for it" without discussion, or are they able to dialogue about their needs and come up with win-win outcomes?

You should take time to explore what each partner thinks and feels about how they decided to commit to each other, asking follow-up questions to learn how this influences the narrative of the relationship for each partner. For example, perhaps a partner who felt forced to commit "or else" now has a narrative that their decisions never really matter and feels a lack of agency. Meanwhile, perhaps the partner who put the pressure on feels as though they were never actually wanted because they had to push for their partner's commitment. You can use this information to then explore how the couple navigates relational processes with each other, how they take responsibility for the choices they make, and how reactive they are to the stories related to commitment.

Next, ask about any other major transitions in the couple's life together, like childbirth, pregnancy loss, job loss, or the loss of loved ones. Here you are continuing to gather information on how the couple makes big decisions and how they respond to stress and change. Do they make decisions as a unit or is there unilateral decision-making? Are they able to be supportive and loving during moments of stress or do they become avoidant or argumentative? You want to hear not only what they remember happening, but also the story they have about why it happened the way it did. Again, are they able to be relational or do you need to help them improve the sense of "we-ness" by teaching them how to create win-win outcomes? Is there any reactivity left from these moments (perhaps due to letdowns and disappointments, betrayals, or other unresolved pain points), and are they able to take individual responsibility for how each transition panned out?

Once you have learned the narrative of the relationship and are familiar with its major milestones, explore how the couple navigates problems. Usually, you can do so by discussing one of the challenges the couple brought up during the relationship narrative. Otherwise, ask questions about where they saw problems or challenges arise and how they navigated these. You may notice that a pattern emerges, or alternatively, that different types of situations or stages in their individual growth brought out different responses. For example, one partner may have responded by giving in to every argument that happened during the dating phase, but wedding planning brought out a new, more assertive or combative side that their partner had not seen before.

Make note of these patterns and exceptions to discuss with their couple during the feedback portion of the session. Highlighting patterns helps you begin to consider the treatment plan—where can the pattern be changed? It also helps the couple conceptualize their issues. Moving forward feels less overwhelming when they can see specific areas that could be changed to create improvement within the relationship.

Kimmie and Selah: The History of the Relationship

"I'm going to take a sharp left turn and ask you to tell me about the history of your relationship," I said. "Let's take a pause on talking about the problem and talk about how you met."

Selah and Kimmie smiled at each other.

"Well," Selah began, "we met at work a really long time ago. Kimmie and I were really good friends at the time."

I nodded encouragingly. "Do you remember what you liked about her?"

"She was just a great friend," Selah reflected. "Really fun to be around, a great listener, easy to spend time with."

"I know you mentioned you were friends—did you have romantic feelings at the time, too, or strictly platonic?" I asked.

> "I definitely had feelings for Kimmie," Selah smirked. "I remember thinking about being with her but stopping myself because we worked together. It just didn't feel like the right time."
>
> Kimmie agreed, "I felt the same. At the time, I didn't know Selah liked me in that way and I didn't want to risk the working relationship or our friendship. But I always thought she was beautiful and I wanted to spend as much time with her as I could."

In Selah and Kimmie's case, it was clear they had very positive memories of the beginning of their relationship and that there was consensus on the memories. Learning that the couple has a positive perspective regarding their early years provides a few data points for the therapist:

- The couple's relationship started with a foundation related to positive experiences and feelings.
- The couple is not in such a state of negative sentiment with each other that they can no longer remember or acknowledge the positive experiences in the past.

When the couple can see the positive in their relationship, you can help them anchor into those positive feelings during difficult moments in session. It also will be something to remember later when exploring with them what was unique and different about the early days compared to their relationship now.

> ## Ron and Andrew: The History of the Relationship
>
> In providing a timeline of their relationship, Andrew and Ron shared that while they'd had ups and downs, they'd always come back to each other.
>
> Andrew recalled, "We'd get in these fights where Ron would threaten to leave, but as soon as the fight was done, we'd sit down with cooler heads and reassure each other we were 100 percent committed to each other."
>
> "It sounds like even though there were big fights, they didn't disrupt your commitment," I reflected.
>
> "Yes, exactly," said Ron. "I've always wanted to make this work, even if sometimes my actions didn't reflect that clearly. After those arguments we would apologize and try to move forward."
>
> "When did you first realize that perhaps that cycle was becoming a problem you couldn't sustain anymore?" I asked.
>
> Andrew's mouth set into a thin line. "At a certain point, it wasn't passionate anymore. At the start, you could come back to the passion and excitement. But eventually you are living real life together. And when you find yourselves fighting over dinner or ruining every vacation, it starts to shake your sense of stability. I would say for me, things really changed after the vacation. It was just awful."
>
> Ron added, "My level of commitment has always felt strong to me, but I realize now my words in fights may have said otherwise. That big fight during our vacation woke me up to changes that need to be made."
>
> "What have the two of you tried in order to improve this?" I asked.
>
> "Andrew says I haven't tried anything," Ron answered, with a pointed glance at his partner, "but I have. I went to see a therapist a few times, but . . . I don't know. We just talked and I didn't know how to really explain my issue. I also talked to my doctor and got a prescription to try to help with my moods."

> "But you didn't stay on the medication," Andrew interjected. "And you didn't even give therapy a chance. You can't go a few times and expect things to improve."
>
> Ron blew out his breath. "I know. I did what I always do and I didn't stick with it. I'm mad at myself too."
>
> "Have you tried anything together?" I asked them. "Previous couples therapy?"
>
> "We took a class together online," Andrew said. "It taught us how to have more effective communication. It works when we're calm but not when we get angry."
>
> I nodded. "You shared that there has been a pattern of ups and downs. Do you remember a period of time when this wasn't an issue?"
>
> Ron smiled ruefully. "Not really. And it has nothing to do with whether I love Andrew or not. I just really struggle to calm myself when I'm upset. I need to work on that."

It was clear that Ron and Andrew had been stuck this cycle since the beginning of their relationship. It had become ingrained in the way they responded to each other during conflict and was often fueled by not knowing how to respond to dysregulation. This meant that the couple would likely need to spend time on repairing past ruptures and learning how to self-soothe.

John and Amy: The History of the Relationship

"We really liked each other," Amy shared, "but, you know, it was college, so sometimes we were stupid." When I asked what she meant by that, she said, "Sometimes partying or wondering what else was out there got in the way. We had a few silly college breakups, but we always came back to each other. John was my person. My best friend."

When a couple describes their early days as a mix of "hot and cold," it's information that the therapist can use to better understand whether this pattern has ever been different. Has the couple always had a mix of feelings of being connected and doubts, and how have they navigated those? How does this "hot and cold" experience impact their ability to trust and feel committed to each other? Ultimately, it's generally a positive sign that they can still see the good even when there is hardship.

After listening to Amy and John describe their "best friends with benefits" status from their early college days, I started to dig into how the relationship developed. "How did you finally decide to commit?"

John smiled at Amy. "Oh, that was all me."

"Tell me more," I encouraged him.

"I think it was halfway through junior year that I realized no one was like Amy," he said. "Not only was she my best friend but I loved being with her as a partner. She's beautiful, fun, smart. We had great sex. I started to realize it was stupid we weren't committing, so I told her it was time for us to settle down." He laughed, a little self-conscious.

Amy added, "I really wasn't thinking much about commitment until he brought it up. But as soon as he did, I realized he was right. We were perfect for each other and I wanted to give us a chance. It's been history ever since. I don't think we ever broke up again after that point. Am I right?"

"Yep, we've been together since then," John agreed.

"And how did you decide to live together and then get married?" I asked.

> "Once we fully committed, we decided it didn't make sense to keep renting different places with our friends," Amy said. "We wanted to be together. When our leases ended, we decided to move in together."
>
> "What was that transition like?" I asked.
>
> Amy gave a wry grin. "Hindsight is 20/20. I remember being shocked by how little he knew what to do around the house and by how messy he was. I had to remind him of basic things like picking up toilet paper from the store when we ran out or switching his laundry. At the time I just thought of it as a quirk, but now it's becoming a problem."
>
> I summarized: "So you remember being frustrated about your differences in how you maintain a home, but overall, you didn't think too much about it."
>
> "Not even frustrated," Amy reflected, "just surprised."

As they continued to share their major transitions and commitments with me, it became clear that Amy and John had enjoyed an overall positive relationship through the years. Once they decided to commit, they made decisions together, respected each other, and worked to show each other love and support. They had fond memories of their wedding and their decision to have children. This told me that the couple likely had a number of strong relationship skills and the ability to show respect and love toward each other.

Because of this positive history, much of my focus would be on learning why it had changed. My theory was that the couple had hit a stressful point in their relationship that took them outside their window of tolerance, making it difficult to connect with each other. I was starting to believe that our work together would be to have John and Amy focus on what they already knew how to do well, help them to repair whatever regrettable moments had caused the breakdown, and support them in developing stress management skills.

Ebony and Karl: The History of the Relationship

In contrast to all three other couples, Ebony and Karl expressed overall negative sentiment about their early days together.

"I know there is so much to talk about regarding the betrayal that's been experienced," I said, "and we are going to come back to it. But for a moment, I'd like us to pause on discussing that. I'd like to hear from you both more about your relationship. Let's start with how you met."

Both were quiet, waiting for the other to begin. Finally, Ebony murmured, "Do you want to go first, Karl?"

Karl sighed. "I mean, I don't remember much. We met on an online dating site. Was it OkCupid?"

Ebony gave a slight shrug. "I dunno, maybe. Either that or Tinder."

As they spoke, I observed low energy. They weren't looking at each other and there was no positive affect. (For example, couples will often smile at each other, give each other empathetic glances, or nod in agreement with each other.)

"Do you remember the first time you connected on the app?" I prompted them.

"Yeah," Ebony's voice was uncharacteristically hard. "Karl was pretty rude, actually. I think he said something offensive veiled as flirty."

Karl stiffened. "I don't even remember that. All I remember is that you said something abrasive about not wanting to waste your time if I wasn't serious about taking you on a date."

Ebony parried, "I mean, you said something weird in the messages and I didn't know if I could take you seriously."

"Where did you end up meeting for the first time?" I asked.

"Karl was constantly busy, so it took weeks," Ebony responded, "but we finally met at some dive bar." She raised an eyebrow. "He was on his phone the entire time."

"Oh my god, that's not true!" Karl protested. "You always say that. There were about 10 minutes I had to be on the phone for work."

"It was still pretty rude," Ebony persisted. "Honestly, I feel so pissed off thinking about it because clearly the writing was on the wall."

I could plainly see that this couple had developed **negative sentiment override**.

> **COUPLES THERAPY DICTIONARY**
>
> ### Negative Sentiment Override
>
> Most couples describe their relationship history with a mix of fondness and bitterness. When a couple describes their early days with negative sentiment, it doesn't necessarily mean it's how they felt at the time; it's also possible that the way they are describing the past is related to how they are feeling in the present. This is called *negative sentiment override* (Hawkins et al., 2002), a state where rather than seeing the relationship through rose-colored glasses, everything is gray. It's an indication that the couple is in high levels of distress and that their relationship is in a highly fragile state.

Karl explained, "I left the date unsure of how I felt. I was really focused on work and didn't know if I wanted a serious relationship, but Ebony texted me that she wanted to see me again and I felt obligated to do it."

Ebony recoiled. "Ouch. I can't believe you just said that. You're so hurtful toward me."

I turned to her. "Ebony, how do you remember it?"

Ebony shook her head and blinked, trying to regain focus. "I remember telling him I wanted to see him again, but he didn't seem *obligated*. To me, the next few dates seemed as if we both wanted to be there and enjoyed our time together."

"What was the next major commitment you made to each other?" I asked. "Did you move in together? Decide to get married?"

Ebony sighed. "I think this is where the problems started. Several months into dating, I got pregnant. Karl and I decided we would parent together and the best way to do so would be to be married. It makes me so sad to think about how I never got a romantic proposal. It was so anticlimactic."

"Did you have a wedding?" I asked.

This question provoked sudden emotion from Ebony. "We did." She held her fingers to her eyes, trying to stanch the tears. "But it wasn't what I'd dreamed of. I didn't look pretty—I was very pregnant—so the dress wasn't what I wanted. I'm sorry . . . it really just makes me so sad."

Karl took up the story. "I think at that point we knew we had to get serious with each other. And we really tried. We had our oldest baby that year. I always wonder if we'd be together if that hadn't happened, but I guess it is what it is."

As Karl and Ebony continued to describe their history, I heard regret, pain, and frustration. Their relationship had started on rocky ground, creating a context in which the couple was never quite sure where they stood. Ebony, in particular, struggled with a deep uncertainty about whether she was genuinely wanted and chosen rather than just becoming a coparent and partner by circumstance. This vulnerability had been living within the relationship, and the discovery of Karl's affair had caused Ebony to double down on that painful belief. This information demonstrated to me that we had a difficult road ahead of us because there was never much of a foundation of trust and commitment for Ebony and Karl. For a long time, both of them had been struggling to feel safe, secure, and grounded; to navigate relational processes by having concern for each person's well-being; and to take responsibility for their choices.

COUPLES THERAPIST RESOURCE

The Art of Assessment

Sometimes the assessment process will not follow the linear path I've laid out for you. Although it will usually be appropriate to follow the steps I've laid out (each partner's view of the problem, attempts to solve problems, the history of the relationship, interactional patterns, family of origin influence, current level of commitment in the relationship, and goals for therapy), sometimes you might decide to rearrange the flow, skip a step, or come back to a step based on how the couple is responding to you or based on their specific needs. For example, as we saw earlier, when Ebony and Karl discussed the issue bringing them in for therapy, Ebony became flooded and we needed to take a break. Although we did spend a bit more time talking about the problem, in order to give Ebony a reprieve, I decided to "dig" a little less and move on to discussing their relationship history with them. Once we had explored their relationship history, I returned to the issue that had initially brought them into therapy.

I thanked Ebony and Karl for rehashing the past with me and asked them to come back to the issue at hand—specifically, to something Ebony had said earlier about starting to notice that things felt "off" in their relationship even before she discovered the affair. I asked her to tell me more about that and how the feeling developed until the discovery of Karl's infidelity. Whenever an affair is part of a couple's presenting problem, I spend more time exploring the impact on the person who was betrayed. Later, in my one-on-one with Karl, I would spend time learning his thoughts on what led up to the affair, but when a couple is still in the recovery stage, it's not effective to ask the shocked and betrayed partner to listen to their partner's side of the story.

After hearing more about Ebony's experience, I asked what the couple had tried so far to navigate the issue of Karl's infidelity.

Ebony answered, "After I found out about the affair, I did ask him to leave initially, so he went to a hotel for a few days. That didn't feel any better."

Karl jumped in. "It felt awful. I really didn't want to be away from Ebony and the kids, and we were still fighting through text message."

"So you tried to get some space from each other to see if it would reduce some of the pain in the home?" I reflected.

Ebony nodded. "Yes, I thought if I didn't have to see him, maybe I would feel better. But then the rage just built up anyway, so it didn't help."

"Have you tried anything else up to this point?" I asked.

"We've both been seeing individual therapists," Ebony answered. "My therapist is constantly telling me to leave Karl, but I don't think that's helpful because I'm not sure it's what I want. I haven't seen her in a few weeks."

Karl added, "We also saw a couples therapist for a couple sessions."

Ebony grimaced. "Yeah, that's an experience I'd rather not remember."

"Tell me about it," I prompted them.

Ebony took a steadying breath. "During the first session, she asked me to listen to Karl talk about what was going on for him leading up to the affair and had him express his unhappiness in our marriage. It was really cruel."

Karl shook his head. "Yeah, I agreed we shouldn't go back. It was really bizarre for her to ask Ebony to show me empathy right now."

Ebony continued, "It's so fresh and he ruined our family, and yet she spent most of the session trying to convince me that I should be understanding of it. It was horrible. She even said to me, 'Do you think there are things you did to contribute to this?'"

I sat back. "Wow."

Ebony looked at me gratefully. "I am not above taking accountability, but Karl was lying to me while I was pregnant. I just can't even think of anything I could have possibly done that would have caused him to do this to me. I'm so devastated I can hardly breathe." She pressed a hand to her chest and breathed deeply.

"It sounds like you weren't able to talk about the trauma you've experienced and that it was seen more as an issue with equal responsibility," I reflected.

Ebony dabbed at her eyes with her fingertips. "Exactly. It was awful."

It's significant that Ebony and Karl's previous couples therapist seems to have skipped a step when it comes to affair recovery. Rather than taking time to process the shock, trauma, and loss as well as to help the partner to atone, she jumped straight into what I see as the second step of affair recovery: better understanding what happened leading up to the event.

Jumping too quickly from assessment to giving feedback or trying interventions can be harmful in any couples therapy, but especially so when there has been a devastating blow to the safety and security of the relationship. Before you can ask a betrayed partner to be vulnerable by extending empathy to the partner who violated their trust, you must first ensure they feel safe. This is done through coaching the other partner to become a safe person in the relationship through regaining trust. I knew I would need to be especially focused on helping Karl to gain the patience needed to withstand Ebony's pain for the time being and support Karl in listening to Ebony, answering her questions, and understanding that this process would not be quick and that it would take time before we could begin to ask Ebony to look at her own role in the dynamic. I would do more of this coaching with Karl during our one-on-one session.

ASSESSING THE COUPLE'S INTERACTIONAL PATTERNS

This part of the first 90 minutes of assessment is different in that the therapist is no longer "interviewing" the couple to learn about them. Instead, the therapist asks the couple to reflect on a disagreement they are having and then discuss it with each other in front of the therapist.

This enactment occurs midway through the assessment, allowing the therapist to integrate self-reported information with observed interaction. It also serves as a way to break up the initial portion of the day by giving the couple an opportunity to talk with each other rather than the therapist.

While the couple has already given you their own narrative of their issues, this narrative is often skewed, as the couple cannot see themselves from the outside looking in. They often describe surface-level symptoms—for example, "We have communication issues"—which may be accurate but is not diagnostically useful on its own. It does not tell you why this couple has communication issues and what would need to change in order to improve them. Observing the way the partners interact with each other provides important information that would otherwise be missed if the therapist were to take their descriptions at face value.

After learning more about the couple's problem and relationship history, the therapist will let the couple know that it is time for the two of them to talk about their issue together. The therapist instructs the couple to discuss one area of conflict for five to seven minutes (Gottman, 1999). Typically, the therapist instructs the couple to select a "low" to "medium" difficulty conflict (not the presenting issue), but they may use discretion if they assess that the presenting issue is mild enough to be safely enacted. During the enactment, the couple should act as if the therapist is not in the room; the therapist acts as an observer of the couple, without helping them along in their conversation at all.

Therapists might wonder if this is effective, as it's likely that couples will be on their "best behavior" during this discussion. However, research has shown that even though couples might show slightly more supportiveness (Foster et al., 1997) and lower reactivity than they would at home, they still tend to show negative affect even when pretending to be happy and therapists are still able to discern whether they are truly happy with each other (Vincent et al., 1979). This is all to say, regardless of the couple taking a more tempered approach to their disagreements, they aren't able to hide their dysfunctional patterns from the observer.

As the therapist observes the couple discussing the issue, they are looking for signs of functionality and dysfunctionality in their communication. Couples who have dysfunctional communication and are unhappy in their relationship tend to (Notarius and Markman, 1989):

- Show more hostility at the start of their conversations
- Maintain hostility during the conversation
- Reciprocate and escalate their partner's hostility
- Do not repair or fix their behavior during the interactional process
- Have longer negative reciprocity loops
- Show **pursuit/withdrawal patterns**
- Show less positive behavior and interactions between each other

> **COUPLES THERAPY DICTIONARY**
>
> ### Pursuit/Withdrawal Patterns
>
> One of the most common dysfunctional interactional patterns to watch for is pursuit/withdrawal (also called demand/withdraw). In this pattern, one partner attempts to discuss a problem, while the other avoids the discussion by being nonresponsive, changing the subject, or ending the conversation (Christensen & Heavey, 1990). Couples who exhibit this pattern struggle to solve problems, have increased anger, and become stuck in negative interactional cycles.
>
> It's worth noting that research has shown this pattern is not related to personality, which means there is possibility for change when interventions are applied to help the couple change their interactional cycles (Heaven et al., 2006).

While watching the couple, the therapist doesn't only want to assess for negative interactional patterns. They want to also look for helpful behaviors—what the couple is doing well. These include the couple being able to:

- Start conversations gently, using a calm tone of voice, curiosity, or affection
- Maintain this gentle demeanor during the conversation
- De-escalate by not reciprocating their partner's escalation
- Repair during the conversation
- Have shorter negative loops due to the repair attempts being given and then accepted
- Show positive behaviors between each other, such as joking with each other, complimenting each other, and showing active listening

> **COUPLES THERAPIST RESOURCE**
>
> ### Interactional Patterns Enactment
>
> The interactional patterns enactment has three steps:
>
> 1. The therapist instructs the couple to decide which disagreement to discuss. This should be a "low" or "medium" difficulty conflict and not the presenting problem. The therapist lets the couple know they have five minutes to discuss and that during these five minutes, the therapist will remain silent and will only observe.
>
> 2. As the couple decides which issue to discuss and then discusses the issue, the therapist only acts as an observer, noticing whether the couple:
>   - Has a harsh start-up or soft start-up to the conversation
>   - Maintains harshness throughout the conversation or is able to neutralize (or never engage in) harshness
>   - Reciprocates/mirrors escalation or de-escalates
>   - Does not offer repair or does offer repair

- Shows pursuit/withdrawal patterns or an ability to stay present with each other
- Gets stuck on negative loops or is able to disrupt negative loops to get back on track
- Shows negative sentiment override or shows positive interactional patterns

3. The therapist then engages in discussion with the couple about their own observations of their interactional patterns alongside the therapist's observations.

John and Amy: Interactional Patterns

When it came time for Amy and John to have their conflict discussion so that I could observe their interactional patterns, I let them know that we would be switching gears. "For most of the session today, I've been asking you to talk to me. Now, I am going to have you talk to each other as I observe.

"Take a moment to think about something you need to discuss or have disagreed about recently. The only two directions I will give are one, to choose an issue that is mild—something that is difficult to discuss but not so difficult that it causes major arguments—and two, I want you to discuss it for five minutes."

Amy hesitated. "Okay . . . so should we talk about the issue that brought us here?"

"The two of you can decide that," I answered. "Go ahead and talk together to figure out what you'll be discussing. I am just here to observe."

> [*While I usually specify that the couple should not discuss the issue that brings them into therapy, in this case I sensed that the issue they would bring up would not be too high conflict to navigate during session, so I decided to give them the option.*]

The couple still hesitated. "Is there a format to follow?" John asked.

> [*Some couples will dive right into discussing an issue, while others will feel self-conscious and ask for more information. Avoid getting involved. Start observing as soon as you've given them instructions.*]

In response to John, I smiled and said, "I'm just observing," then sat back and gestured for them to begin.

"Okay, um . . ." John looked to Amy. "I think we could talk about planning the vacation for this summer. We haven't had time to talk about that, and I'm pretty sure we still disagree on what to do."

Amy agreed, "Yeah, that's fine. We can talk about that one."

They both shifted in their seats to face each other.

"So, what do you want to do for vacation?" John asked Amy, his voice a bit stilted.

Amy answered, "I've already said this. I want to make it easy this year and just drive to the beach for a week."

John nodded. "Okay, but we've talked about this. Driving to the beach is easy, but our time there isn't usually great. It's overly expensive and Jacob is always grouchy."

Amy gave a slightly forced smile, clearly hearing a familiar argument. "Kids get grouchy."

John gave a forced smile of his own. "Why are you so against us taking the flight out to Montana?"

Amy sighed, "Because it's way more for me to plan. You don't think about anything related to the trip, so I think I should be the one to make the choice."

They both sat in silence for a moment. Finally, John raised his hands and said, "Fine, whatever. We'll just go to the beach, then."

Amy turned to look at me. "See? This is what happens. I guess we'll go to the beach, but I don't know where to go from here." She waited for me to respond. "Has it been five minutes yet?"

I shook my head but did nothing else.

"Well, I guess we figured that out pretty quickly," John tried to joke.

Amy rubbed her temples with her fingers. "We didn't figure anything out. You just decided you didn't want to talk about it anymore, as always."

John rolled his eyes. "I decided I don't want to talk about it because we won't get anywhere."

The five minutes continued to tick on in silence until, suddenly, Amy laughed.

Surprised, John smiled. "What?"

"We are ridiculous." She threw up her hands. "This is an argument about a *beach trip*."

She giggled again. John grabbed her hand and squeezed it.

> [*As I listened to John and Amy discuss their vacation, I began to see why they were having difficulty working through issues. They struggled to negotiate or show curiosity, and they became shut down or critical. However, I also saw that they did have the capacity for repair with each other. Amy recognized the conversation was getting heated, made a joke, and laughed—all cues for de-escalation of the conflict. John, in turn, accepted Amy's attempts to de-escalate by offering physical affection.*
>
> *When a couple's five minutes are up, I stop the interaction and discuss my observations with them, also asking for their input. This collaborative approach encourages the couple to make their own assessment, so they do not feel as if I am authoritative and in judgment of them. It also begins the important process of waking them up to their own dynamics, as they have to begin to articulate them in a way they haven't before. This exercise not only reveals real-time dynamics, but also introduces the couple to a central theme of the intensive: the power of observing and shifting their own patterns. Finally, it prepares the couple for the kind of feedback they'll receive during the final portion of the day's session.*]

"Was this conversation similar to the conversations you have at home?" I asked John and Amy.

Amy smiled sheepishly. "Pretty much . . ." With another laugh, she corrected herself, "Probably more mild."

"Definitely more mild because you're here," John agreed.

"If I had taken video of the conversation and you were watching it, what would you notice about how you talk when you're trying to make a decision?" I asked.

John thought for a moment. "I think we just kind of repeat ourselves and get shut down and don't get anywhere."

Amy added, "Yeah, I recognize we don't even hear each other out. We shut each other down."

I followed up with another question: "Did you notice anything you did like about your conversation?"

"I will say that John and I still try to mostly respect each other," Amy ventured.

"Yeah, we recognize when it's getting too ridiculous or going too far," John agreed, "and I think we're good at stopping ourselves before it goes there."

"Yeah, like John will always offer me a hug," Amy said.

I leaned forward. "If you're open to it, I'd like to share my observations."

Both of them leaned forward as well, their faces eager and apprehensive.

"I definitely noticed the same positives you mentioned," I began. "I could see that you both recognized that the conversation was escalating and you did a really nice job of de-escalating. Amy, you did something called 'offering repair' when you made a little joke. That means you did something to signal to your partner that they are safe with you and that you don't want things to get worse.

"John, you accepted that repair. Both of those actions are really important. If one person offers repair and the other person doesn't accept it, then you're more likely to escalate. So you did a great job there."

I paused for their reactions.

John looked at Amy. "Yeah, I like that we can do that. We really do notice when we're being ridiculous and I think we both try to stop ourselves from making it worse."

"Yes, it's a great communication skill," I affirmed. "Here is where I see that you get stuck. The first thing I noticed is that you quickly jumped into solutions. As soon as you brought up the topic of vacations, you both gave your solution. You didn't really discuss anything."

Amy nodded. "Yeah, I think we both have strong personalities and just present what we want to do without much conversation."

"And that can be an issue, right? Because then you're not really taking the time to be curious about the why. For example, at the end of the conversation, I didn't really understand what either of you are looking for in a vacation. I wonder what would have happened if you had started from a more curious place—for example, asking each other what you hope for in a vacation."

Amy blinked. "That's true. I don't really know exactly what John wants in a vacation other than knowing where he wants it to be."

"You can avoid a lot of arguments by really understanding what's underneath because then it's easier to negotiate with each other," I pointed out, before continuing, "The next thing I noticed was there was this dance of blame, assumptions, and criticism and withdrawal."

John grimaced. "I hate that we do that. I really don't want either of us to shut each other down."

"Is there anything I missed?" I asked. "Anything else you noticed?"

John and Amy looked at each other, then shook their heads in tandem. "I don't think so," said Amy.

"Okay," I said, "that was helpful. Thank you for doing that. Now, I'd like to spend a little bit of time learning about your families."

THE INFLUENCE OF FAMILY OF ORIGIN

Following an enactment like the one above, it can be helpful to briefly explore the influence that each partner's family of origin has had on the couple. Gathering the family history comes after the enactment for three reasons.

First, it gives the couple a mental reset. When a couple has been interviewed about the problem and then their relationship history, it often feels necessary to change the energy in the room. An enactment does that by moving the energy away from therapist-to-couple to partner-to-partner discussion.

Second, the enactment brings to light frustrating communication patterns. When the couple begins to discuss their families of origin, they might have a fresher perspective on how they've been impacted by the way they were raised and how their family members currently treat them.

Lastly, having the enactment in the middle of the 90 minutes allows the therapist to contain the enactment by redirecting the couple to the next portion of the interview. Rather than getting stuck on whichever disagreement the couple was having, the therapist can simply state that it's time to move on to the next part of the assessment.

During this portion of the interview, the therapist is learning more about how each partner was impacted by their family of origin growing up (in a relational sense) and how they see each other's family having an influence on their relationship now. The families of origin have a large impact on the interactional patterns within a couple's relationship. Clients who describe positive interactional patterns in their family of origin tend to manage the demands of their adult partnerships more effectively, while those who have an internal working model of a dysfunctional family of origin tend to experience more difficulties in their adult relationships (Sabatelli & Bartle-Haring, 2003).

This information matters for the therapist because it provides a hint regarding which type of work might need to be done in the second day of the intensive session. Couples have transference in their relationships in which they attempt to define their relationship based on an internal working model from their childhood experiences. Each partner has had unique childhood experiences and has therefore developed their own internal working model, which can create strong and polarized experiences amid relational conflict. The partners unconsciously fight with each other over what it means to be in a relationship based off their personal templates from childhood (Meissner, 1978).

The couple might find that they are struggling due to unhelpful internal working models of relationship, which means that much of the work might be related to helping the couple develop new ways of seeing themselves within a relationship and better conceptualizing what it means to be in a healthy relationship. In this case, the therapist might also decide to work with the couple to create a more securely attached system in their adult relationship, bringing to recognition that they did not have that as a child.

By understanding the clients' families of origin, the therapist can also begin to connect the dots between pain points in childhood and trigger points in adulthood. The therapist should keep these connections to themselves during assessment and share them with the couple during the feedback portion. Highlighting these enduring pain points can help the couple to build empathy for each other and understand why events within the relationship that might have otherwise been forgettable were particularly activating for one or both of them.

For clients who report having seen more effective interactions growing up, the therapist might begin to develop a hypothesis that the clients will need less support regarding the impact of their families of origin on their relational skills. In this case, the therapist might focus more closely on any occurrences in their relationship that have made it difficult for them to use the effective forms of communication that were modeled to them. For example, the couple might have a healthy sense of what it means to be in a relationship but find themselves having a difficult time being intimate with each other after one of them experienced a traumatic event recently. This isn't necessarily because of family of origin issues; rather, they were met with a challenge they did not have the skills to overcome.

Helpful questions to ask the couple during this portion of the session include:

- Tell me what it was like for you growing up in your family.
- What do you think you learned about relationships from your family?

- What do you think is one really helpful thing you learned about relationships from your family growing up?
- What is one unhelpful habit in relationships you've inherited from your family?
- How do your families play a role in your lives now? What do you think about the role they play?

As you hear each person's narrative of their own family of origin, pay close attention to their partner's reactions. If you notice the partner has more to add or seems to disagree, ask them directly what their thoughts are on their partner's perspective. This will give you a more holistic view of each partner's family of origin—after all, the truth often lies in the middle of what someone says about their own family and what the other person observes.

Ron and Andrew: The Influence of Family of Origin

After going through an interactional patterns enactment with Andrew and Ron, I announced our move to another topic. "I'd like to learn a little more about the families you grew up in. What was it like for each of you growing up in your family?"

"Ron should go first," Andrew immediately proposed. "He's got a lot going on with that."

To my surprise, Ron agreed. "Yeah, I definitely am the one that brings all the family baggage into this relationship."

Making a mental note of how both partners had identified Ron as the one with family baggage, despite Andrew's own admission that his parents' divorce still impacts his perspective on love and commitment, I said, "Tell me more."

Ron took a breath. "I grew up in a super broken home. When I was born my dad apparently disappeared. I don't really know what happened, but I do know it was really traumatic for my mom, just based on stories I've heard. When I was around two years old, though, he showed up again and my family played house for a few years."

"'Playing house'—what does that mean?" I asked.

"Well, my parents pretended to want to be a family, but that's not really what ended up happening," Ron explained. "My dad's heart was never in it. As far back as I can remember, he was angry and completely absent, even though he lived there."

Andrew added, "The stories are really sad. His dad was such an asshole."

"Anytime he'd get angry with my mom, he'd just walk out," Ron recalled. "He was so aggressive too. He'd say the worst things to all of us. I will say, my mom was our saving grace."

Andrew broke in, "I don't know. She's got issues too. He won't tell you this, but his mom really made Ron be an adult way too young."

Ron frowned. "That's not true. She did her best."

"Was there any pressure put on you, whether from your mom or just from yourself, to step into your dad's role?" I asked Ron.

"Andrew thinks so," Ron said, looking at his partner, "but I don't see it. I just think I did what had to be done."

I turned to Andrew. "What about your family? What was it like growing up with them?"

"My childhood was difficult. As I mentioned, my dad was never around; my parents divorced when I was pretty young. With that being said, my mom was a very loving and giving person. Beyond my dad being completely unavailable, I had a really nice and secure family growing up."

Ron looked down. "Yeah, I feel like I drag Andrew down with all my baggage."

"What are some lessons about relationships you both learned from your families?" I asked. "Maybe share one positive characteristic you learned from them and something you learned that isn't so positive?"

Ron began, "It's clear as day to me that whenever I get upset I don't know how to handle it, so I just withdraw. I definitely learned that from my dad. And I think the belligerence part comes from both parents, honestly."

"What about positive?" I prompted him.

Ron gave a weak smile. "That's hard to say. I think I learned how to recognize when I've done wrong and apologize. My mom was really good at that, and she also made it clear she wanted me to grow up to be someone who can take accountability. Watching my dad never take accountability had a big influence on me. I am a work in progress, but when I know I've done wrong, I own it."

"How about you, Andrew?" I asked.

"I think I learned how to be generous and understanding from my mom and grandparents," he replied. "I watched them be kind to others and to each other, and they were always very forgiving."

"Anything you've inherited from them that you'd like to work on?" I pressed him.

"Hmm..." Andrew considered. "I don't think so. Do you think there's anything, Ron?"

Ron hesitated. "I love your family, so I don't want you to think I'm criticizing them. But sometimes, I do think they don't have great boundaries. It can be frustrating when they get involved in our lives, and I think it sometimes makes you question your own decision-making."

Andrew shrugged. "Well, we are all just really close to each other. I don't think it negatively impacts me."

"Okay..." said Ron, sitting back.

Not wanting him to withdraw, I pressed the issue: "Do they play a role in your relationship now? Either family?"

Ron ventured, "Andrew's family is very connected to us. We spend a lot of time with his mom and grandparents on holidays and sometimes even vacation. I really love his family, but recently I think they've been playing a role in telling him to leave the relationship. I guess I can't really blame them, but it also makes me feel a little hopeless they would ever accept me again."

"They accept you!" Andrew argued. "You don't have to worry about that. But they're not happy with how often we fight."

"How about your family, Ron?" I asked.

"My mom is around, but she can't do much for us. We tend to take care of her, which can be a strain sometimes," he admitted. "She usually comes with me to Andrew's family's gatherings for holidays. She really loves Andrew."

Andrew agreed, "Ron's mom is really sweet. We do give her money and sometimes she gets in predicaments that we end up having to fix, so that's a little stressful. I don't think we've ever figured out what our boundary is with her."

I decided to explore a potentially sensitive topic. "I know you've mentioned that sometimes alcohol plays a role in your arguments—was alcohol ever a factor in your families?"

"Not mine," Andrew replied. "We don't really have any issues with alcohol in my family."

"My dad was definitely an alcoholic," said Ron in a dull tone. "I think it contributed to his moods and to him leaving."

As I continued to learn more about Ron and Andrew's families of origin, a picture emerged of two people who were very much influenced in relationships by the way they grew up. Much of their current conflict seemed to be related to how they had felt in childhood. Ron, who had witnessed a parent withdrawing and becoming belligerent, had unconsciously modeled himself in this way during conflict. Andrew, who had also experienced abandonment by a parent at a young age, felt especially sensitive to the ways in which Ron would withdraw during conflict. Andrew also highly valued kindness, and so when Ron became belligerent, he felt as if their values did not align. Ron, meanwhile, felt deep shame about the family "baggage" he brought to the relationship, which only served to make him want to withdraw more.

This information helped me begin to formulate why the couple was stuck in a pursuit/withdrawal cycle with each other and why their arguments seemed to be so big—they were about much more than the here and now. As I continued to work with Andrew and Ron, I would be able to help them understand the context that was making it hard for both of them to maintain neutrality with each other, be relationally minded, and take responsibility rather getting caught up in co-escalatory responses based in their respective childhood pains.

LEVEL OF COMMITMENT IN THE RELATIONSHIP

After discussing family of origin influences with a couple, it's time to move on to learning their levels of commitment in the relationship. I often investigate this by directly asking them, "When it comes to commitment, where do you each stand? Are you fully in the door? Are you all the way out of the door? Or do you have one foot in and one foot out?" Here, you're looking to understand whether the couple is on the same page about commitment and if they are not, what they are each hoping for from the intensive in regard to their commitment.

While the couple might have already shared their level of commitment with you by this point, or at least dropped hints, it's important to directly ask the question. This question is saved for this point in the session so as to allow the couple to first take time to discuss their issue, the history of their problem, their interactional processes, and the impact of their families of origin. If asked about their commitment at the very start of the session, clients might respond reactively by saying they want to end the relationship even if they don't—perhaps because they are still upset from a recent argument or are nervous and in a mode of being withdrawn. Alternatively, clients might hide their desire to leave a relationship, as they don't want to disappoint the therapist early in the session or they are afraid of how their partner might react. By this point in the session, hopefully each partner feels joined with the therapist and has had time to reflect on how they truly feel regarding commitment in the relationship.

You also don't want to save this question for last. If the question is not asked before the couple describes their goals, then the couple might describe goals that do not align with how they actually feel about their level of commitment in the relationship. For example, a partner might continue to "go with the flow" by agreeing to goals to improve the relationship even though they want out. The timing also provides an opportunity for someone who said they want to end the relationship earlier on in the session to clarify or change their stance if they'd like that opportunity.

With all of this being said, even when asked at this point in the session, some people will still not be fully open about their level of commitment in the relationship. Therefore, it is important to talk more about commitment during the individual sessions as well.

> ### Ebony and Karl: Level of Commitment
>
> "How committed are you both feeling to the relationship right now?" I asked Karl and Ebony.
>
> "I so deeply want to say I am fully committed," Ebony answered. "We have a family and a life and I'm about to have a baby. I can't imagine doing that alone. I don't want to be a single mom or have my kids go through a divorce. But I just don't know if I can ever trust Karl again."
>
> Karl shared, "I'm 100 percent committed if I can see that we can make some progress. I'm not willing to put Ebony through a situation in which she feels tortured all the time, and it's not right for the kids to have all of this conflict in the house."
>
> Ebony looked at him in disbelief. "So, you're putting it all on me? You're committed if *I* have better behavior?"
>
> Recognizing that if that conversation continued, it would likely escalate, I broke in. "Karl, what do you think Ebony is feeling right now?"
>
> Karl gestured at her. "She's mad. And this is what I'm saying. If we can't talk about things without Ebony having this type of reaction, then I don't know what to say."
>
> "I think," I ventured gently, "that what Ebony is saying is that your answer does not sound like commitment to improve the relationship. It sounds more like a strings-attached commitment—'I will be with you if you change' instead of 'I know I caused immense pain and I am committed to doing what I need to do to fix it.' My assumption is your answer created a sense of uncertainty for her."
>
> Ebony nodded vigorously. "Yes, that's exactly it. I never hear him say that he is committed; it's always with strings attached."
>
> "I *am* committed," Karl insisted. "I'm just frustrated, but I'm committed."

Despite Karl's insistence, it was clear to me that both partners were questioning their commitment to the relationship. At this moment in the session, I made the decision to move on to the next step, making a note to explore this topic more with each of them during our one-on-one sessions. If I had pressed on in that moment, it likely would have resulted in an argument; I wanted to ensure that I contained that possibility until I'd completed my assessment, both because I do not intervene during the first day and because I'd already seen what I needed to in terms of the ways in which Ebony and Karl interacted during conflict.

During the commitment portion of the session, it might become unclear whether the couple is truly committed or just afraid to admit that they are not willing to do the work required for improvement. Sometimes, the couple is able to talk about this honestly during the joint session, but at other times, you will need to recognize the uncertainty or withheld information and put a pin in it to explore further in individual sessions.

Not all couples express doubt regarding commitment. Many couples will clearly state that they feel highly committed to their relationship and are willing to do the work to improve it. When it is straightforward, the commitment portion of the session is often short.

You will use the information regarding commitment to help the couple create goals and to begin to plan for day 2, as it is important to know the couple's level of commitment when considering interventions.

GOALS FOR THERAPY AND FOR THE RELATIONSHIP

After discussing commitment, you will guide the couple to describe their goals for therapy. This is saved for the end of the joint assessment because information can arise throughout the interview process that informs the couple toward what they would like their goals to be. You will ask the couple to identify the goals they have for the intensive weekend and the goals they have for their relationship.

Helpful prompts for assessing the couple's goals for the intensive include:

- Now that we've talked about your relationship and what you're experiencing, I would like to know what you're hoping to accomplish this weekend.

- What are your goals for our work together? If I am helpful this weekend, how will you know?

- You might both have different answers for this, but what do you really hope to get from our time together?

- Let's say that after our weekend, you go home and go to bed. When you wake up in the morning, you discover there was a miracle and suddenly you feel exactly as you hoped you would in the relationship. How do you know there was a miracle? What is different?

As you ask the couple to detail their goals for the intensive, dig deeper with them if they struggle to give descriptive answers. For example, if a client responds to the question regarding their hopes for the weekend with something like "I hope we can communicate better," the therapist should coach them to elaborate on what this means by asking them to describe the thoughts, feelings, and behaviors that would occur if they were to communicate better.

Goal setting serves the purpose of building consensus with each partner regarding their desires for how their problem will be solved. It is also influential in the development of the treatment plan or "roadmap" that the therapist will develop and discuss during the feedback session (Woods, 2019).

Kimmie and Selah: Goals for Therapy and the Relationship

"Based on everything we've discussed, I'd like to hear more about your hopes for our time together," I said. "If I'm helpful to you both this weekend, what would you hope to see happen?"

"I know we both really love each other," Kimmie said, taking Selah's hand. "I think I want us to just be more aligned and connected again. I want Selah to feel loved and supported by me, but I also want to feel more prioritized."

Selah added, "I agree with Kimmie. I really want to better understand why I'm having such a hard time showing her that I prioritize her and setting boundaries, and I don't want to always feel so guilty when I'm dealing with family stuff—it's really hard and I don't understand why we keep arguing about it."

"It sounds like you both are really committed and are looking to this weekend to help you get on the same page again," I said, "and also to figure out how you can support each other without deprioritizing your own needs."

Kimmie replied, "Yes, that's what I'm hoping for" at the same time that Selah said, "Exactly," covering Kimmie's hand with her own.

Although Selah and Kimmie had different goals related to their own needs, overall, they built consensus together regarding meeting those goals with each other. They both agreed that they would like to create a relationship in which they both win. We established several specific goals related to Kimmie and Selah supporting each other to get what they need, with the ultimate relational goal being a happier relationship that functions better because each partner feels cared for.

Ebony and Karl: Goals for Therapy and the Relationship

For Ebony and Karl, their goals were not easy to pin down. Both of them had already expressed confusing messages regarding their level of commitment to each other and their belief in the possibility of repair. Throughout the morning the couple waffled—at times affirming their commitment to do whatever it takes to stay together and at other times expressing doubt and hesitancy.

"We've talked about some hard stuff today," I said, "and I know it's already been a lot. I've heard you both share some mixed feelings. Ebony, I believe I've heard you share that part of you is hopeful that the relationship can be repaired and that this weekend can relieve some pain. But another part of you is questioning whether repair is worthwhile or even possible. And Karl, I've heard you say you're 100 percent committed to making things right, and I've also heard you doubt whether you can—"

"Yes, that's why we need your help," Ebony cut in. "Do *you* think it's possible to fix this, or should we just break up?"

"Is that a goal for you?" I asked. "To figure out if you should break up?"

Karl looked over to Ebony and then to the ceiling. He huffed in exasperation, smirked at me, and shook his head. "Ebony, if you just want someone to tell you we should break up, then just say it now. Let's not go through all of this if that's what you want."

I paused for a moment as they both sat in silence.

"It's not what I want," Ebony finally responded. "It's not what I want at all."

"What do you want?" I asked gently.

"I don't know! This is all so overwhelming."

"It's so hard," I validated.

> [*It was clear that both Karl and Ebony were unsure of their goals, feeling torn between wanting to "save" the relationship and questioning whether that was even possible. This isn't unusual. Even as I started the goal-setting conversation with Ebony and Karl, I sensed that we would not end this particular part of the morning with any clear goals. Rather than put any pressure on them, I allowed them to discuss their ambivalence and confusion and made a note to myself to continue to explore goals with them during our individual conversations and throughout the rest of the first day. Sometimes a couple's only goal might be to gain clarity on the situation, particularly when there have been incredibly upsetting or chaotic events.*]

"Everything is so confusing right now. It's hard to know what to think or feel," I posited.

"Well, my goal is to not hurt anymore," Ebony said. "And to not lose my family. My goal is for this to get fixed." She looked sadly at the ground and then toward Karl to assess his reaction.

> "And Karl," I turned toward him, "what's your goal?"
>
> "I really don't know," he said.
>
> "It can be hard to know your goals when you're in the midst of so much pain," I validated.
>
> Karl exhaled. "Yeah. Even thinking about it feels overwhelming right now."
>
> "I understand that," I said. "We can take our time thinking about the goal. Maybe, for right now, the goal is to explore what you're both feeling and thinking. A lot has happened, and sometimes it can help to take a step back by reflecting on and exploring the events before making any big decisions about next steps."
>
> Karl looked at me, relieved. "Yeah, I think I need time to figure out what we're even doing here. Although, I do hope you can give me some direction on how I should try to repair with Ebony, if that's even possible."
>
> "I hear you're not sure of your overall goal, but you're looking for some direction. Am I getting that right?"
>
> Karl nodded. I turned to Ebony, "And you don't want to hurt anymore. You're also trying to figure out if you want to continue in this relationship—if it's even possible to get the type of healing you would need?"
>
> "That's right, I think," Ebony replied.

While some couples attend an intensive with very clear goals in mind, many will struggle to articulate what it is they actually hope to get out of the session. This difficulty regarding goal setting lives on a spectrum. Sometimes a bit of prompting and reflection from the therapist is enough to help the couple along. Other couples need more time to discuss their concerns out loud together and as individuals. While the purpose of the goal-setting conversation is to clearly understand what the couple is working toward, sometimes the conversation itself doesn't result in any goals; however, it can still be used as an assessment tool by the therapist. In the case of Ebony and Karl, I learned that they were still in the eye of the storm and that they both needed more information before creating any goals for the relationship.

Observation

As you directly inquire about the couple, their relationship, their family, and their goals, you are not just taking in the information they give you; you will also be reading between the lines of their interactions. This means paying attention to the couple's described and exhibited communication strengths and weaknesses, each partner's position in the relationship, their level of connection and attunement, and how they navigate boundaries in the relationship.

Communication Strengths and Weaknesses

Throughout the first 90 minutes, you should observe how the couple communicates with each other as they answer your inquiries. Does one person talk more than the other? Do they show each other respect? Do they interrupt each other or become argumentative? And, of course, during the enactment portion you will observe their communication habits as they interact solely with each other, without your involvement.

Position in the Relationship

As you observe the couple, make note of the position of each partner within the relationship. Are the partners on an equal plane with each other, or is one partner grandiose and in a one-up position while their partner is in a depressed, shamed, one-down position?

Connection and Attunement

You should also observe the couple's level of attunement through nonverbal and verbal communication. Do the partners seem to be connected to each other or disconnected? Are there moments when it is easier for them to connect and attune, whereas other moments create disconnect and misattunement? For example, you might note that when one person becomes distressed, their partner reaches for their hand in an attempt to soothe them—in this case, they are still showing connection although they are facing conflict. Another couple might show the opposite, not seeming to notice each other's distress or respond to it. You might see attunement when the couple has a capacity to be playful with each other, even when things are hard. This might show up in the therapy session by the couple sharing an inside joke or a moment of laughter.

Boundaries

Watch for the ways in which the couple navigates boundaries within their relationship and in their larger community. In regard to each other, do they tend to be boundaryless (which might be apparent in the way they speak and treat each other with disrespect)? Or are they walled off with each other (exhibited by a lack of vulnerability and sharing between them)? Or perhaps they navigate boundaries well with each other by being able to express their own needs and feelings while also showing respect toward the other person's needs and feelings.

In regard to their larger community, is the couple able to have healthy boundaries with their friends, family, work, and so on? For example, do they both agree that they maintain healthy boundaries with in-laws or has one partner felt violated due to a lack of boundaries with in-laws?

Understanding these areas helps inform you regarding how differentiated the couple is, whether they are able to live relationally, and what type of boundary work they might need to do.

Closing the Joint Session

As we have seen, during the first 90 minutes of an intensive, the therapist guides the couple to share their definition of the problem, what they've tried before, their relationship history, their family history, and their goals. The therapist also observes the couple's interactions informally throughout the session and more formally during the interactional exercise.

By this point, the therapist should have learned more about the couple to put any previous written assessment results into context. The therapist better understands the systemic context of the results because they now know what the couple has been through within their relationship and within their families. This helps the therapist create a fuller narrative regarding the problem and gives them a deeper sense of what might help the couple overcome their issues. The therapist also understands the couple's goals for therapy, which can put into perspective any issues reported prior to the session.

The therapist should also be able to identify how the couple fares in the areas of assessment mentioned earlier: the ability to maintain neutrality, the ability to navigate relational processes, and the ability to take appropriate responsibility. As the therapist considers whether the couple struggles in any of these areas, they can use the contextual information to describe the "why," first to themselves and then later as feedback to the couple. What's more, the therapist can begin to consider how the couple can overcome these challenges by having a clear understanding of the issue and the context of the couple.

Before splitting into individual sessions, the therapist will close the first portion by asking the partners to turn to each other and share why it is important to each of them to go through the intensive couples therapy session together. This provides the couple an opportunity to close out the session with gratitude and appreciation. It also gives the therapist another opportunity to observe the couple's interactional process, specifically: Is the couple engaged, affectionate, and cooperative? If so, they have positive sentiment toward each other, which is a positive sign for their ability to improve their relationship. If a couple is not engaged, affectionate, or cooperative, change will be more challenging (although still possible). The therapist will want to explore further with each individual why it is difficult for them to be engaged, cooperative, and affectionate and what would need to change in order for it to be easier for them.

Kimmie and Selah: Closing the Joint Session

"Before we take a break and go into our individual sessions," I said, "I want you to turn to each other and look at each other."

Kimmie and Selah turned toward each other and immediately started to giggle. "Uh-oh, what are you making us do?" Kimmie joked.

I smiled back. "I want you to share with each other why doing this intensive is important to you. This is a big commitment—you're agreeing to spend a lot of time being vulnerable to solve these issues. Tell each other why this is important."

Selah smiled at Kimmie. "I know this isn't how we are. I love you very much. I'm really sorry we've been fighting so much and we've been so distant. I really want to figure out how to change that because I know we can be happy together." As she finished speaking, she reached for Kimmie's hand.

Tears glinted in Kimmie's eyes. "I feel the same. I'm really so sad about how things have been, and I know it can be different and I want to see that again. I feel like we can do that with the help we'll get in here."

Kimmie and Selah are an example of an engaged, affectionate, hopeful, and cooperative couple. I would go on to highlight this as a strength to the couple during the feedback session, as having positive sentiment toward each other is a sign of a healthy relationship.

Ebony and Karl: Closing the Joint Session

When I asked Karl and Ebony to turn to each other and look at each other, neither of them moved to do so. Ebony stared ahead while Karl rubbed his forehead.

I added, "I want you to share with each other why doing this intensive session is important to you. This is a big commitment—you're agreeing to spend a lot of time being vulnerable to solve these issues. Tell each other why this is important."

Ebony turned tentatively toward Karl, who hadn't yet looked at her. Ebony glanced back toward me with wide eyes as she continued to wait for Karl to follow my direction. Finally, she burst out, "Karl, are you seriously doing this? You've ruined my life and you can't even look at me and say something?"

Karl sat stiffly. "I don't really know how to answer it. I don't understand the question."

Ebony's rage grew. "We are spending all of this money and time, I am pregnant and agreed to do this with you even though it's killing me, and you can't even answer the damn question of why this is important?!" She looked back at me for help. "Should we even be here? Is there any hope if he can't even say why fixing this is important?"

I gently interjected, "Karl, you shared earlier that your goal is to get direction on how to repair your relationship with Ebony. Can you share with her why you want to do that? Why is this relationship important to you?"

> [*Although I instructed Karl to turn toward Ebony, I did not intervene when he chose not to. Remember, during the first day, I am not intervening. When directions are not followed (unless they are related to safety), I only observe and begin to consider what this might mean about the couple. In this case, I made a note to follow up with each partner, during our one-on-one sessions, to explore what they were thinking and feeling in this moment.*]

As therapists, we can ask the client to do something, but if they choose not to we can't force them. However, we can use the information to inform future exploration or intervention.

Karl bit his lip. "Obviously, I don't want the relationship to end, and I want to save our family. That's why it's important. I think I've repeated that several times at this point." He continued to look at me, rather than at Ebony.

Rather than press him to follow the direction, I simply reflected, "Okay, you are here because you want to save your family and repair the relationship. And that's important to you. What about you, Ebony? Why is this important?"

Ebony blew out her breath. "Honestly, this is just awkward now. I don't even think he wants to be with *me*. He just doesn't want our relationship to end so he can save face and because he's afraid the divorce will cost money. It's clear I don't matter."

"I can see how painful it is," I assured Ebony. "I am hopeful our work together can help the two of you reach the goals we discussed and that you can have some relief from that. I think this is a good time to switch to our individual sessions."

> [*As Ebony and Karl attempted to share why the intensive weekend was important to them, I observed that they seemed to become physiologically flooded. Once this was apparent, I knew I had likely obtained all the information I could get with both of them in the room. It was time to move into the individual sessions.*]

Ebony and Karl are an example of a closed-off, cold, unhopeful, and argumentative couple. As the therapist, this information was important to me, as I would use it to inform further exploration during the one-on-one sessions. Specifically, I wanted to learn why Karl was closed off when I asked him to turn toward Ebony and I wanted to better understand how Ebony felt when Karl did not turn toward her and how she placed this into the greater context of the relationship. This information would inform the work I would do with the couple—as I continued to assess them, it became clear they would both need a lot of support and guidance regarding self-soothing to stay present, rather than becoming closed off and argumentative.

Individual Sessions

Once the therapist has completed the joint portion of the assessment, they will meet with each partner individually, typically after a short break. Depending on the clients' and the therapist's own needs at this time, the therapist might ask the couple to give them 15 minutes to regroup or just a moment to grab some water and go to the bathroom before jumping into the first individual session.

To determine which partner will have their one-on-one first, I observe whether they are exhibiting signs of flooding. If so, I will usually ask the person who is more outwardly distressed to stay for the first one-on-one so I can help them process how they are feeling. If neither partner is exhibiting signs of distress, I will ask the partners to decide among themselves who should stay first.

> [After noticing that Ebony and Karl were becoming flooded and recognizing it was time to end the joint session, I needed to decide who would stay first for their one-on-one. I usually begin with the person who is more outwardly distressed—Ebony, in this case—but there was an additional factor to consider: I had the sense that Karl hadn't been telling me everything I needed to know. Meeting with him first could help me ensure I had the entire picture of the relationship. Still, it seemed cruel to send Ebony out into the waiting room so distressed. Moreover, I was hopeful that what she shared privately about their relationship could help me better understand why I was getting the distinct feeling that Karl wasn't being honest. I decided I would still meet with Ebony first.]

Individual sessions during day 1 of the intensive take anywhere from 45 minutes to two hours. Ideally, they are about an hour long. The amount of time you spend with each individual is related to the current issue they are facing, how much or how little they talk, and whether you need to collect special information regarding a specific issue (e.g., if suicidal ideation becomes apparent, you will need to spend more time with the person).

During the individual sessions, the therapist is continuing to join with each partner while also offering an opportunity for each partner to share anything they might have censored or not had time to share during the joint session. The therapist will also follow up on anything that was shared in the joint session that they want more information about and will learn more about each partner as an individual.

> ### Ebony and Karl: Individual Assessments
>
> First, I laid out the plan for the individual sessions with Ebony and Karl: "During our one-on-ones, I will spend about an hour with each of you to learn more about you as individuals and to hear more about how things are going for you in the relationship. Just as a reminder, I won't keep secrets from either of you. This doesn't mean I will blurt out something you share with me, but it does mean that if it seems integral to our work together, I will encourage you to share it with your partner."
>
> I continued, "Ebony, I'll have you stay here with me first. Karl, I encourage you to go do something for about an hour. I really think it benefits people to leave my office and go for a walk or get something to eat. You're also welcome to stay in the waiting room. I can have Ebony send you a text when it's time for you to come back here."
>
> Karl seemed relieved. "Okay, sounds good." He got up and headed for the door. "I'll be back in around an hour unless I hear otherwise."

During the individual meeting, I am assessing the following:

- **The individual's narrative of the problem:** Often, each partner describes the problem almost exactly as they described it during the first 90 minutes of the session with their partner present. However, there are times that an individual takes the opportunity of being out of earshot from their partner to disclose other information. In these cases, the individual interview provides the therapist imperative information to accurately assess and then treat the couple. Depending on how much the client has to share, this portion might take a few moments or up to an hour.

- **The individual's level of commitment:** Again, most people will repeat what they shared during the joint session and this question will therefore only take a few moments. However, sometimes a client will admit they were too nervous to say what they really feel in front of their partner and will give you new or more detailed information about their level of commitment to the relationship.

- **The individual's relationship history:** I ask each person to give me a summary of their relationship history prior to the current relationship. I usually do not dig too deep, unless I believe I need more information based on what has been shared. During this time, I am looking to understand if their past relationship issues and successes mirror the current relationship or if they are different. This helps me to understand any patterns of interaction that they've experienced before (indicating that these patterns might be more deeply entrenched, requiring extra support to change) or to understand that their current reactions in this relationship are different (and therefore are more grounded in what is specifically happening now in this relationship).

- **Mini genogram:** I ask each person to complete a mini genogram with me. Within this genogram, I am exploring their family of origin: who they grew up with, what their role was in the family, if there was a history of mental health or substance use issues, and if there were any individual or family traumas they would like to disclose to me.

- **The individual's mental health history:** I ask the individual to talk about their own mental health history and their relationship with substances. At times, therapists try to get this information by beating around the bush or by hoping the client will disclose it on their own, in an attempt to avoid making the client uncomfortable. However, these topics are taboo to many people—if the therapist does not ask about them directly, it's possible that the client will never bring them up and therefore the therapist will be missing important information about the client related to their mental health and its impact on the relationship.

- **The individual's theory on each partner's responsibility:** I ask each person to tell me their theory on what is going on in the relationship and who holds the responsibility. I want to see if there is recognition of each person's role and whether the client has insight on both the other person and themselves.

- **Psychoeducation:** At times, a therapist might want to use some of the individual time to provide psychoeducation. For example, you'll see in the following vignette featuring Karl and Ebony that I spent some time talking to Karl about common responses to betrayal. The therapist might also provide psychoeducation to the client on how their own family history might play a role in how they've learned to navigate relationships, how diffuse physiological arousal influences the ability to communicate, or how their mental health might be impacting their ability to connect with their partner. In cases of abuse, the therapist might utilize the time to provide psychoeducation on intimate partner violence.

Although I am looking to get information for each of the areas listed above, it's rare that I work through each category as a checklist. The client might divert from one question to share other information with me, or I might choose to dig in deeper regarding something they have brought up. This means that I either creatively collect the information by asking questions within the context of what we are discussing or pick and choose what I won't have time to get to.

Ebony and Karl: The Individual Interviews

Once Karl left the room, I checked in on Ebony's comfort. She took a few moments to get some water and go to the bathroom before we started on the individual interview portion of the assessment.

"When I'm meeting one-on-one with someone," I began, "I like to start by asking if there was anything else they wanted to share from the first part of our day that they didn't yet have a chance to share."

Ebony, already seeming more relaxed with just the two of us in the room, smiled bleakly. "I'm glad you asked that. Yes, there are things I want to share but didn't want to bring up in front of Karl because he'll just deny it."

I nodded. "What would you like to share?"

"I don't think he's stopped the affair," Ebony murmured. "I found an extra phone in his sock drawer that looks like he still uses it, and there have been other weird things. I just think he's lying to me."

"When did you find the phone?" I asked.

> [*When a client shares shocking information like Ebony just did, therapists should remain grounded rather than responding with reactivity. This stance allows the therapist to get more information without becoming inappropriately allied with the client or inadvertently expressing something that sounds like judgment to the client.*]

"I found the phone while I was cleaning earlier this week." She took a deep breath to steady herself. "When I saw it, I wanted to just leave right then and there. But we already had this session booked, so I thought I might as well come and maybe we could talk about it."

"Have there been any other signs you've seen that perhaps Karl isn't being honest with you?" I pursued.

Ebony's eyes welled up. "I wonder if I'm misreading things. But the other day I ran into one of his coworkers and she was so weird with me. It made me feel awful. I don't know if she knows something about what happened or if she knows something is still going on. He's also been taking money from the cash pile, and I don't know what it could be used for."

I handed her a tissue. "When you notice these things, what do you find yourself feeling?"

Ebony sighed. "I feel so anxious and really mad. And then crazy—I doubt myself because he's good at making me think things are normal."

"Tell me about that." I encouraged her. "What has he said or done that makes you believe things are normal?"

"He's become really transparent about a lot of things," Ebony said. "He's given me the logins to the bank accounts so I see what's happening with money. I have access to his email. He spends most of his time at home if he's not at work. All of those things make me want to believe nothing is going on. But the one thing I asked him to do, he hasn't done yet."

"What's that?"

"I told him I wanted to see the message he sent Aviva—the affair partner." Her voice was hard. "He told me no, that it would be violating her privacy, and then he told me he deleted the message and blocked her anyway. That doesn't feel right to me."

"Have you shared with Karl that these things don't feel right?"

Ebony hesitated. "At first, I let him know I didn't feel as if he was being fully honest. But then he started to tell me I wasn't giving him a chance and that I needed to try to trust him so we could move forward. I've been trying."

"When you let him know that you're uncertain that you can trust him, he shuts it down?"

"Exactly," Ebony said, "and then I feel really stupid for even thinking it."

"Do you want to tell Karl what you found?" I asked her.

Ebony shook her head slowly. "I'm not sure."

I watched her facial expression for clues. "What makes you hesitate?"

Ebony lifted and dropped her hands. "I think he'll tell me I'm wrong, and it won't matter anyway."

I nodded, showing understanding. "If you don't tell him that you have suspicions today and tomorrow, what do you think could happen in our work together?"

"I'm not sure," she admitted. "I guess I wanted to see if he'd admit it on his own. That might help me to see if he's starting to be honest."

I paused to let the situation settle, then continued: "I completely understand the desire to withhold this information. It sounds like in the past when you've brought up your concerns and suspicions, you've been told you're wrong and made to question yourself. Here is the conundrum: Now that I know there is extra information that brings about suspicion that the affair hasn't ended, I can't proceed without that information being on the table for discussion. If I pretend that I don't know, I am being dishonest to Karl, but also all our work will be ignoring a very big, but quiet, elephant in the room." I paused again. "What do you think about what I am saying?"

Ebony murmured, "I hear you. I think you're right. If I don't say anything about it, then I might not get any more information and I'll leave here wondering if he's lying to me anyway. I don't even know how to bring it up."

"Let's play it out," I suggested. "Let's say that tomorrow morning when we all sit down together, I ask you to start by sharing with Karl what things have been like for you recently. What would it be like to take that opportunity to share what you've noticed?"

Ebony winced. "I'm really nervous . . . he's going to get so angry at me for going through his stuff."

"He might," I acknowledged. "What happens if he gets angry?"

Ebony sighed in frustration. "When he gets angry, he tells me I need to move on or things won't work out between us."

"So, he might say to you something like, 'We've talked about this a hundred times. Maybe we won't ever get through it and there is no point?'"

Ebony nodded. "Exactly."

"And if he does that, then what?"

She reflected for a moment. "I guess then I'll try to apologize so he doesn't walk away. I want us to work."

I assured her, "I will be there—you won't be alone in the room. And I'll be helping both of you to talk in more effective ways. I'll coach Karl toward respectful responses if he struggles to do so."

Ebony scowled. "Even with all that, I don't know if he'll be honest with me."

I smiled reassuringly. "You get to be an observer. You get to see if he can be honest with you, be empathetic with you, and work toward repairing with you. You're not sure yet if he can, and you don't need to know—what you can do instead is observe how he responds and then consider what that means to you."

For the first time, Ebony brightened a bit. "I like thinking of it like that. I can watch to see how he responds."

I nodded. "That's right."

"Okay," Ebony drew a deep breath. "I can do that."

"Do you need us to spend a little more time talking about how you're going to bring this up to Karl?" I asked.

"No," she answered, "I think I know what I will say."

> [*When Ebony shared with me her suspicions, I let her know that it would be important that we share these things with Karl, while also being gentle with her by asking for her buy-in to sharing, exploring how it would feel to share, and helping her to play out what that conversation might look like.*]

By asking up front whether Ebony had withheld some information during the first part of the day, I ensured we had enough time to talk more about what she had withheld and why, and I was able to coach her toward bringing this information up with Karl. With that resolved, we still had time to continue to explore the areas of inquiry during our one-on-one session. Ebony shared openly with me about her past relationships, family of origin, and theories on what was going on in her relationship with Karl. She would often become tearful and want to pause to discuss some of the painful moments she and Karl had experienced since the discovery of the affair. Because this was very fresh for Ebony, I followed her lead and allowed her to take time to explore this.

Once I recognized we would need extra time for our one-on-one, I asked Ebony to send Karl a message letting him know the new time frame so that he could plan accordingly. Ultimately, we spent about two hours in our one-on-one session—twice as long as my rule of thumb. However, given her uniquely painful situation (an imminent pregnancy, doubts about her partner's honesty), it seemed appropriate.

Once Ebony and I finished our time together, I welcomed Karl into the office for our individual meeting. I started by thanking him for his patience while Ebony and I spent so much time together, then asked how he was feeling.

Karl shifted in his seat. "I feel okay. I'm still not sure how this weekend can help us when it seems she doesn't want to move forward."

"Something I like to ask people when we first sit down is if there was anything they didn't have a chance to mention during our time as a group," I said, watching his face carefully for any clues his reaction could reveal.

Karl remained impassive. "No, I think I mentioned everything I needed to."

From here, I asked Karl about his level of commitment to the relationship (half in, half out), his relationship history (no serious relationships before Ebony), his family history ("everything was fine, but my parents divorced"), and his mental health history ("I think I'm fine other than the stress of this situation"). Finally, we reached the part of the session where I ask for the client's theory of each partner's responsibility.

"I mean, I take total responsibility for my actions," Karl said. "What I did was messed up—I hurt Ebony and damaged our relationship. But look, I didn't want to say this earlier, but the reality is that at this point it's Ebony who is causing the issues."

I nodded encouragingly. "What do you mean?"

"I think she needs individual help," Karl told me. "I don't think this is really what we need. I agreed to it because she wanted it, but she's not well. She's depressed or something and it's coming out at the relationship. I think she doesn't know how to manage her emotions and just move forward."

"Tell me more about your perception on how people get through betrayal in a relationship," I suggested. "What do you think they should do and how should they act?"

Karl sat back. "I know you probably think I'm a jerk. I think it makes sense for her to be upset about it, but this has been going on for weeks. I've said I'm sorry, I've given her access to my email, she sees the bank accounts. What else could I really do? At this point she's just choosing to be mad."

"It sounds like you feel as if you've put in a lot of effort to make it up to her but nothing has worked?"

Karl nodded vigorously. "Yes, and so I think she needs to work on herself."

I paused, sensing the moment had come for psychoeducation. "Karl, I want to give you some information about how affairs impact a person and what it tends to look like following the discovery."

I talked to Karl about how the violation ruptures trust and creates a deep sense of insecurity in the partner who has been betrayed. When someone learns that the person who was supposed to be their safe landing in the world was harming them, it rocks their sense of reality. Most people, after they've learned of an affair, will start to question the past and their own ability to see things accurately. I explained that there are often trauma responses to affairs and that it takes a long time to recover. I let him know that the person who betrayed their partner has the onus of repair on them at the start and that rebuilding trust requires that person to be a steady rock, empathetic, transparent, and remorseful.

Finally, I broached the topic I'd been wondering about myself. "Karl, something that is pivotal for affair recovery is the whole truth. Sometimes people won't tell their partner the whole truth because they are afraid it will hurt them more and cause bigger problems. Here is what I know as a couples therapist: The truth really does always come out. And if you withhold it during the period of recovery, then your partner will have an even harder time trusting you again when it does come out. It's best to get it all out in the open. Is there anything you haven't shared with Ebony?"

> Karl remained impassive. "I don't think so. She keeps asking me things, but I've shared everything."
>
> I nodded. "Okay, that's good to know. During the session tomorrow, we will likely have a period where Ebony will want to ask you questions. That's a very common aspect of affair recovery. I encourage you to make sure you answer her as clearly as possible because that really helps to recover the foundation of trust."
>
> Karl's jaw set. "I've answered everything."
>
> "I understand," I said, "and the nature of betrayal is that people will often need to ask something many times to do something called *safety seeking*—this is when we keep looking to make sure everything is okay. The more you can answer directly, honestly, and with love, the more possible it will be for Ebony to recover trust."
>
> Throughout the rest of the individual session, Karl and I discussed what led to the affair, what the affair was like for him, and how it felt to have to end things with his affair partner. I still sensed that Karl was not being completely up-front; he often showed frustration when asked about the affair. At the end, I again reminded him of the importance of rebuilding trust with Ebony and the level of commitment that would be needed to do that.

Once you've finished both individual sessions with the couple, it will be time for a break. The length of the break is dependent on how much time you have left in your day, how much time you need to prepare for the next part of the day, and how much time the couple needs. Breaks usually range from 15 minutes to an hour. I suggest making sure you have your food prepared in advance so that you can eat during this break and still have time to look over your assessments and think through how you'll offer feedback in the final portion of the day.

During the break, you can use the following therapist assessment worksheet to help you gather your observations. I've also included an example of a filled-in assessment worksheet to help guide you.

COUPLES THERAPIST WORKSHEET

Joint Intensive Couples Therapy Assessment Notes, Intensive Day 1

Couple's names: _____ Date: _____

Couple's View of the Problem

Partner 1: _____
_____
_____

Partner 2: _____
_____

Major Ups and Downs in the Relationship/Turning Points

Ups: _____
_____
_____

Downs: _____
_____
_____

Notes regarding past stressful experiences: _____
_____
_____

Interactional Impressions

_____
_____
_____

Communication Weaknesses

- ☐ Jumping to solutions without dialogue
- ☐ Difficulty sharing information (conversation is very short)
- ☐ Grandstanding
- ☐ Passivity in one or both partners
- ☐ Argumentativeness
- ☐ Inability to negotiate or come to agreement
- ☐ The Four Horsemen (criticism, defensiveness, stonewalling, contempt)
- ☐ Getting off track (bringing up other topics instead of finishing a conversation about one)
- ☐ Kitchen sinking (piling on other issues or complaints)
- ☐ Interrupting each other
- ☐ Harsh start-up
- ☐ Pursuit/withdrawal

Notes: _____
_____
_____
_____
_____
_____

Communication Strengths

- ☐ Curiosity
- ☐ Empathy
- ☐ Listening skills
- ☐ Soft start-up
- ☐ Assertiveness
- ☐ Agreeableness
- ☐ Ability to negotiate
- ☐ Repair techniques (affection, humor, ability to apologize)
- ☐ Responsibility taking

Notes: _____
_____
_____
_____
_____

Family History

Partner 1: _____
_____
_____

Partner 2: _____
_____
_____

Couple's Goals for Therapy

Partner 1: _____
_____

Partner 2: _____
_____

Overall Assessment of Three Areas for Relational Effectiveness

Relational regard: _____
_____
_____
_____
_____
_____

Individual regard: _____
_____
_____
_____
_____
_____

Regard of other: _____
_____
_____
_____
_____
_____
_____

Neutrality versus reactivity: _____
_____
_____
_____
_____
_____
_____

Self-responsibility: _____
_____
_____
_____
_____
_____
_____

Relational problem-solving/responsibility: _____
_____
_____
_____
_____
_____
_____

SAMPLE

Joint Intensive Couples Therapy Assessment Notes, Intensive Day 1

Couple's names: Andrew and Ron   Date: xx/xx/xx

Couple's View of the Problem

Partner 1: Andrew believes that the biggest issue is the cycle of arguments between him and Ron. He thinks that for anything to improve, Ron would need to improve the way he communicates and manages his emotions. Andrew believes the major issue that needs to be solved is whether they should stay together.

Partner 2: Ron agrees with Andrew that the problem is their cycle of fighting. He believes that the issue is related to his struggles with conflict management and self-regulation. It also seems as if he believes that Andrew's family involvement contributes to a negative narrative about their relationship. Ron agrees that they need to decide on whether to stay together; however, he is more confident than Andrew that the relationship could improve.

Major Ups and Downs in the Relationship/Turning Points

Ups: Positive start to the relationship, moving in together, buying their first home, wedding

Downs: Several major arguments that resulted in Ron leaving or threatening to leave, difficulties navigating Ron's mother's mental health and physical health needs

Notes regarding past stressful experiences: The couple reported that their biggest stressors have been related to conflict within the relationship, particularly major arguments that often occur after drinking. The most upsetting experience is related to a recent vacation.

Interactional Impressions

The couple chose to discuss whether they should pay for Ron's mom's car debt. They started the conversation with curiosity and patience. When they were unable to come to an agreement, they became frustrated. Ron withdrew and told Andrew he could just make the decision. Andrew rolled his eyes and accused Ron of always doing the same thing. Ron apologized "for being such a burden."

Communication Weaknesses

- [x] Jumping to solutions without dialogue
- [ ] Difficulty sharing information (conversation is very short)
- [ ] Grandstanding
- [x] Passivity in one or both partners

- ☐ Argumentativeness
- ☒ Inability to negotiate or come to agreement
- ☒ The Four Horsemen (criticism, defensiveness, stonewalling, contempt)
- ☐ Getting off track (bringing up other topics instead of finishing a conversation about one)
- ☐ Kitchen sinking (piling on other issues or complaints)
- ☐ Interrupting each other
- ☐ Harsh start-up
- ☒ Pursuit/withdrawal

Notes: *Ron withdraws and Andrew pursues. They get into conflict when they realize they are not coming to a consensus.*

Communication Strengths

- ☒ Curiosity
- ☒ Empathy
- ☒ Listening skills
- ☐ Soft start-up
- ☐ Assertiveness
- ☒ Agreeableness
- ☐ Ability to negotiate
- ☐ Repair techniques (affection, humor, ability to apologize)
- ☐ Responsibility taking

Notes: *The couple shows empathy and curiosity and can listen until they become frustrated. They also tend to be mostly agreeable toward each other in session.*

Family History

Partner 1: *Andrew reports that his parents separated when he was young and that his father was hardly ever around. This created a sense of abandonment. However, he also reports that his grandparents and mother were a stabilizing force in his life.*

Partner 2: *Ron's parents separated when he was very young and then continued to have an unstable relationship throughout his childhood. He reports a history of substance misuse. He also reports belligerent conflict in the home.*

Couple's Goals for Therapy

Partner 1: *Andrew wants help discerning whether he and Ron should continue their relationship. He would also like help trusting himself and managing his reactions to perceived abandonment.*

> Partner 2: Ron wants help better understanding himself, improving his communication skills, and improving the relationship with Andrew.
>
> **Overall Assessment of Three Areas for Relational Effectiveness**
>
> **Relational regard:** Andrew does not have a positive view of the relationship and has begun to have a negative outlook on the relationship as a whole. Ron has a high level of regard for the relationship, but his actions often harm the relationship unit as a whole.
>
> **Individual regard:** Andrew seems to have positive regard for himself but he may struggle to set and keep boundaries. He has a high level of empathy, which might cloud his view on where to draw the line. Over time, this has led to resentment in the relationship. Ron does not regard himself highly. He seems to struggle to express his needs and points of view and is quick to be self-deprecating. Ron likely needs help expressing his feelings and needs in a clear and respectful manner so things are not bottled up.
>
> **Regard of other:** Andrew has a history of high regard toward Ron, often feeling empathetic toward Ron after their fights and being open to forgiveness and understanding. Due to the number and escalation of fights, Andrew has begun to be closed off in order to protect himself. Ron has high regard for Andrew and is concerned for how Andrew feels. He is open to hearing Andrew's thoughts and feelings; however, he might struggle to understand how to explore those thoughts and feelings and how to align his actions in a way that shows positive regard to Andrew.
>
> **Neutrality versus reactivity:** The couple is able to maintain neutrality during many of their conversations; however, they become reactive when they are not able to make a decision and when they have been drinking.
>
> **Self-responsibility:** Andrew seems to have a high level of self-responsibility. He reports a history of taking action when he notices issues with how he is navigating a situation. He knows how to apologize. Ron is developing self-responsibility. Historically, he would apologize for his actions but not take steps to consistently improve after the fact.
>
> **Relational problem-solving/responsibility:** The couple struggles to solve problems together. On a large scale, they are having difficulty deciding whether to stay together or end the relationship. On a small scale, they often become frustrated when unable to make a decision. They need support developing skills of negotiation.

Providing Feedback and Goal Setting

The feedback portion of day 1 is an opportunity for synthesizing information and helping the couple to feel seen, heard, and hopeful. Your job during the feedback session is to be honest about what you've seen (even if it's hard) and to talk about what you believe will help them. It's truly an art form to learn how to infuse hope within reality. We don't want to be too optimistic and mislead couples who are struggling into believing the intensive will work magic for them, but we also don't want things to seem too dire, as this increases overwhelm and can reduce motivation.

I always start the feedback session by thanking the couple for time they've spent with me and for how much they've shared. I then let them know that using any assessments they've completed and what I've observed in our time together, I have come up with some feedback I would like to give them.

John and Amy: Feedback

Once our break time was over, I invited John and Amy to rejoin me in the office. I started by explaining what this final portion of our day would look like.

"During this part of our time together, I am going to be talking to you a lot." I smiled. "This is likely the most I will talk during our time together. I'm going to share my observations of your relationship, including areas I see as strengths as well as areas I see as challenges for you both. I'm also going to share with you what I think can be done to improve your relationship. Does that sound okay?"

"Yes," Amy answered, while John nodded.

"While I'm going to be sharing a lot with you, I do want you to be involved," I continued. "So please let me know your thoughts on what I'm saying, interrupt me if you disagree, or share with me if you agree."

John said, "Sounds good."

Amy added, "I'm looking forward to hearing what you think."

Getting out my notes, I began by talking about the important measurements in Gottman Method Couples Therapy, the modality I practice. (If you practice according to a different modality, you will want to give the couple a general overview of what your feedback is based on.) Since I'd be providing feedback based on the Sound Relationship House and their Gottman Assessment, I wanted them to understand that throughout my comments, I would be weaving in those three areas of strength that the Gottman Method looks for: relational regard (for themselves, each other, and their relationship), the ability to maintain neutrality, and problem-solving capacities.

"First, looking at the Sound Relationship House, I want to bring your attention to trust and commitment," I began. "At first, I was unsure of the level of commitment because I knew there had been some threats to end the relationship. However, after talking with you both, I've learned that you're both very much committed and would like this relationship to work. It sounds like the threats to the relationship were more about being upset and not knowing how to express it.

"With that being said," I continued, "it's important to avoid threatening the relationship. It can break trust because it creates a sense of uncertainty. As you can see on the Sound Relationship House, it's pivotal to the relationship to build strong commitment and trust." I paused. "What do you think about what I'm saying?"

Amy nodded slowly. "I need to work on that. I just get so upset sometimes and I want a reaction. But I know it's not right."

"I understand where it comes from," I assured her. "I'd like to help you learn how to express your own feelings and hold boundaries, so you don't get to that place. This is what we call *self-regard*. From what I heard, you are very overwhelmed, and I think you have a difficult time asking for help. So you get more overwhelmed and then resentful about how much you've extended yourself."

"That's true," Amy agreed. "I do so much for everyone, and I need help sometimes. I think part of it is that I don't ask for help. But sometimes I do, and John doesn't seem to care."

I turned. "John, this is where I come to you. When we are looking at areas of trust and commitment, Amy has impacted trust by threatening divorce, but you've impacted her feelings of trust and security in the relationship by abandoning her at times. Do you know what I mean by that?"

John frowned. "I don't think I abandon her."

"You don't abandon her in that you don't leave her in the house alone for days at a time," I agreed, "but sometimes you might as well. What I learned from both of you is that although you both have full-time jobs, yours takes precedence. Amy ends up working 40 hours a week, but she also has to flex her work hours to make everything with the kids work, to keep the house clean, to do laundry, on and on. It's too much."

"She does a lot, but her job is more flexible," John pointed out.

"It might be true that her job is more flexible," I told him. "But Amy has been screaming from the rooftops that she is unable to continue on this way. So not only does she feel abandoned in the physical sense, but she also feels abandoned in the emotional sense when you dismiss her."

At this, Amy started to cry. I looked at John.

"What do you think Amy is thinking right now?"

John looked uncomfortable. "That you're right and that she is exhausted."

I leaned toward him. "I know you love Amy. To improve this relationship, you'll need to build more awareness of her life, what she is carrying, and you'll need to consider how you can take on some of the load too. This is what we mean by *other regard*.

"To rebuild some of the trust in this relationship," I continued, "I want to help Amy learn to express herself and self-soothe when she is upset so she doesn't threaten divorce. And John, I want to help you learn to be more attuned to Amy and to what's going on around you in the home. I will help you to do this tomorrow by supporting you to have conversations in which you're more curious about her thoughts, feelings, and needs.

"I'd also like to help both of you look at the tasks in your home and think of actions you can take to make it more equitable. This is the *problem-solving* piece I mentioned. So tomorrow, we will spend time talking about the load at home and then we will explore possible solutions."

I made sure to wrap up the feedback portion with several minutes left to bring the session to a close. "It's been such an honor to learn more about each of you," I told them, "and I really look forward to diving in tomorrow. Before we finish today, there are a few things I'd like to talk about. First, I want to give you a brief overview of tomorrow. We will all meet at 9 a.m. and we will spend most of the day with all three of us. Tomorrow will be different from today. I will be here with you, guiding you, but you'll be talking with each other through the bulk of the day.

"Tonight, when you go home, I want you to prioritize rest. I also encourage you to not continue talking about the issues we've discussed today. Your brains need a break! I also suggest that you stay away from alcohol. I've had so many experiences where couples go out to dinner after their session, drink some wine, and get into an argument. Then the next day we must process that argument. I would love to avoid that.

"Lastly, I'd like you to turn toward each other and share what you're grateful for today. What do you appreciate about your partner?"

Amy, still looking at me, began, "I'm really grateful that John..."

I stopped her. "Let's start practicing for tomorrow. I want you to tell John, not me."

> Amy smiled sheepishly and shifted to face her partner. "John, I am grateful you agreed to come today. I know this isn't your type of thing, but I feel better already knowing you're committed to understanding what's making me so unhappy."
>
> John responded, "Amy, I really appreciate you and all the work you put into getting us here. I think I'm starting to better understand how much you do. And I appreciate that you're giving me a chance to do better. I love you."
>
> With that, the first day of the intensive was over for John and Amy.

As demonstrated in my feedback session with Amy and John, with each piece of feedback I offer a couple, I explain how my perspective is informed by my therapeutic modality, then let them know how I think I can help. I also continually check in with the couple by asking, "What do you think about what I've just said?" or "Do you agree?" or "Does this surprise you?" I ask these questions as an opportunity to learn where I've gotten it wrong, where they are in misalignment, or what seems to trigger them or be difficult for them to hear. I also learn positive information, like which types of feedback help them to feel motivated and hopeful and which strengths make them feel proud. This inspires couples to have confidence in me as the therapist and to feel hopeful about the plan I have to help them.

At the end of the feedback session, I give a brief overview of the next day and some directives for the evening, including prioritizing rest, avoiding discussion of the issues in their relationship, and avoiding alcohol (which often leads to said discussion). Then I ask the couple to turn toward each other and show gratitude for going through such a long day together. There are times that I choose not to do this part—for example, if the couple is particularly flooded or incredibly angry with each other. However, asking the couple to offer gratitude can serve as a positive transitional moment from the hard work of the intensive into the world. It reiterates to each person that they are loved and safe with their partner, even when things are hard.

This affirming conclusion helps the couple to stay regulated and motivated to resume our work the following day.

CHAPTER 4

The Intensive, Day 2

> ### John and Amy: Day 2
>
> When Amy and John returned the next morning for day 2 of their session, they looked rested and ready to go. Just like day 1, I took time to join with the couple, check in on their comfort levels, and set an agenda for the day.
>
> "How was your sleep last night?" I asked them.
>
> "I was so tired when we left here," Amy admitted. "I fell asleep as soon as we finished dinner."
>
> "Same here," John said. "I was on kid duty, but as soon as that was done I hopped right into bed."
>
> "Are you both ready to get started today?" I asked. "Do you need anything, like water or a run to the bathroom?"
>
> "I think we're good to go," Amy replied. John nodded in agreement.
>
> "Fantastic." I opened my notes. "I'd like to give you a quick overview of the day and then we can get going. Today is going to be different from yesterday. Yesterday I spent a lot of time asking you questions and speaking directly to you. Today, I am going to be helping the two of you talk to each other. I'll be an observer on the outside as you have these conversations.
>
> "The second thing that will be different about today is that I will be intervening. Yesterday, I was just observing because I wanted to better understand the status quo of your relationship. Today, however, if I notice either of you doing something that isn't getting you to your goals, I will step in and give you feedback or help you do it differently.
>
> "We will have time for breaks during the day and I'll certainly suggest times for those breaks as we go based on my observations of energy and time, but I also invite you to ask for them if you need anything at any point." I paused. "Do you have any questions?"
>
> John shook his head. "No, that sounds good. I'm ready to get started."
>
> "I'm all set," Amy agreed.

Once you've rejoined with the couple and given them the day's goals and agenda, you'll begin to lead them through a series of guided interactions to help promote change in each of the three key areas you explored during the assessment on day 1:

- **Relationship regard:** During your work with the couple in an intensive session, you are helping them to build regard for themselves, the other person, and the relationship. The individual is being supported as they better understand their own feelings and needs and learn to express them. They are also being supported as they set boundaries and make decisions. Within the session, each individual is encouraged to also have a sense of awareness and regard for their partner, learning how to better attune with what their partner thinks and feels even if it is different and having a desire to create a relationship that works for both of them. Lastly, the couple is working toward developing skills and making decisions that honor the relationship—whether that means staying together or separating.

- **Neutrality:** During day 2, you will give special attention to reactivity and use interventions to help bring clients to a place of more neutrality. You might utilize interventions that support the couple as they navigate flooding or that help them express themselves without blame, for example.

- **Responsibility:** As you work with the couple, you'll help each of them develop insights into their personal responsibilities. You will also coach them on how to build confidence regarding solving problems together. This might include coaching them on how to bring up issues or what it means to negotiate.

There are three main types of guided interactions you'll use for this work:

- **Enactments:** As discussed in earlier chapters, enactments are interactions between couples prompted by the therapist. Whereas the first day's enactments were only for observation, on the second day of the intensive, the therapist may use different intervention techniques or exercises during the enactment to help the couple create change.

- **Exercises:** Exercises are activities that your couple will be directed to do during the session. An example of this is directing them to have a specific conversation, play a game, or answer a set of questions.

- **Interventions:** Interventions are actions you take to shape the interactional patterns and help the couple make progress. This includes psychoeducation, restructuring, and more.

Enactments

The magic in day 2 is the enactments. While enactments are also utilized in traditional couples therapy, they are harder to set up and complete effectively due to time restraints. Enactments are the foundation for most of the work that will be done during the second day of the intensive. While the first day relied heavily on therapist-to-couple communication, the second day will primarily involve partner-to-partner communication, with the therapist as observer and coach.

Throughout day 2, you will be setting up enactments with the couple and then utilizing interventions within those enactments. Enactments move the couple into their interactional patterns and provide opportunities for the therapist to then intervene when the couple becomes mired in their dysfunctional patterns.

Because these enactments are designed to help the couple improve their interactional patterns, there may be some day 2 sessions where it does not make sense to focus on enactments, or even to use them at all. For example, if the couple has decided they would like to end the relationship, then the therapist might forgo enactments and spend more one-on-one time with each partner, since the clients are no longer focused on changing their patterns but looking for support regarding which steps to take next.

Enactments have several main purposes, including the following (Butler & Gardner, 2003):

- **Assessment:** When having the couple participate in an enactment, the therapist can act as an observer of their interactional patterns, as we saw in the enactment used on day 1. The use of enactments during day 2 provides an opportunity for continued assessment in which the therapist can note any previously unseen challenges or new growth between the partners and utilize this information to continue to inform treatment of the couple.

- **Facilitation of communication skills:** When a couple is in an enactment, the therapist can provide them with guidance on how to use new communication skills and the couple is also able to practice these skills. This helps the couple use effective communication in real time.

- **Redirecting relationship processes or patterns:** During an enactment, the therapist will be present when the couple begins to fall into dysfunctional relationship processes or interactional patterns. The therapist can then intervene by asking the couple to pause and redirecting them toward more effective processes and patterns.

- **Promoting secure attachment:** During the enactment, the therapist can guide couples toward opportunities for facilitating deeper attachment. These opportunities include disclosing vulnerable thoughts or feelings (which often hide behind more aggressive behavior or combative language), sharing memories or hopes, and experiencing emotions together.

Enactments are divided into three phases (Davis & Butler, 2004).

Phase 1: Initiation

While enactments are helpful tools for relational change, the ways in which they are managed can lead to either a successful or unsuccessful outcome. Successful outcomes result in a couple engaging in higher levels of emotional vulnerability, trying a new communication skill, or changing a process or pattern within the enactment. An unsuccessful enactment is an enactment that was not managed well and therefore might have increased the clients' anxiety outside of the window of tolerance. Unsuccessful enactments also occur when the therapist manages the enactment on one of two ends of an extreme—either taking a laissez-faire approach and providing little to no containment, which often leads to the couple being unable to maintain neutrality and becoming reactive, or micromanaging the couple to the point that they are not able to fully express themselves emotionally or create a stronger attachment with each other due to the frustrating interruptions (Davis & Butler, 2004).

To increase the likelihood that an enactment is successful, the therapist must do four things: introduce goals and roles, specify the topic, set expectations, and establish structure.

INTRODUCE GOALS AND ROLES

First, the therapist will explain the purpose of the enactment, the role of each member of the couple, and the role of the therapist. The most basic example of this is when a therapist asks the couple to talk with each other about a difficult topic. The therapist instructs the couple to look at each other and explains that the purpose of having the conversation about the difficult topic is to work toward understanding each other more clearly. They then explain to the couple each of their roles; in the case of this enactment, the therapist might explain to partner A that their role is to be the speaker while partner B is the listener. The therapist might go into more depth describing the responsibilities of each of those roles—for example, the speaker is responsible for sharing their own perspective, speaking for themselves, and avoiding criticism and blame whereas the listener is responsible for hearing the speaker's perspective without interruption, working toward understanding their position, and being able to summarize their position.

Lastly, the therapist should let the couple know what their own role is during the enactment. They might say something like "I will just be an observer during this conversation; please pretend that I'm not in the room" or "I have two roles. One role is to observe and the second role is to intervene. If I notice that you are interacting in an unhelpful manner with each other, I will step in to help you try it in a new way."

SPECIFY THE TOPIC

After the therapist describes the goals and roles, they work with the couple to specify the topic. It is important for the therapist to direct the couple in this, as the decision should not be random. Rather, the therapist should consider how the content is going to help the clients reach their goals. The therapist might choose a specific piece of content for many reasons. Perhaps they choose low reactivity content to make it more likely that the couple will be able to practice new skills without becoming overwhelmed. The therapist might also choose content that is higher reactivity—for example, when a couple is overcoming a betrayal, at some point they will need to be given instructions on how to discuss the impact of the affair. The therapist will help the couple to do this by choosing that content at the right time, usually after teaching them some more basic skills first.

SET EXPECTATIONS

Once the topic has been decided upon, the therapist should set ground rules regarding communication. For example, the therapist might remind the couple to refrain from interrupting each other and to avoid the four horsemen. The therapist should also coach the couple on expectations for attachment-based responses to each other. Responses to help develop a secure attachment include the use of empathy, validation, and curiosity.

ESTABLISH STRUCTURE

Structure is established by directing and arranging the couple (e.g., having them turn toward each other or move their chairs), coaching them to speak for themselves using first-person language, and reminding them that you are removing yourself from the interaction, verbally and nonverbally.

The goal of couples therapy is to help the couple function without the therapist. Helping the couple to physically experience the communication as being between the two of them instead of being between the three people in the room begins to build their confidence for having conversations together. Arranging the couple helps the therapist to resist triangulation, as it serves as a physical reminder to the therapist that they are an observer—they can intervene, but they are still the outsider.

John and Amy: Enactment

The previous day, when I had asked Amy and John to choose a mild disagreement of theirs to use as a brief enactment, they had discussed a disagreement regarding a vacation. Afterward, they affirmed that their struggle to slow down, show curiosity, and be flexible with each other was like other disagreements they'd had.

Because this disagreement mirrored their pattern but had little reactivity associated with it, I decided to use it in the first enactment I wanted to try with them on day 2. During the day 1 enactment, I did not specify a topic and I did not provide much structure. I typically choose to give the most basic instructions on the first day because I want to assess reactivity and observe a more natural conversation experience between the two partners. On day 2, however, I want to give them an opportunity to build skills and feel successful.

After getting John and Amy settled in, I explained what we were going to do and set out the goals and roles. "We are going to start today by having a conversation using the speaker/listener model. The purpose of this is to begin to lay a foundation for healthy communication between the two of you. In this exercise you will both have an opportunity to be the speaker and the listener. When you are the speaker, your job will be to express yourself without blame. Instead, talk about your own thoughts, feelings, and needs. When you are the listener, your job is to be present with your partner. Whenever you notice yourself wanting to interrupt, becoming defensive, or getting distracted, your job is to come back to what your partner is saying. As you listen, you want to notice not just the words they say but also how they feel. Once they finish speaking, you'll summarize what you heard and show empathy by letting them know what makes sense about their perspective."

I paused. "I know I'm saying a lot. Are you still with me?"

"Yes . . ." Amy hesitated. "I'm just worried I'll forget the instructions."

"No worries," I assured her. "If you forget the instructions, I will help. As you talk, I will be observing. If needed, I'll hop in to help you do it differently. There is no expectation that you get this perfect—you're here to try new things and learn some new skills. If I notice it's becoming difficult for either of you to follow the speaker/listener roles, I will help you."

Next, I specified the topic of the enactment and established expectations for how they should communicate. "I'm going to have the two of you talk about your vacation again. Today it will be different because we are using this model. Your job is to work hard to slow down, show curiosity, and be open and flexible with each other. Remember to follow those speaker/listener roles. You also want to work to be a source of secure attachment for each other—just like yesterday when you noticed that things were getting heated so you made a joke or grabbed each other's hands."

Seeing comprehension on their faces, I gave them directions to establish the structure of the exercise. "You're going to talk about your vacation together. Amy, how about you speak first? John, you'll be the listener. Amy, talk about your perspective on the vacation, using 'I' language—really just talking about what you think. John, you'll try to listen and be curious about Amy's thoughts. Try to understand how she's feeling and what she needs.

"Amy and John, could you turn toward each other on the couch so you can see each other's faces? Okay, wonderful. I'm going to stop talking now, and Amy, you go ahead." I shifted my chair backward to indicate that I was officially removed from the interaction.

Phase 2: Intervention

As the couple engages with each other in the enactment, there will be times when the therapist needs to intervene. This is for two primary reasons:

- **Sustaining the interaction:** While the primary goal for the therapist is to observe the enactment, it's also the therapist's job to make sure the couple never runs out of fuel. *Sustained interactions* occur when the therapist provides the couple with positive and motivating feedback (e.g., "Wow, that was really beautiful how you responded to your partner there"), interrupts demotivating patterns ("Let's pause for a moment because if you keep interrupting your partner, you aren't going to get anywhere"), or encourages the couple to keep going ("I know this conversation is challenging, but let's keep going").

- **Coaching:** When the couple is struggling and doesn't know what do to, the therapist will intervene and provide some feedback to the couple or teach them a new skill to try. For example, the therapist might say, "I hear what you're trying to express, but it's not coming across that way. How about you try it this way instead?" Coaching often involves helping the couple build skills related to communication, self-soothing, and problem-solving. This helps to support the goals of relationship regard, neutrality, and problem-solving.

As you read the following enactment with Amy and John, notice where these two interventions come into play.

John and Amy: Enactment Intervention

Amy began, "I think we should go to the beach for our vacation this year. I know that's annoying to you, but it's just my opinion and…"

I held up my hand. "Amy, I'm going to ask you to take a pause. Remember, right now I just want you to speak for yourself. When you share your assumption with John that he thinks it's annoying, he's going to get distracted thinking about whether he finds it annoying. If you're wrong, he will likely interrupt to correct you, which will take this off track. Can you try to just let him know your perspective here? Focus on why you want to go to the beach, your ideas about the beach trip, how you feel about it."

Amy nodded eagerly. "Yes, I can try again." As I sat back, removed once more, Amy turned back to John. "I think we should go to the beach," she repeated. "I have a lot of reasons for it. First, I really like the beach. It's fun for me to play in the sand with Jacob. When I do get a few minutes of relaxation, I love to sunbathe and listen to the waves. Second, it's close to our house. It's so much easier to hop in the car for a few hours than it is to deal with airports … in my opinion, at least."

"You're doing great, Amy," I said softly.

Amy glanced at me, then continued. "Recently life has been so busy, and I feel really overwhelmed. I have a hard time imagining a vacation that makes me think about too much."

John stepped in. "This is the thing that frustrates me. I already told you that it won't be stressful. We've flown before—it'll be okay!"

"Okay, John, pause," I said. "Right now, you're listening to Amy. I understand you might have a different perspective of the trip than Amy's, but if you interrupt right now, then Amy is going to feel unheard and you're just going to fall back into your cycle. It's completely normal to get distracted by your own perspective and thoughts, but for now I want you to just notice that you're having the thought or urge to interrupt and then let it float by. You'll have your turn next." I gave them both a thumbs-up. "Let's keep trying."

John took a breath. "Sorry about that. Keep going, Amy."

"Okay, I got a little distracted, so let me think . . ." Amy looked up at the ceiling, focusing her thoughts. "Okay, yeah . . . so the main thing is that I'm incredibly stressed with our home life, parenting, and work. I just don't want a vacation that adds more work for me. I want it to be simple. Even thinking about planning a big vacation with a flight and hotels and a new city makes me anxious."

Seemingly to her own surprise, Amy started to cry. Seeing it, John immediately reached out and grabbed Amy's hand.

"Beautiful, John," I murmured. "You're reminding Amy you're there for her."

Amy steadied herself with a breath. "Okay, I think I'm done talking now."

"Okay, John," I said, "go ahead and summarize what you heard from Amy."

"It makes sense to me that if you're stressed out, you'd want an easy trip," John said. "I get that."

"Now, ask Amy if she has anything else to add."

John turned toward Amy and asked her if he'd missed anything or if she'd like to add anything more. Amy shared that she felt as if John understood her.

"John," I directed, "it's your turn now. Why don't you share with Amy your perspective?"

"Well, I do want to say I understand how Amy feels. I guess if it's going to be such a fight, we can just do what she wants," he said.

> [Sometimes, a partner will attempt to prematurely end the enactment by saying they don't need to discuss their own perspective. In this instance, I didn't believe that John felt completely on board with Amy's idea for a trip. My concern was that if I allowed the conversation to be over, John would later resent Amy. Therefore, I decided to encourage John to discuss his perspective anyway, using motivating feedback to help him sustain the interaction.]

"John, that's really kind of you to hear Amy's perspective and to offer her the opportunity to lead the way in planning the trip," I said. "However, I would still like you to discuss your perspective, as I think it's good practice for each of you to get comfortable sharing what you think and having healthy dialogue around disagreement."

John nodded and turned to Amy. "Amy, my perspective is that while the airport travel might be stressful, we will be happy with the ultimate outcome. I've always imagined being able to travel with my family and I think it's important to show Jacob the world. I don't get a lot of time off from work, so when I do have the time I want to use it to try new things."

John looked over at me and I gave him an encouraging nod. Amy continued to listen to John as she kept her body turned toward him and maintained a gentle face.

John went on, "I guess I just feel frustrated that you're letting your anxiety about airports control our experiences." With this, I saw Amy's relaxed face move into a grimace as she made an exasperated chuckle.

"You've got to be kidding me." Amy looked at me with an incredulous smile.

"John, what you just shared was more about Amy and less about you. Try to speak for yourself and not about her. Amy, you've been doing a beautiful job—can you try to turn back toward John and give him another chance to express himself?"

> Amy nodded and John tried again. "Sorry about that. I won't talk about you, I'll talk about me. It's important for me to have adventures and go to new places, and not being able to go makes me feel stuck. It's not a feeling I like. If we could go, I do imagine that I could manage Jacob so you could rest on the plane, and I could see us making wonderful memories together."
>
> I waited a moment to see if there was more that John wanted to share. When it seemed clear he was finished, I turned to Amy and, with a hand gesture, encouraged her to continue the enactment.
>
> "Well, it all makes sense to me, John. I know you love to travel and it's something we used to do together. I understand that part of you wouldn't go away just because we have a child now. I guess where I get the most frustrated with this entire thing is when you say you feel trapped . . ."
>
> "Amy," I cut in, "this is about focusing on John's perspective and trying to understand where he's coming from. When you started to share your own frustrations, the focus moved away from him and toward you. Could you try to focus on him again?"
>
> Amy took a deep breath and nodded. "Sorry, this is hard," she said to me.
>
> "I know it can be. You're doing well. Keep trying."
>
> Amy turned back to John and apologized. She then went on to share with him that his perspective made sense and that she understood his desire to travel to new and adventurous places. "I really do understand, John, and I don't want you to feel so bad. I want you to have the types of trips you need, too."
>
> "Now, Amy, could you ask John if there is anything else he would like to add?"
>
> "Sure," she said with a smile. "John, is there anything else you'd like to add?"
>
> John took a moment to think and then shared, "I just want you to know that I want us to both have what we need, and I do think there's room for compromise."

Phase 3: Reflection

Once the enactment has concluded, the therapist will guide the couple toward reflection on the process. This involves four key steps:

1. **Review goals and roles:** The therapist reiterates the goals of the enactment that was just completed and reminds the couple which roles they played. This helps the couple recall the purpose of the enactment.

2. **Connect the process to overall therapy goals:** The therapist connects the enactment to the couple's overall therapy goals. For example, if the goal is for the couple to learn how to better manage conflict, the therapist might remind the couple that they discussed their disagreement during the session to practice having effective conflict with each other.

3. **Reflection:** Next, the therapist encourages the couple to reflect on the enactment: what went well during the enactment, what they noticed that their partner was successfully able to do, and what, if any, challenges they still came across. The therapist will also offer their feedback, especially related to areas of growth or change that they've already noticed in either partner or that the couple still needs to work on. During this reflection, the therapist should be focused on process over content, encouraging the clients to notice how the interaction went instead of discussing the actual specifics of the content.

> **COUPLES THERAPY DICTIONARY**
>
> **Process versus Content**
>
> Couples therapists differentiate between process and content. Both are important to therapy.
>
> *Content* is the material that the couple discusses—for example, where they want to go for vacation, how the betrayed partner learned about the affair, what happened during a big argument, or a story about a partner visiting their family members. Content is important because it allows the client to feel seen and heard and helps the therapist understand the bigger picture. However, if the focus is exclusively on content, change will not occur.
>
> *Process* is about interactional patterns and the clients' internal worlds. It has to do with what is happening and how it happens. For example, the content being discussed might be information about a big argument, but to really create change the therapist will need to explore with the couple what was happening during that argument: Where was the couple? How were they feeling? What was happening internally? What were they doing?
>
> The therapist should redirect the couple to look toward their process when they are talking about a past event. They should also direct the couple to notice their processes during an enactment.

4. **Commitment:** Finally, the therapist encourages the couple to make a commitment related to the process or content of the conversation. This might involve committing to changing a pattern of communication or learning to respond toward attachment needs more effectively. For example, a partner might say, "I realize that I can become critical quickly, and I want to commit to trying to say things in a gentler tone. I will keep working on that."

In regard to content-related commitments, it's possible that the enactment brought about new information that the couple would like to apply to their lives. For example, a client might say, "I finally understood what you meant by needing me to set better boundaries with my dad, and I'm going to try to do that this week."

Let's take a look at how John and Amy concluded their enactment.

John and Amy: Conclusion of an Enactment

"We started this conversation to really practice speaking and listening with each other," I said. "You both got an opportunity to be a speaker and a listener when talking about something challenging. Our goal was to work on slowing down and being more curious and open to flexible problem-solving. This connects to the bigger goals of learning how to discuss difficult topics and find a way to be on common ground and come up with win-win outcomes.

"Now," I continued, "I'd like to take a moment to hear what you noticed about the conversation. Let's start with what you think went well."

John spoke first. "I think we did a pretty good job of slowing it down this time. I definitely feel like I shared more about why I wanted to go on the bigger trip. I'm also glad I stopped interrupting Amy and just listened. I don't think I realized before how it connects to her overall stress."

"I agree," said Amy. "We did better slowing down and not just jumping into problem-solving."

> "What do you appreciate about what your partner did?" I asked her. "Turn to John and tell him directly."
>
> Amy shifted to face her partner. "I appreciate that you took Liz's feedback and quickly went back to listening to me. That felt good. Also, I always appreciate when you're affectionate."
>
> John took his turn. "I really appreciated that you spoke for yourself and didn't talk about your assumptions of what I would think or feel. That felt much more productive for me. I also appreciated how you listened to me."
>
> "I am glad you noticed those things about each other," I said. "Is there anything you think still needs some work?"
>
> Again, John spoke first. "I realized I have a really hard time listening if I disagree, so I need to work on that."
>
> Amy added, "I think I need to work on how critical I get when I'm frustrated, as well as how much I assume. I was able to stop myself after you pointed it out, but I want to continue paying attention to that."
>
> "Do you think you have any agreements regarding the vacation that you'd like to make sure you remember?" I asked.
>
> "I think we can agree we need to keep talking about it," Amy answered, "and I feel committed to finding a middle ground for both of us."
>
> "I'm committed to finding a time to continue the conversation if it's not today," John said.
>
> "What about commitments you want to make regarding your communication?" I pursued.
>
> "I'm committed to working on how much I assume," Amy said with a wry grin. "I really am going to try to not do that so much."
>
> John added, "I feel really committed to learning how to listen better."
>
> I nodded, then offered encouragement of my own. "You do really well with this already, but perhaps you could also make a commitment to continue to show affection whenever either of you is having a hard time."
>
> Amy took John's hand. "Definitely."

Exercises

Enactments can be created through a variety of exercises, including those described next. This is not an exhaustive list; I encourage you to weave in your own exercises that you commonly use.

Regardless of which exercise you use, most enactments will look similar to John and Amy's if they focus on content that is not highly reactive. Sometimes, though, enactment can result in reactivity due to emotional flooding. These can still be moments that help guide the couple toward more functional behaviors if the therapist recognizes there is flooding and intervenes within the enactment to help the couple change that process by encouraging them to take a break or by implementing a soothing routine, like a breathing exercise. This will be illustrated further through vignettes with our other example couples.

Exercise 1: Speaker/Listener

Like Amy and John, many couples need to practice basic speaking and listening early in the intensive. While they might understand the concept of speaking and listening, the "muscle" to do it is often atrophied in conflictual relationships.

I typically use a speaking and listening exercise as my first enactment because it builds the foundation for the rest of our conversations. If a couple isn't able to speak and listen effectively, any interactions will be challenging.

When using this enactment exercise, introduce the couple to the speaking and listening model and let them know they'll use it throughout your sessions. Begin with a low-intensity issue so that the couple has the opportunity to practice without high levels of reactivity. As the couple's skills with speaking and listening grow, you can utilize the exercise for more difficult content.

When introducing the speaker/listener enactment, I often pair my verbal directions with a handout of written instructions, as some people are more visual learners than auditory learners. You are welcome to use the speaker/listener instructions I've provided on the next page.

Couples Handout

Speaker/Listener Exercise

Instructions for the Speaker

1. **Get consent:** Ask your partner if it's a good time to talk. Respect their response and agree on a time within 24 hours.
2. **State your intent:** Start by expressing that you care about the relationship and want a constructive conversation.
3. **Allow feedback:** Pause regularly for your partner to mirror back what you've said so they do not get "lost in the sauce" of what you are sharing.
4. **One topic:** Stick to one topic and avoid side issues.
5. **Speak for yourself**: Share your feelings without blaming. Use phrases like "I feel . . ." followed by a feeling, not a thought (for example, "I feel sad," not "I feel like you don't think about me"). Avoid pointing fingers or using criticisms.
6. **Maintain a safe tone**: Speak calmly. If you can't, self-soothe.
7. **Use your wisdom**: Avoid blame, labels, or absolutes. Focus on expressing your feelings.
8. **Let them be successful with you**: Acknowledge when your partner gets it right.
9. **Close and invite**: Thank your partner for listening and ask if they'd like to share their thoughts.

Instructions for the Listener:

1. **Listen:** Let your partner speak without interrupting. If your mind starts to drift, work on bringing it back to your partner. Withhold your own agenda.
2. **Reflect**: Reflect back what you heard without adding your own interpretation. Ask, "Did I get that right?"
3. **Summarize:** Briefly summarize the main points and check for accuracy.
4. **Validate:** Acknowledge that their perspective makes sense, even if you don't fully agree.
5. **Empathize**: Express understanding of how they might feel. Ask, "Is that how you feel?"
6. **Ask to switch roles:** Finish by ensuring your partner has said everything they need to, then politely ask if you can respond, taking your turn as the speaker.

The previous example is not the only speaker/listener exercise available for enactments. The following are two other popular exercises. I also encourage you to research other options to find the best fit for your own clinical style.

THE IMAGO DIALOGUE

Developed by Harville Hendrix and Helen LaKelly Hunt as a core technique utilized in Imago Relationship Therapy, the Imago dialogue process is informed by four key principles (Hendrix, 2007):

- **Safety and respect:** The partners are asked to make a commitment to speak calmly; to avoid attacking, blaming, or criticizing; and to listen without interruption.

- **Mirroring:** The partners are asked to practice paraphrasing and repeating back what they heard in order to ensure understanding.

- **Validation and empathy:** The partners are expected to be able to put themselves in their partner's shoes. They show their ability to do this by offering validation and empathy.

- **Intentionality:** The partners are encouraged to express their thoughts, feelings, and needs clearly.

COUPLES THERAPIST RESOURCE

The Imago Dialogue

- **Setting the stage:** Before the conversation starts, the couple creates a calm space. Distractions are removed.

- **Sender and receiver:** Rather than "speaker" and "listener," the roles in this dialogue are known as called "sender" and "receiver." The sender expresses their thoughts and feelings as clearly as possible while the receiver listens.

- **Mirroring:** Next, the receiver summarizes what they heard from the sender.

- **Validation:** The receiver validates what they heard from the sender.

- **Empathy:** Lastly, the receiver offers empathy by identifying the sender's feelings and showing compassion.

- **Switch roles:** The couple then switches sender and receiver roles.

THE RAPOPORT FOUR RULES CONVERSATION

Anatol Rapoport, a mathematician and psychologist who was an expert in game theory and conflict resolution, developed several assumptions related to how conflict manifests between people and what you can do about it. His work has been used to help people navigate conflicts disrupting international relations as well as interpersonal conflicts. In the Gottman Method, clinicians utilize Rapoport's four rules to teach their couples speaking and listening skills.

One of the most powerful assumptions in the Rapoport conversation is that there are two subjective realities, both of which are valid to an extent. Within this model of conflict resolution, we do not look for absolute right or wrong, but rather varying perspectives. The partners are encouraged to develop deeper understanding of each other by focusing on perceptions more than arguing over facts (Rapoport, 1960).

Couples are also taught Rapoport's Assumption of Similarity: When you identify a negative quality in your partner, try to see that very quality in yourself, and when you identify a positive quality in yourself, try to find that quality in your partner (Gottman, 2011).

Daniel Dennett (2013) summarized Rapoport's four rules as follows:

1. Restate the other person's position fairly and clearly.
2. List points of agreement.
3. Mention what you've learned from their perspective.
4. Offer your counterargument.

> **COUPLES THERAPIST RESOURCE**
>
> ### Rapoport's Rules
>
> When a couple is having an argument, they should follow the four rules laid out by Rapoport (and consolidated by Dennett). The goal of using the four rules is not to win an argument but to increase empathy, understanding, and the capacity for problem-solving.
>
> 1. **Restate the other's position clearly and fairly:** After listening to the other person's perspective, restate what they've said in a fair, clear, and neutral manner to show you've really heard them. Avoid reacting with your own opinions or arguments or asking "gotcha questions" like "Isn't it true, though, that you said something different last week?" Respond from a place of genuine care and curiosity.
>
> 2. **List points of agreement:** Let them know which aspects of their perspective you agree with. Even if you only agree with a small part of what they've shared, starting with agreements creates a sense of collaboration rather than conflict.
>
> 3. **Mention what you've learned from their perspective:** Share what you learned as you listened. This might include what you've learned about the other person's thoughts, feelings, or experience, or even a new fact that you've learned.
>
> 4. **Offer your counterargument:** After you've restated the other person's perspective, shared where you agree, and discussed what you've learned, you can present your own perspective. Remember, the goal is to foster collaboration, and so sharing should be done with respect, kindness, and owning that it is your own perspective and not necessarily an objective truth.

Exercise 2: HARD Conversations

Many couples will be able to utilize the speaker/listener structure over and over throughout the intensive to begin their conversation about various issues that they'd like to address. However, some issues will cause high levels of reactivity and escalation and will require an enactment that includes mindful attention to emotional states, frequent pauses for self-soothing and reassurance, and reorientation to the goal. The HARD Conversations exercise helps couples navigate a disagreement that has escalated.

> **COUPLES THERAPIST RESOURCE**
>
> ## HARD Conversation
>
> - **Halt:** Ask the couple to pause and take a break.
> - **Attend to attachment needs:** Help the couple briefly attend to their attachment needs. For example, one person might share with their partner that they just need a moment but still love them. If they cannot do it, you can by saying something like "Let's take a break here. You are both here to improve things and I know that matters a lot to you, so taking a moment is important toward that goal."
> - **Repair:** When the couple is able to "cool down," help them repair with each other by offering an apology.
> - **Debrief:** Ask the couple to talk about what happened (process), rather than what was talked about (content). Help them to describe their observations of the interaction and what would make it better next time.

When the first day of the intensive involves particularly difficult subject matter, this exercise is often the best choice to help couples develop skills for navigating complex issues together. This ended up being the case with Ebony and Karl—as you'll see below, I ultimately pivoted to the HARD Conversation model as the better enactment for helping them work through their significant barriers to communication and trust. As you read through their enactment, look for the moments where these four elements—halt, attend, repair, and debrief—show up.

Ebony and Karl: HARD Conversations

When Ebony and Karl arrived for the second day of their intensive, Ebony looked as if she had spent the morning crying, while Karl looked exhausted and forlorn. Before starting the day, I checked in on their comfort needs—did they need the bathroom? Water? A blanket to wrap around themselves? Then I asked how they were both doing. They expressed that they were tired and emotionally drained but ready to start the day.

I started with my usual speaker/listener exercise. After describing to the couple how we would do the enactment, their roles, and my role, I introduced the topic for their interaction.

"I'd like the conversation to focus on how you're feeling today. Ebony, I'll have you go first; Karl, you'll listen. Go ahead and turn toward each other. I will be here if you need any support."

Ebony began, "I'm very nervous this morning. I feel like so much is riding on what happens today. I'm also so emotionally drained. And incredibly sad. I feel a lot of things. I don't really know what else to say."

"I know you feel those things," Karl responded dully.

I encouraged him, "Karl, could you summarize what you heard from Ebony and offer her some validation? Let her know what makes sense."

Karl obediently added, "I hear you're feeling a lot of things—that you're really worried about what will happen and that you're sad. I know you feel all of these things. I get why you feel them."

Ebony's voice was hard. "I guess I just don't hear any empathy in your voice. I know I've been talking about this a lot, but I don't understand why you're being so dry with me."

They both remained silent for a moment.

I decided it was time to give Ebony an opening to share her discovery of Karl's second phone, as we'd discussed the day before. "Ebony, is there anything else you want to let Karl know about how you're doing?" I prompted.

Ebony blew out her breath. "I'm not okay. I want you to know you've ruined my life. I can't even enjoy my pregnancy. It's all so awful. You're being so dry right now—I think you're still lying. I don't know why I'm here."

Karl's dull affect fell away and his voice rose. "You think I'm still lying? What the hell? Where do you get that from? This is nuts."

"I don't even want to say," Ebony answered through gritted teeth. "But I've seen some things and I know stuff. I really think I hate you."

I held up my hand. "Let me pause you there."

Karl stood. "No. No way—this isn't fair. I need to take a break and leave for a minute."

"Okay," I assured him. "Let's pause for a moment. We can all take a break and then we'll come back together. Ebony, would you like to go get some water?"

"I can do that," Ebony answered tightly.

"And Karl, you're going to go take a walk?"

"I guess so," said Karl. "When do you want me back?"

"How about in five minutes?" I proposed.

"Fine." He left, shutting the door firmly behind him.

> [*Karl's request for a break was timely. Along with giving them both a chance to settle their emotions, it was a good opportunity for me to reevaluate my approach. It was clear that the couple had become critical and flooded and that they both needed to take a break. In some situations, the break is enough for the couple to move back into the speaker/listener exercise. However, based on my understanding of Ebony and Karl, they needed to practice repairing and debriefing after their difficult conversations. For that reason, when they returned, I pivoted to the HARD Conversations exercise, using the pause they had taken as the initial halt step.*]

"I know that was a really hard conversation," I began. "Is that what tends to happen when the two of you are talking about something upsetting?"

Karl answered definitively, "Yes, I feel attacked."

"I wasn't attacking you!" Ebony shot back.

I held up my hand. "Okay, let's take a deep breath." As they complied, I went on, "It seems like when you're having that type of difficult conversation, you both become overwhelmed by your feelings and it's hard to stay in the conversation with each other. I'm glad we took a break. Today we're going to be having some difficult conversations, and I want you both to try to speak without attacking each other and to try to listen even when it's hard. Instead of going back into the conversation you were just having, I'd like us to talk about what just happened."

"Okay," said Karl. For the first time, he seemed eager to continue the process—perhaps, I thought, to get it over with.

"Before we do that, Karl, I think Ebony needs to feel safe sharing with you," I said. "Can you let her know you're ready to listen?"

Again, Karl followed my instructions. "Ebony, I do want to listen. I am here to listen and to try to figure things out."

"Ebony," I turned to her, "are you open to having a conversation with Karl?"

"Yes, I am," Ebony replied, her voice somewhat aloof.

"I'd like you to talk to each other about what just happened," I said. "In particular, address what you noticed you each did that took the conversation off track. What do you think you're individually responsible for in that interaction?"

Ebony began, "I got really overwhelmed with emotion and I started attacking Karl."

"Tell Karl," I prompted her.

Ebony turned to look at Karl. "I got really overwhelmed and started attacking you. I'm sorry for that."

Karl nodded in acknowledgment. "I'm sorry too. I wasn't patient or empathetic, and I was having a hard time listening. I need to work on being more patient with you. I know this is really hard for you."

"Now," I continued, "I'd like you to talk to each other about what happened during the conversation we just had. What did you notice about the pattern? About what you each were feeling?"

Ebony offered, "When I was sharing how I felt, I noticed that I began to think Karl was checked out. And anytime I feel that, I start to get completely overwhelmed and really angry."

Again, I directed her to tell Karl rather than me.

Ebony sighed but complied. "When I was sharing, I was watching your facial expressions and you seemed checked out. Then when you summarized, you didn't seem to feel anything about what I said. I get so upset when that happens."

"Karl, why don't you repeat what you heard from Ebony," I suggested. "Tell her what you heard."

"Ebony, I heard you say that you thought I was checked out," Karl said, "and that it makes you really upset when you're sharing important feelings with me and I check out."

"Exactly," Ebony answered, a mix of grief and bitterness in her voice. "It makes me feel like you don't care."

Karl's voice unexpectedly softened. "I do care, Ebony. I'm just overwhelmed."

Encouraged by this, I said, "Karl, can you share what you noticed happened during the interaction?"

He answered, "I noticed that when I heard Ebony start to share how hurt she is, my heart started beating really fast and I started to feel angry. I'm not angry at you, Ebony. I'm angry at myself. But in the moment, I just get completely overwhelmed by it and I shut down and then—if Liz hadn't stopped me, I would have probably gotten mean. I don't like that about myself."

"Ebony, could you repeat back what you heard from Karl?" I asked.

She bit her lip. "I can try. I feel overwhelmed."

I nodded. "Let's take this as slow as we need to. Take deep breaths. Take a sip of water."

Ebony did as I suggested. "Okay, thank you. I needed a moment." Turning to Karl, she went on, "I heard you say it's hard to hear how upset I am. That you get angry and that it comes out at me but really, you're angry at yourself. And that you see if the interaction hadn't stopped, you probably would have gotten mean to me."

Karl nodded. "Yeah, that's how I see it. That's what happens."

> I let them both rest in quietness for a moment before continuing. "What do you think we need to pay special attention to during the rest of our day to try to make the rest of our interactions different? Can you talk to each other about that?"
>
> Karl spoke first. "It really helped that Liz had me take a break. Or let me take the break. And Ebony, I appreciate you letting me do that. I'd like to try to take breaks before I get too upset, so I don't say things I don't mean."
>
> Ebony nodded. "I'm going to try to express myself without accusing you of things. I do have questions, but I need to bring them up differently so we can actually get through a conversation."
>
> "Okay, so today, I am going to pay close attention to when you need breaks," I assured them. "And let's all be mindful of going slow and paying attention to it whenever someone gets overwhelmed. I'll also pay attention to how you talk to each other. If I notice it starts to verge on criticism or attacking, I'll intervene more quickly and help you say it in a new way. I'd also like to encourage you both to notice those things, too, and to ask to take a pause and try again. How does that sound?"

In Karl and Ebony's enactment, the HARD conversation played out like this:

- **Halt:** When the couple became flooded and highly critical and argumentative, we paused the enactment to allow both partners to take a break.

- **Attach:** I asked Karl to help Ebony feel safe after the break. Usually, I would ask both partners to offer some form of attention to each other's attachment needs, but in this situation, Ebony had been so violated by Karl's betrayal that it would not have been appropriate for her to comfort Karl.

- **Repair:** I asked both Ebony and Karl to reflect on their own responsibilities for how the conversation went.

- **Debrief:** Both Ebony and Karl discussed what happened with each other and then followed it up by exploring what they needed to be cognizant of moving forward in order to avoid these issues in the future.

Exercise 3: Emotions and Feelings Wheels

The concept of the emotions wheel was created by American psychologist Dr. Robert Plutchik. Plutchik identified eight basic emotions: joy, trust, fear, surprise, sadness, disgust, anger, and anticipation. He further posited that these basic emotions could combine to create a near infinite number of emotions. Noticing, identifying, and expressing one's emotions can be overwhelming, as it requires a person to have an understanding of their physiological responses and cognitions related to the emotion while also having the vocabulary to express it. To reduce the overwhelm, Plutchik designed a structural model for emotions by creating a wheel in which emotions were depicted around a circle and opposite of each other (pleasant vs. unpleasant emotions).

A few years after Plutchik introduced his emotions wheel, Gloria Willcox introduced the feelings wheel in response to recognizing that her clients often seemed at a loss for words to describe their emotions (Willcox, 1982). Willcox's wheel follows the same concept; however, it only has six primary emotions: joyful, scared, mad, sad, peaceful, and powerful.

Whether utilizing Plutchik's or Willcox's wheel, the therapist is supporting the clients to develop a stronger vocabulary in response to "Racket Theory" (Erskine and Zalcman, 1979), the theory that families have a limited range of "acceptable" emotions, so children learn to express some emotions more easily than others and only have a vague sense of what they are feeling when it comes to "impermissible" emotions. This is often perpetuated by their socialization outside of their family as well.

It is no surprise, then, that many of the couples we work with will struggle to articulate their feelings due to a lack of awareness and vocabulary. When encouraging a couple to discuss a specific event, you might ask them to start the discussion by looking at the feelings wheel and sharing the feelings they had during that event with their partner. This can reduce overwhelm regarding emotions and help the partners be more vulnerable with each other.

Using the emotions or feelings wheel will help clients to express their emotions with more specificity than they could before. Not only does this help the client make sense of their internal world, but it also elicits empathy from their partner, who might be hearing about these emotions for the first time (rather than just witnessing them through their partner's behaviors). I find this to be such a helpful exercise that I keep a feelings wheel pillow in my office—it sits right between the clients for easy access.

Let's take a look at how the feelings wheel helped Andrew and Ron during one of their enactments. As with the other enactments, notice how I introduce goals and roles, specify the topic, and establish the structure before beginning. You can also keep an eye out for the moments when I step in to help sustain the enactment and offer coaching to the partners.

Ron and Andrew: Feelings Wheel Exercise and Enactment

As you might recall, Andrew and Ron were attending therapy due to a history of explosive arguments that had, over time, caused the breakdown of the relationship. On the second day of their intensive, I had them begin by using a speaker/listener exercise to discuss the highly upsetting argument they'd had on a recent vacation. That enactment did not go well. Neither Andrew nor Ron could clearly articulate their feelings, and because of this Andrew became withdrawn and Ron became explosive.

After taking a short break, I decided to engage the couple in an enactment using the feelings wheel. My hope was that providing Andrew and Ron with words they could use to describe their internal world might reduce the activation and shutdown that they seemed to experience when discussing difficult issues.

"We are going to have a conversation about feelings," I began. "This exercise will help you to better understand what the experience of the big argument on your vacation was like for each of you on an emotional level. In this exercise you'll each get a turn to share the feelings you were having during that time. When you are the one sharing, you will just share the feelings you were having, not your assumptions about what the other person was feeling. When you're not sharing, work hard to try to listen to your partner and put yourself in their shoes. The goal is to understand each other and have empathy for each other's experiences. I will be here watching the two of you talk, and if I see you're having any trouble I'll intervene.

"So," I went on, "I'd like you both to think back to your vacation and specifically to the argument you had. Remember, you're working to be good listeners and kind speakers. Ultimately, your goal is to remind your partner they are cared for and loved and understood. To start, I'd like you to turn toward each other. Andrew, I am handing you this feelings wheel. Go through it and find any feelings that you felt during that event. Ron, you'll just listen, and then once he's finished you'll repeat back what you heard."

Andrew took the handout from me. "Okay, so you just want me to start picking feelings I felt?"

I nodded. "Exactly."

Andrew's brow furrowed in concentration. "Okay, hmm . . . I see a lot of feelings here that I was feeling. I think at the start I was feeling angry—to break it down, I was feeling frustrated with you. I wanted us to go grab dinner that night, but we didn't because you drank a little too much and I guess didn't care about . . ."

I stopped him. "Andrew, try to focus on the feelings *you* had, not the feelings Ron had. Try to avoid accusing him of anything right now. Just talk about the feelings."

Andrew nodded and refocused on the wheel. "Okay, so I was frustrated. I really wanted to go to a special dinner together and we didn't. When I tried to wake you up and you wouldn't wake up, I felt pretty disrespected and furious. It was as if my feelings didn't matter and spending time with me didn't matter.

"After that, I just got really sad," he went on. "And then when you woke up and didn't address the issue, I was really mad again, but that time I kind of got quiet and withdrawn. I didn't want to talk to you."

A silence fell. "And what else?" I gently prompted Andrew.

He examined the wheel again for a moment. "I also noticed I started to feel like everything was out of control . . . and also kind of scared when you started yelling at me. It was overwhelming. I didn't know where it came from."

"Any other feelings?" I asked.

Andrew took a breath. "Probably a lot more, but the other big one that sticks out is disappointed. I felt super disappointed in how that night ended. I wanted a nice night with you, Ron. Actually, at the start of the night I was really excited, but I ended up sad and disappointed and uncertain."

I turned to Ron. "Ron, how about you summarize what you heard and perhaps share what makes sense about what Andrew said."

Ron stared at the floor. "Hearing how much I hurt him is a lot to take in—I don't really know what to say."

"It can be so hard to hear the ways we've hurt people," I agreed. "It feels really overwhelming right now. Is that right, Ron?"

"Yes, I feel overwhelmed," Ron murmured.

I leaned forward. "Ron, I want you to just close your eyes for a moment and take a deep breath if you can. In through your nose . . . and out through your mouth . . . how does that feel?"

Ron went through the motions as I led him, then looked at me. "I'm still pretty overwhelmed," he admitted.

It seemed clear that Ron was showing signs of physiological flooding. Wanting to intervene in this aspect of their cycle, I suggested a short break. "How about you get up and get some water and come back?"

When he returned a few minutes later, I asked, "How are you feeling now, Ron?"

"Better." He sat down.

"Andrew, thank you for giving Ron a moment," I said. "Ron, I noticed that you started to look overwhelmed and what we call *flooded*. Flooding happens when we start to experience some sort of threat—not necessarily a physical threat, as it could be an emotional threat too. Our body will start to pump all sorts of stress hormones into our system that can cause us to go into fight-or-flight mode. I asked you to take a break so you wouldn't get stuck in a frozen state or start fighting with Andrew. It's kind of a reset to the system."

Ron gave a slight smile. "It was helpful. I was definitely overwhelmed. I feel much better now."

"Great," I said. "I'd like you to go right back into the exercise. Can you turn back to Andrew and let him know what you heard earlier?"

Ron took Andrew's hand. "I am so sorry. I hear the feelings you had. I understand why you would have been frustrated with me that I passed out before our dinner, and why you'd be really angry when you couldn't wake me up. It makes complete sense to me that you'd be really pissed about that. And I understand why you were disappointed. I'm disappointed in myself. I hear you and I hear how awful it was."

"Andrew, how did that feel?" I asked. "Did Ron get it right? Anything else he should understand about your feelings?"

Andrew covered Ron's hand with his own. "That was right. Thank you for listening."

"Before we switch to Ron sharing," I said, "I want to point out that you both just did a beautiful job there. Andrew, you expressed your feelings without criticism or blame, and you were able to give Ron space to take a break. Ron, thank you for listening to Andrew even though it was hard, and for taking that break when you started to get flooded. I also saw you hold Andrew's hand, which really builds that sense of connection and attachment."

As the couple continued the enactment, now with Ron sharing his own feelings from that night, Andrew was able to be responsive and warm toward Ron's experience as well. By the end of the enactment, both partners seemed more attuned to each other's experience during the event and less reactive to each other's perspective of the night.

This enactment helped the couple move toward those three overarching goals I have for all of my intensive sessions: First, they were able to move toward neutrality and away from reactivity by working to identify their own feelings and express them in a differentiated manner. When Ron became flooded, they were able to take a break, which maintained that safe and neutral stance. Second, the couple was able to become more relational—they had insight about their own feelings and could express them while also being present and empathetic toward their partner's experience. Lastly, they each took responsibility for their own role in the interaction by validating their partner's experience and at times even sharing with each other what they were sorry for.

Leading with the feelings wheel helped the couple to start their conversation from a softer place than they usually do. They also were able to articulate themselves in a way that was less frustrating. This changed the trajectory of the conversation and began to change the way both Andrew and Ron were feeling about possibilities for their relationship. Andrew shared that he was starting to wonder if perhaps the relationship could improve, if they could continue to learn how to be more emotionally vulnerable and safe with each other.

Exercise 4: "My Favorite Story" Guided Imagery

Asking couples to reminisce is standard practice in many modalities of couples therapy. The Gottman Method and Integrative Behavioral Therapy utilize reminiscing on good times as a way to elicit positive emotions about the relationship during the session (Gottman, 1999; Jacobson & Christensen, 1996).

Studies have shown that recalling happy memories elicits positive feelings and is a positive strategy for coping with stress because it dampens cortisol, reduces negative affect, and increases the likelihood of emotional regulation (Speer & Delgado, 2017).

When couples have been struggling with stress, are developing negative sentiment toward each other, and have expressed during their assessment that their early years were good, the "my favorite story" guided imagery can help them regulate their emotions and increase positive emotions about the relationship. Reminiscing about the past can remind them of both good feelings and good times. It can also bring about conversation around what needs to change in the relationship here and now to have good times again.

However, there are two things I would caution you about when considering this exercise. First, if the couple described their relationship as mostly negative in the early years, this exercise may be counterproductive. While you might feel drawn to get them to discuss "the good times," in my experience, this only creates more conflict. Couples in negative sentiment override tend to struggle to think of a favorite story or, if they do think of a story, they find a way to disparage it through contemptuous statements about the memory.

Second, people who rely too heavily on emotional nostalgia can create homeostasis in the relationship, which reduces the likelihood for change (Mallory et al., 2018). The hyperfocus on nostalgia might also mean that the couple is avoiding what is not going well in the present. Couples who seem overly invested in their past might benefit from this exercise, *and* the therapist should be mindful that relating to the past cannot be their only path forward.

COUPLES THERAPIST RESOURCE

"My Favorite Story" Guided Imagery

Ask the couple to close their eyes, then say:

With your eyes closed, I want you to rewind the videotape in your mind. Keep rewinding until you hit a memory that brings up positive feelings about your relationship and your partner. Go ahead and rewind until you find a good memory.

Pause to let the couple reflect.

Once you've found your memory, I want you to imagine that you are there observing yourself and your partner. Notice first how you're feeling in your body in that moment. Just notice.

Pause again.

Now, notice how you look. What are your face and body doing?

Pause.

Look at your partner and notice them.

Pause.

Notice your surroundings—the colors, sounds, objects.

Pause.

Notice the good thoughts you have about this moment.

Pause.

Good. Now, breathe in deeply and allow those good feelings to fill up your body and your heart. Exhale. Good.

Pause.

Inhale again, breathing in those good feelings. Hold on to them. Exhale, releasing anything that feels tense. Inhale the good feelings again. In your mind, take a look around again at this happy moment between you and your partner.

Pause.

Now, very slowly, let's come back. Start to notice the temperature of the room.

Pause.

Now, notice what you hear.

Pause.

Notice what your body is sitting on and how that feels.

Pause.

Slowly, open your eyes and look around the room, and then at your partner, holding on to those good feelings.

Follow-Up Questions for Couple Discussion

- Tell each other the story of the good time you had together. Share in as much detail as you can what you remember.
- Do you have ideas for how you could bring those good feelings into your relationship again?
- What do you wish was happening in your relationship now to have these good experiences again?
- When you think back to that memory, what really sticks out to you about what made it possible?

Kimmie and Selah: "My Favorite Story"

When Kimmie and Selah arrived for the second day of their intensive, I wanted to begin with an activity that would help ground them into the good times of their relationship.

[I chose to do this with Selah and Kimmie for a few reasons:

- *It was clear that the early days of their relationship elicited fond memories for both. I believed that the exercise would not result in a "pulling teeth" experience or cause either of them distress.*
- *Much of what was making it difficult for them to feel connected was related to the stress of some major life transitions. Thinking about positive memories is a helpful coping mechanism for stress.*

- *While Kimmie and Selah were beginning to develop a negative sentiment toward each other, they were not in negative sentiment override. Thinking about positive memories could serve as a momentary counterbalance to the difficulties they were currently facing, while also reminding them that the current stressful period was only temporary and that their story was much bigger than that.*
- *I hoped to open up a conversation between Selah and Kimmie regarding what they could do in the here and now to begin to make time and space for connection with each other.]*

After going over the agenda for the day with Kimmie and Selah, I let them know we would be doing an exercise together.

"First, you're going to close your eyes," I explained, "and listen to me do a little guided imagery with you. Then we will have a conversation. While I'm doing the guided imagery, you both will just relax and listen to my voice. So get in a comfortable position."

Kimmie and Selah both closed their eyes and leaned back against the couch. Kimmie reached for Selah's hand and they continued to hold hands as I gently led them through the "My Favorite Story" guided imagery.

Once Selah and Kimmie had opened their eyes and reoriented themselves to the room, I checked in with them.

"Okay!" I smiled, taking a deep breath and a long exhalation. "How are you both feeling?"

Selah smiled. "Relaxed."

"The same," Kimmie agreed.

"Now," I continued, "I'd like you to turn to each other. I see you're holding hands, so keep doing that. And I want you to tell each other the story of the good time you had together. Share in as much detail as you can what you remember."

Kimmie's eyes misted up. "I was remembering our wedding day." She went on to share with Selah her memories of their wedding. In turn, Selah described a special memory from Christmas when their daughter, Maisie, was younger.

After they finished sharing, I rejoined the conversation. "I have a few questions I'd like you to discuss with each other. Here, let me hand them to you, and the two of you can just talk back and forth with each other."

I offered the couple a sheet with the follow-up questions for the "My Favorite Story" exercise.

[*I provide couples a list of the questions so they can ask them of each other rather than having me become a part of their system by asking them. On day 2, the couple should be interacting with each other as much as possible, with the therapist on the "outside" acting only when intervention, direction, or psychoeducation is needed.*]

"I'd like you to ask each question back and forth to discuss the good memories you shared. As you do, I'd also like you to begin to think about how those good memories can get you closer to your goal of reducing conflict in your relationship and feeling more connected to each other."

Selah turned to Kimmie and said, "I'll ask first. So, what do you think we could do to bring these good feelings back into our relationship? I know that one idea you have is basically for me to set better boundaries so we have more time together—is that right? Is there anything else?"

Kimmie looked relieved, as if she finally felt Selah had been listening to what she needed. "Yes! I think I need that time with you. I also recognize you won't be able to give as much as you could before the last few years. I understand that. When I think back to our wedding day, I think the feeling that sticks out most is that I felt prioritized. I really felt like I mattered. And I miss that. What about you—what do you think we need to do to bring back some of the feelings you thought of with your memory?"

Selah took Kimmie's hand and paused to think. "Well, when I think back to how I felt during the Christmas memory, I just felt like I was having so much fun with you. And I don't really think we have much fun anymore. It's not your fault. I don't think it's really my fault either. It's like life has gotten in the way. We're so stressed that we don't have those types of moments now. We've got a difficult teen, my family—just so much is going on. Somehow, we have to make time for fun."

Kimmie nodded in acknowledgment and agreement. Their ability to agree stood in contrast to the disconnect they'd described, but perhaps this moment was a glimpse of their deeper connection resurfacing. They both looked at me to get some direction for whether they should continue. I just nodded and smiled, then looked down at the ground to indicate that I believed they could work out what to do next on their own.

Kimmie turned back to Selah and said, "Well, I think we've kind of answered the other questions just through those answers we gave. I think I'm looking to feel like a priority, and you're looking for some lightness. And I guess we both recognize that we're between a rock and a hard place. Life is just hard right now, so maybe it's not possible to have exactly those feelings now, but I think we could make it happen in some small ways. Honestly, having this conversation is making me think that I also need to work on just having some patience for this season of life."

> [As you might have noticed, Kimmie and Selah didn't follow the question sheet verbatim. That was okay. I didn't need to micromanage their enactment exercise. They were doing a beautiful job—speaking with each other from a place of neutrality, being relational, and being responsible for themselves—so I sat back and let them have their conversation.]

Once Selah and Kimmie had completed their discussion, I guided them to take some time to reflect. First, I asked what they had noticed about their interactions during the conversation.

Kimmie responded, "It felt easy."

"What does that mean? Tell me more," I encouraged.

Selah cut in, "I agree with Kimmie. It felt easy to talk, like it used to. We used to be such good communicators. I think what made it easy was that we spent so much time yesterday and today talking and hearing each other's perspectives. I've really been able to recognize that we aren't against each other and that we've just got a lot going on. So I think we went into this conversation with less blame. What do you think, Kimmie? What is making this easier?"

"Just having your attention, I think," Kimmie replied. "I'm realizing more and more that this is what I'm craving. So when we have this time to sit and talk, I feel better almost automatically."

"And what would you like to take from this conversation?" I asked. "Any commitments you'd like to make with each other for moving forward?"

Selah looked at Kimmie. "I've really heard you today, and yesterday too. I know that you need to feel like a priority, and I need to stop being so defensive about that. I commit to working on setting boundaries with my family. Liz, if it's okay with you, could that be our next discussion today?"

"Sure, Selah. If that's okay with Kimmie, we can take a break after this part and then come back and talk about that."

Kimmie responded that this would work for her too.

> I reengaged the couple in the exercise at hand by asking Kimmie to reflect on any commitments she would like to make following the conversation. She responded, "Yes, I think it's two things. One, I want to make a commitment to be clearer about what I need. If I even just start asking you to have non-distracted conversations with me more often, I think I'll feel better, and I'm sure you'd say yes most of the time.
>
> "I also want to be committed to developing more patience for this temporary time in our lives. We have a really beautiful life together with so many good memories. Right now it's stressful, but isn't that the point of a relationship sometimes—to be able to be there for each other even when it's hard? So I want to commit to being there for you without asking for so much."
>
> The enactment, which started by reflecting on the good times between them, resulted in both Kimmie and Selah having a stronger awareness of each other's needs and a willingness to respond to them through personal commitments.

Exercise 5: Expanding Intimacy

Sex and intimacy issues are among the greatest taboos for couples to discuss. Findings show that even though intimacy conflicts tend to be recurrent and of high importance to the relationship, intimacy is discussed less often than other hot topics like children and finances (Papp et al., 2013). Couples therapists often meet with partners who are struggling with some form of intimacy but are unable to discuss this with each other.

One of the reasons that couples don't discuss intimacy is because, like emotional vocabulary, they do not know how to discuss their thoughts, feelings, and needs related to closeness. In fact, many couples think intimacy only means sex; as a result, they are not able to articulate all the interconnected areas of intimacy that might be influencing sex or other forms of closeness with each other.

While the topic is difficult to discuss, it's highly important to do so. When a couple expresses that they do not have enough affection, love, and closeness in their relationship, it is hard for them to sustain high levels of relational functioning and the relationship then faces a higher risk of dissolution (Huston et al., 2001). Therefore, it's imperative that the therapist helps them discuss these issues by providing them with some foundational language and structure to begin the conversation.

In response to recognizing deficits in being able to identify and communicate about intimacy issues in my couples therapy sessions, I developed an intimacy wheel. I share this with couples to help them identify the different areas of intimacy and then assess how close they are feeling in each area.

This exercise helps couples enter an enactment where they discuss intimacy in a way they have not done before. It can help couples who aren't quite sure why they aren't committing, who are having less sex, or who feel distant from each other begin to better understand where they are doing well in terms of intimacy and where they are facing challenges. Because it is a structured way to discuss intimacy, couples tend to feel safer than they would if they were given a more open-ended prompt. It also encourages the couple to discuss specific areas they'd likely avoid otherwise.

You can use the following steps with couples to explore the intimacy wheel. You can also find a full-color, dry-erase version of this exercise in my *Couples Therapy Flip Chart* (Earnshaw, 2024a); this format allows the couple to write directly on the intimacy wheel while you are able to view the therapist script and other notes for the exercise.

COUPLES THERAPIST RESOURCE

Intimacy Wheel Exercise

To begin the exercise, hand the couple the intimacy wheel and provide a brief definition of each type of intimacy:

- **Sexual:** Physical pleasure and desire
- **Physical:** Nonsexual touch and physical closeness (e.g., hugs, kisses, cuddling)
- **Emotional:** Sharing feelings and a sense of trust
- **Spiritual:** Connecting on beliefs and values
- **Intellectual:** Sharing thoughts and stimulating conversations
- **Experiential:** Novelty, creating memories, shared activities

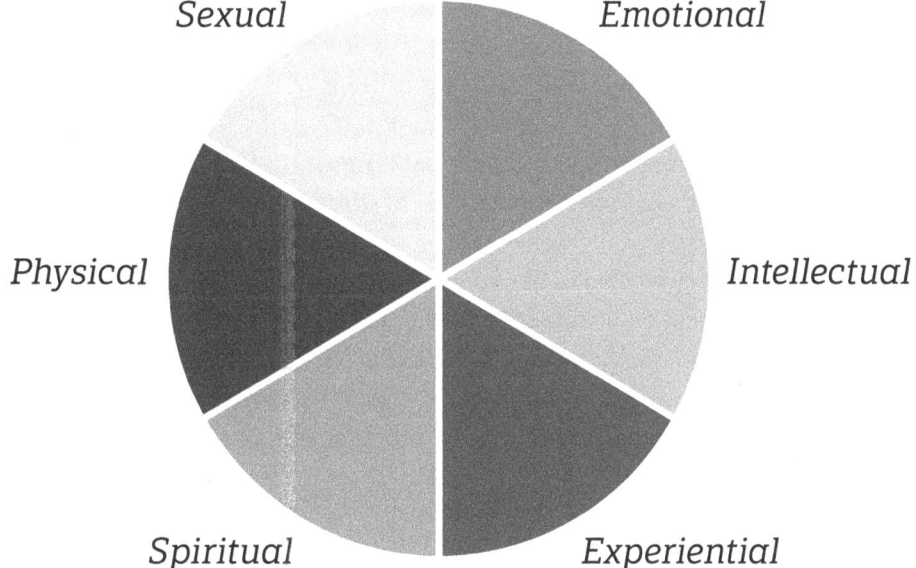

Explain to the couple: "No one person will fulfill all types of intimacy for an individual. For example, you might have deep intellectual closeness with a friend while experiencing strong physical intimacy with your partner. When a relationship feels lonely, it often means a crucial intimacy type is lacking. Identifying these areas and taking small steps can help enhance intimacy and reduce loneliness. In addition, not everyone desires the same types of intimacy in a relationship. For example, one partner might desire more experiential intimacy while the other might desire more emotional intimacy. Partners should work together to support each other's desired needs for closeness."

Ask each partner to rate their satisfaction with each area of intimacy in their relationship on a scale of 1 to 10 and share their ratings with each other. Then ask them to choose one intimacy area that they would like to improve together. Help them plan a small step toward building that intimacy that would add one point to the current rating. Once that area is improved, the couple will move on to the next area for improvement. Emphasize gradual, consistent progress.

Kimmie and Selah: Intimacy Wheel Exercise and Enactment

After Kimmie and Selah finished the "My Favorite Memory" exercise, they spent some time discussing boundary setting with Selah's family. They came up with some solutions for setting boundaries with Selah's family members while still being supportive and helpful toward them. The outcome felt like a win-win.

We took a short break and when we returned, I wanted to spend some time addressing intimacy in the relationship. Throughout our time together, it was clear that Kimmie was craving more emotional intimacy. And after our "good times" conversation, I could see Selah was also craving closeness and intimacy—particularly experiential intimacy, as she seemed to be yearning for more fun with Kimmie. It seemed important to provide structure for having a conversation about intimacy and closeness in their relationship, so I decided to introduce the intimacy wheel exercise.

"Now that we've had an opportunity to talk about some of the challenges you both have faced, I'd like us to spend some time talking about intimacy. A lot of people think intimacy just means sex, but it really means closeness and there are a lot of areas of intimacy—one is sex, but there is also experiential, emotional, spiritual, and physical intimacy. Over the last few years, you've been so busy and I think you've had to put intimacy on the back burner, so let's look at it together. Building intimacy and closeness can act as a buffer during times of stress, like all the stressful transitions you're experiencing now with family."

I handed them the intimacy wheel. "I'd like you to face each other and, using the intimacy wheel, go through each area and rate it on a scale of 1 to 10. A rating of 1 indicates that area of intimacy is mostly nonexistent in your relationship, while a 10 would mean it's reached your ideal. It's okay if you each have a different rating. Once you rate the area, talk with each other about what would need to happen to improve it by one or two points, if it needs improvement. Okay, go ahead."

> [During a "traditional" 50- or 90-minute session, I ask the couple to rate each area and then choose one to focus on while saving the other areas for later. I do this so the couple can be focused on a specific area during our short amount of time together. During the intensive with Selah and Kimmie, however, I asked them to discuss each area as they went through the entire wheel. I made this decision based on my observations of Kimmie and Selah's ability to dialogue effectively with each other and because we had more time to discuss in general.]

Selah examined the wheel for a moment. "Hmm, I don't know what some of these mean. What's experiential intimacy?"

I explained, "It means that you find closeness together when you're experiencing things together. For example, the memory you had about Christmas—that was a special experience you had with Kimmie that brought you closer together."

Selah nodded. "Okay. For me this is like a 5. I do enjoy when we do things together, but we don't do much together with just the two of us anymore."

"I agree with that," said Kimmie.

They both paused and looked at me, still unsure of how to proceed.

"Okay," I said, "You both individually rated experiential intimacy as a 5. Now, you'll ask each other, 'What would make this area get one or two points higher—what would we need to do?'"

"Well, to make this a point or two higher I think we need to find a way to get more time together." Kimmie looked at Selah and laughed helplessly. "I don't know how to do that, though."

"What do you think gets in our way the most?" Selah asked.

"Life. Not to kick a dead horse, but certainly all the work that's gone into your dad and brother. Plus we have a kid. We have lives that have to be tended to. It's just so busy," Kimmie responded.

"Do you think the boundary setting we just discussed will help anything?" Selah asked.

"I do," Kimmie answered. "I think that it will open up more natural time for us to connect. I think then we'll have more opportunities to experience things together. Is there anything you've been wanting to do that we haven't had time for?"

"Honestly, it's always important for me to have a lot of time with you over the holidays. I really wish I had more time this year to decorate and go to different holiday events, but I haven't," Selah shared.

I continued to watch Selah and Kimmie as they conversed. They were doing a good job of managing the conversation between them. If they had started to become frustrated with each other, critical, or defensive or had completely gotten off track, I would have intervened. However, it was not necessary at this point.

As they continued to discuss experiential intimacy, it became clear that they would need to make more time for it and become more intentional with how they used that time to have experiences together. Kimmie offered to help Selah get all of the holiday decorations out of the basement and to plan an evening for them to decorate.

Once they finished discussing experiential intimacy, they decided to move on to emotional intimacy. Selah rated this as a 6 and Kimmie rated it as a 5. Together, they determined what they would both need in order to raise the scale a point or two higher. Selah needed more support and understanding while Kimmie needed more heart-to-heart conversations.

By this point, Selah and Kimmie had been discussing intimacy for 45 minutes. It was clear they understood how the intimacy wheel worked and were equipped to have productive conversations about it. I decided to end the exercise and enactment.

"Selah and Kimmie, I think you both did a beautiful job with that exercise. Can you share your reflections with me?"

They shared that the exercise showed them that they needed to work on intimacy but that they were both willing to do so. They described enjoying the exercise and believing they needed to make more time for structured conversations about closeness in their daily lives. When I asked them to share more about the commitments that arose from the exercise, they expressed that they wanted to commit to being more mindful about emotional and experiential intimacy. Kimmie committed to helping Selah get the experiential closeness she was missing by being more proactive about planning special time together. Selah pledged to offer Kimmie more undistracted conversation time to help her feel more emotionally connected.

The intimacy wheel exercise had addressed Kimmie's goal to feel more like a priority and both of their desires to feel less withdrawn in the relationship. I encouraged them to take a copy of the intimacy wheel home with them and to continue to use it to discuss each area.

Exercise 6: Repair and De-escalation Exercise

Rupture and repair are common aspects of functional relationships. However, many couples experience ruptures in their relationships and do not know how to initiate or accept repair in order to restore their bond. In fact, dysfunctional relationships almost always exhibit a lack of repair processes.

There are several reasons why a lack of repair processes causes or maintains dysfunction in an intimate partnership. First, when there is conflict and no repair (or the repair fails), studies have shown that there is a physiological impact, including a heart rate that stays high or even goes up. When people are in this type of physiological state, continued escalation or withdrawal is likely (Gottman, 1993). Second, when there is no successful repair, each partner feels abandoned in their feelings and will react to this. This causes each partner to move into their dysfunctional self-protective stance, which could be withdrawal or pursuit. A lack of repair therefore keeps people physiologically aroused toward a flooded state and maintains the negative conflict cycle. Over time, this will result in a negative sentiment override.

Repair is especially difficult when the conflict at hand is not based solely in the present moment but is also related to family of origin wounds and transference. The couple will be less likely to offer or accept repair because they are not only fighting in the present but also being influenced by what has happened in the past.

When working with a couple who has escalatory conflicts due to a lack of repair, it can be helpful to introduce them to the following exercise so that they can begin to generate a new model of navigating conflicts that uses healthy repair and de-escalation. During this time, you can also help the couple to see how their internal working models from their families of origin are influencing the escalation and making it difficult to repair, pointing out the areas in which they might want to begin to respond in a more conscious way to each other in order to change the legacy of family conflict patterns.

Like feelings or intimacy, repair might be a language one or both partners don't speak. They may not have seen it modeled effectively and might struggle with the structure and vocabulary. This exercise offers a structure to practice repair. As in other exercises during the intensive, you should set up the enactment by describing the instructions and goals, then allow the couple to have the conversation. You should only intervene when the couple gets stuck or needs help changing their interactional pattern.

You can use the following steps with couples to develop skills for de-escalation during a conflict and repair afterward. You can find a full-color, dry-erase version of this exercise in my *Couples Therapy Flip Chart* (Earnshaw, 2024a) or use the reprinted worksheet that follows.

COUPLES THERAPIST RESOURCE

De-escalation and Repair Exercise

To strengthen the relationship and maintain a healthy conflict cycle, partners must develop skills for de-escalating conflict in the moment and pursuing repair afterward.

De-escalation skills begin with both partners monitoring the intensity of conversation during a conflict. When either one senses themselves approaching dysregulation, they can use tools like humor, apologizing, affection, asking for a redo, or taking a break to reduce the emotional charge and communicate more effectively. The therapist can guide the couple in discussing their individual preferences for which tools they find easiest to use and respond to.

Repair skills include addressing conflicts equitably (i.e., each couple taking responsibility for how their actions/words made the other person feel), reconnecting emotionally (offering actions/words that reassure the other person and reassert their commitment to the relationship), and moving toward resolution (proposing steps that can help them solve the conflict or simply discuss it more productively and sensitively). Again, the therapist can guide the couple in exploring which types of repair each partner finds most effective and coaching the other partner in how to pursue that type of repair.

To begin the exercise, ask the couple to talk about past arguments so that you can identify patterns regarding repair or lack of repair.

Using the first column on the worksheet that follows, help the couple identify their individual physiological and behavioral symptoms of escalation. Guide them in identifying what they need from their partner to de-escalate.

Next, provide psychoeducation on what repair is, why it is important for breaking a negative cycle, and how it can make conflicts more functional and less destructive.

Using the second column on the worksheet, ask each partner to share what type of reconnection they find most effective. You can also invite them to share what types of reconnection are not helpful for them.

Many people become defensive when they are encouraged to pursue reconnection. You might hear, "I won't do that until my partner does it too" or objections that certain types of reconnection feel inauthentic or "weak" to the person offering them, or patronizing to the person receiving them. Be open to their concerns and empathetic regarding any hesitation they feel; provide guidance for seeing reconnection and repair skills in a different light. Explain how it is both partners' responsibility to be the change they want to see in the relationship.

Then, use the third column to help the partners identify what they need from each other after an argument. Ask each partner how they feel about giving the other partner what they need, and work through any reservations they might have (e.g., perhaps one partner needs time and space after a conflict, but the other partner gets anxious in the meantime).

Finally, reinforce de-escalation and repair skills by asking the couple to utilize them in real time.

COUPLES WORKSHEET

Repair and De-escalation

ADDRESS	RECONNECT	RESOLVE
When I am escalated, I notice....	When I am upset, it helps if you do this....	After we escalate, I need....
☐ Increased heart rate	☐ Give me time to calm down	☐ Affection
☐ Fast-paced breathing	☐ Let me have a redo	☐ Space or time to decompress
☐ Raised voices	☐ Notice where we agree	☐ Solutions
☐ Blame	☐ Use humor	☐ To talk about what happened
☐ Aggressive body language (e.g., stiff muscles, clenched fists, large movements)	☐ Give me physical affection	☐ Time for fun and play together
	☐ Offer verbal affection	☐ An apology
☐ Fidgeting or pacing	☐ Let me have alone time	☐ To move my body
☐ Harsh language	☐ Apologize in the moment	☐ Time to reflect or process
☐ Feeling activated or shut down	☐ Listen to what I have to say	☐ Intimacy and closeness
☐ Flushing in the face	☐ _____	☐ _____
☐ _____	☐ _____	☐ _____
☐ _____	☐ _____	☐ _____
☐ _____		

Ron and Andrew: Repair and De-escalation Exercise

Over the course of their second day, Andrew and Ron worked on getting through conversations in a more regulated manner. They also practiced expressing themselves more clearly and listening more intently. It was clear that they had benefited from utilizing the feelings wheel, as they were beginning their conversations by sharing their feelings rather than launching into blame. Halfway through the day, I brought up the concept of repair. In the past, the couple had struggled to repair with each other following an argument.

It was my belief that this was related to the negative cycle they were in—both were so hurt that they were struggling to extend goodwill or accept it—as well as their childhood histories of not seeing much repair being offered or accepted. From a young age, Ron saw co-escalatory arguments in which the adults would eventually explode and then withdraw. He did not see repair during or after these conflicts. And while Andrew described his family as loving and warm, he also hadn't witnessed effective repair. The adults in his life had tended to avoid repair by sweeping issues under the rug—a working model he had inherited and used at the start of the relationship. Whenever Ron would escalate, rather than addressing it, Andrew tended to "move on with a smile."

Unconsciously, they both believed that what they had witnessed was the way people should handle conflict. Ron's working model was that when people were mad they would explode; then they would either leave and never return or come back and pretend nothing had ever happened. For Andrew, his working model was to avoid making anyone feel uncomfortable—even if they said or did something hurtful, he shoved his feelings deep inside and offered them forgiveness without repair.

Even if Andrew and Ron decided not to stay together, it was important for them as individuals to change the way in which they navigated conflict by learning to repair.

After returning from our lunch break, I introduced the topic. "I'd like you both to go over this sheet together and discuss repair. Repair is what we do with other people to bring down the heat of an argument and to protect the bond and prevent rupture. Historically, the two of you have struggled with repair. To navigate your conflicts in a healthier, less escalatory way, you'll need to work on offering and accepting repair attempts with each other. Even if you decide not to stay together, you'll need to learn how to do this in your future relationships."

I handed them the repair and de-escalation exercise sheet. "I want you to each look at the three steps on this sheet and fill in the blanks for each other. Ron, you can go first. Talk to Andrew about what you notice about yourself when the two of you are in conflict—what you tend to need during the conflict and what helps you reconnect after the conflict. After Ron goes, Andrew, you'll go next."

Ron and Andrew took a moment to review the sheet, looked up at me, and then intuitively turned toward each other.

> [As you do enactments throughout the day, the couple will come to understand they are no longer talking through you but rather talking with each other, with you there to guide them when needed.]

Ron began, "Okay, so looking at this chart, I can tell I struggle with this. When I get upset, I use harsh language and all of these things happen to my body—my heart is racing, it's hard to breathe, my face is hot. I feel awful physically. In those moments, I think it's hard to get through to me. I think you've tried to in the past, but I haven't really accepted what you do."

Andrew nodded. "I think in the past I tried to be more gentle when you would get into one of your moods, but over time I stopped trying because nothing ever worked."

"Yeah, I'm noticing that. I think I need to get better at letting people give me a clue that I need to calm down. I just get so in my head and so obsessed with winning. But I need to let people help me calm down."

To get Andrew and Ron back on track, I gently redirected Ron back to the column 2 of the sheet: "Ron, it sounds like you've reflected on how you're feeling when you're upset, and you've noticed that you often don't let anyone help you calm down in those moments. Perhaps read from the second column and see if there is anything you could let Andrew know that might help in the future." I gestured for them to continue their conversation.

"Looking at this list," Ron said, "I think that what helps the most is if you say something affectionate to me and then give me space. It doesn't say it here, but I also think if you told me something like 'I need you to calm down,' it might help to clue me in on how I need to de-escalate."

Andrew nodded as he continued to listen. "What about the third column? Is there anything I could do in that column to help after the fact?"

"Well, you're not usually the one who needs to apologize at that point," Ron laughed ruefully, "but I do think I need some sort of affection. I know it's a lot to ask after the fact, but just some sort of cue to remind me you still care about me—that really helps."

"That's naturally what I like to do. I guess the hard part is that in the past, you'd withdraw for so long that you didn't give me the opportunity. By the time you came back, I'd be too upset to want to offer it anymore," Andrew responded.

"Okay, well, this is what's frustrating," Ron said. "If I withdraw, it's because I don't want to keep arguing—I'm trying to make things better—but you can't let me have that space. You're putting me in a no-win situation."

Hearing Ron begin to exhibit defensiveness, I stepped in. "Ron, are you feeling defensive?"

"A little bit," he admitted.

"What happened? Did you feel criticized?"

"Yes, I feel like Andrew isn't giving me a chance to be different and just keeps piling on the past."

"Andrew, it sounds to me like you're sharing with Ron what has been difficult in the past and perhaps you're wondering if things will be different this time. You're wondering if you should take the risk to be vulnerable with him again and offer affection when it's been rejected in the past."

Andrew nodded. "Yes, that's exactly it."

"Ron, I know it might be hard to hear Andrew's experience and concern," I acknowledged. "I don't hear criticism in his words. I'm wondering if you could try to take a moment to take in his concern and respond to it."

Ron took a deep breath. "I'm sorry. This is just all overwhelming to me. I'm really sorry, Andrew." He took Andrew's hand and squeezed it.

I quickly cut in: "Ron, what you just did was repair. There was an escalatory moment, and you offered affection and an apology. I wanted to take a moment to point that out. Go ahead, continue the conversation."

Andrew squeezed Ron's hand back, accepting his repair attempt. "I understand. We've been in a lot of conflict for a long time, so I think it's easy for us to get caught up in it. I wasn't criticizing you. I was trying to see what's different this time because I can't keep trying if things won't be different."

"Andrew," I said, "You just accepted Ron's attempt to repair with you by squeezing his hand back. What you both just did right now was exchange repair attempts. By doing that, you communicated to each other that it was safe to stay in the conversation."

They both smiled and sighed in relief.

"I want you both to keep trying to give and receive repair," I told them. "It keeps the heat down and increases the likelihood the conversation can continue. Andrew, how about you go through the exercise now while Ron listens. Talk to Ron about what happens to you when you're upset, what you need in the moment, and what you tend to need afterward. Ron, just listen to Andrew so that you can learn about him."

After Andrew finished sharing his answers to the repair exercise, I reminded the couple that we completed this exercise because of their cycle of escalatory conflicts to help them learn to repair in the moment and after the fact. I then asked them to reflect on what happened during the exercise.

"I noticed that we were able to de-escalate," Andrew replied. "That's huge. Usually, once one of us gets defensive the whole thing goes off the rails."

"I agree. It felt much better to offer repair and accept it," Ron shared.

"I'm also wondering if you could reflect on how this is different from what you experienced growing up," I inquired.

Ron turned to me and said, "My family never offered any repair. Not to the other adults, not to the kids. We just got into big fights and then everyone had to suck it up."

I gestured toward Andrew to remind Ron to talk to his partner and not to me.

Ron shifted to face Andrew. "Growing up, people got into huge fights, and no one ever tried to make it better in the moment. I don't remember affection or apologies or anything. I don't want to do that in this relationship. It's not healthy."

Andrew sighed. "In my family, things weren't as loud as yours, but when people messed up and hurt each other they just kind of swept it under the rug. No one ever wanted anyone to feel bad, so no one ever got an opportunity to talk about what happened or offer or hear an apology. I think that's why at the start of our relationship I was such a doormat. And then when I couldn't take it anymore, I started to become mean because it was all pent up. I'd rather be able to deal with how we've impacted each other as soon as possible, instead of letting it simmer."

"What are your commitments to each other from this conversation?" I probed.

Ron responded first. "I'm committed to accepting repair. I'm going to work really hard to notice that when you're telling me to calm down or try again or when you're being affectionate, it's your attempt to make things okay between us. I also need to do a better job at coming back after I withdraw and letting you know that I'm sorry—really apologizing for the impact and hearing you out—because I know you haven't had that from me. Or anyone in your life."

"And I'm going to be better at accepting your repair attempts," Andrew said. "To be honest, even when you have tried, I've been shutting them down because I've been so closed off to the relationship. But if we decide to stay together, I need to give you an opportunity to make things right with me."

After this conversation, Andrew and Ron had a deeper understanding of how to repair with each other and were committed to putting it into practice.

Exercise 7: Negotiation

When couples are faced with decisions that need to be made, they often struggle to come to consensus because they become competitors rather than collaborators. Instead of trying to find win-win solutions, couples spend a great deal of time attempting to convince the other person to do it their way. Teaching couples how to use negotiation helps them to develop a more relational lens for solving problems, as it increases productive communication and decreases destructive communication (Bütz, 1991).

> **COUPLES THERAPIST RESOURCE**
>
> ## Negotiation Exercise
>
> Many couples therapy techniques, including brief couples therapy and the Gottman Method, teach negotiation. In particular, they tend to utilize Fisher and Ury's (2012) negotiation process. This four-step process teaches clients how to advocate for themselves while still caring about what the other person wants, needs, and feels.
>
> The four steps are:
>
> 1. **Separate people from the problem:** The therapist encourages both partners to focus on the issue rather than the other person. For example, instead of saying "You're so selfish!" (which attacks the person), a partner might express, "I feel unsupported when I ask for help around the house" (which focuses on the issue). The idea is for the couple to depersonalize the conflict and avoid attacking or blaming each other.
>
>   I often introduce this to my clients by saying, "Let's stop making your partner the problem and focus more on how the problem is the problem. When we focus on what the problem actually is, people can move from offensive and defensive positions to create a solution together. It allows for more constructive and respectful dialogue."
>
> 2. **Focus on interests, not position:** Often couples argue about specific positions rather than really understanding the reasons behind each partner's position. The therapist can encourage the couple to explore the underlying interests that are driving their positions—their needs, dreams, fears, and so on. Helping each partner express how the issue at hand is related to something bigger than them makes it less about the specific argument and more about getting the person what they need on an existential level.
>
>   For example, say a couple is mired in an argument over how much time they spend together versus having separate "me time." The partner who wants more alone time may have the interest of recharging and reducing stress, while the partner who wants more togetherness may have the interest of feeling connected and secure.
>
> 3. **Generate options for mutual gain:** The therapist helps the couple to generate options for solving the problem in which they both gain something. During this stage, the therapist encourages creativity and asks each person to consider the interests of their partner (instead of the positions) to create win-win outcomes. The partners brainstorm potential solutions that allow them to meet both of their needs.
>
>   For example, the aforementioned couple might find a compromise where one partner gets designated "me time" while the other enjoys shared activities with their friends, and then they spend quality time together as a couple afterward when both are feeling recharged.
>
> 4. **Use objective criteria to make decisions:** Ask the couple to consider objective realities. For example, if they are arguing about whether to send their child to public or private school, ask them to look at their finances to see how much money they have to spend on school.

Questions the couple can ask themselves to explore these objective criteria include:

- What has worked well in the past?
- What is fair to both partners?
- What are the needs of each partner, and how can they be balanced?
- What external standards (such as social norms, family needs, or work commitments) might help inform the decision?

Teaching couples the art of negotiation promotes collaboration and respect, reduces blame, encourages creative problem-solving, and ultimately helps the couple see their ability to be successful in solving their own problems.

In order to do this exercise, I provide the couple with a piece of paper and a pen. I ask them to first write down how they would define the problem and what the ultimate goal is for solving the problem.

Then I ask them to talk to each other about the underlying needs related to their positions. This often starts with something like "I want a sense of . . ." For example, someone might want their house to be clean because they want a sense of peace.

Once they have reflected on the underlying interests, I ask them to consider how they could create mutual gains in which both of their interests are met.

Finally, we look at whether these ideas hold up to objective realities before making a temporary decision for next steps. Telling the couple their negotiation outcome is only temporary reduces rigidity and increases the likelihood that the couple is open to trying out the solution they've identified.

Like all exercises, this is set up as an enactment. The couple communicates directly with each other and the therapist intervenes only when necessary to improve communication or clarify any areas of confusion.

John and Amy: Negotiation Exercise

Through the enactments we had completed so far during day 2 of their intensive, Amy and John had improved their listening and curiosity skills. However, they still hadn't been able to decide where they wanted to go on vacation. A low-intensity issue that was nevertheless at the top of their minds—it was a perfect opportunity for them to practice negotiation skills. I planned to have them practice negotiating with each other regarding the vacation and then, later, use the same skills to discuss how they would manage tasks around the house.

"I've noticed that a big difficulty the two of you have is coming to a solution together that feels like a win-win," I said. "In this exercise, you're going to practice negotiating—it's a skill I think you could both improve to feel better about your communication and to make decisions more efficiently and fairly. Because we've been talking about the vacation here and there, let's make that the focus of the conversation."

I pointed to the pads of paper and pens sitting in front of them. "First, I want you each to write down your goals for solving this issue regarding the vacation. We've talked about this part, so I think you both already have a sense of your goals."

Amy and John took a moment to write.

"Okay, now I want you to turn to each other and discuss the goal you wrote down. Share with each other the 'why' behind your goal. Remember, we did talk about this a little earlier, but I want you to talk to each other about what you each hope to get from meeting this goal—which need will be met? What will you have a sense of?"

Amy shared that her goal was to go to the beach because she wanted to relax and have no stress involved in their trip. "I just want a sense of peace," she expressed.

John shared that his goal was to go somewhere new, specifically somewhere they would have to fly to. He hoped for excitement and novelty—"a sense of adventure," as he put it.

I then instructed the couple to write on their pads of paper any ideas that would meet the needs and interests of both partners. I explained that it's important to find outcomes with mutual benefit, especially during these hard-to-solve conflicts. "Take a moment to consider every realistic option for the vacation you can think of," I said.

They spent a few moments writing down ideas, and then I instructed them to turn toward each other and share. "I want you to talk about your solution ideas together. I'm going to be watching to see the two of you really working on those speaking and listening skills. Try to get curious about the options. After you do that, I'll let you know the next step."

Amy started by offering an alternative to the beach: a trip to the woods to stay in a cabin. It was the same amount of driving but it was somewhere new and novel. John shared his original idea but offered a solution to reduce Amy's anxiety: perhaps they could bring a babysitter with them on the plane so Amy could have a break.

Their discussion was much improved from earlier in the day. They both asked questions and showed interest in each other's ideas. Once they finished talking, I guided them to the next part of negotiation: "Now I want you to keep talking with each other, but start to talk about how your ideas are similar. Where are you on the same page?"

"I think we're both on the same page about wanting to reduce the stress," Amy ventured. "I agree that having a sitter with us on the plane would be nice. Then I could rest."

John added, "I think we also agree that we want to go on the trip and that we want to do it to have fun, make family memories, and spend time together, but also to rest. We agree on a lot. Just not location."

"Okay!" I smiled encouragingly. "Considering your similarities, I want you to try to come up with an idea that combines the things Amy wants with the things John wants. And remember, coming up with the idea and agreement right now doesn't mean you can't change your minds later. You can research it and start to plan it and then have a new idea together. But let's just try to come up with something. Be creative."

Amy and John spent about ten minutes coming up with creative ideas that would meet both of their needs. Together, they decided that the best option would be to rent a cabin in the woods. The drive wasn't far, John hadn't been there before, and there were adventurous activities to do. Amy also agreed that the following year, she'd be open to looking into a bigger trip with John.

Because the couple was able to come up with this solution easily, we did not need to move on to discuss objective realities. Instead, I allowed them to explore how they would take next steps toward this agreement. They agreed to do some planning as a team once they were home.

At the end of the exercise, I asked them to reflect on how it went.

"This was much better," said John. "I think we just need to use this format whenever we get stuck on a decision. Our problem tends to be that we get really stuck in wanting to win. I think this was good because it never made me feel like I was losing and it didn't make Amy lose, either."

Amy agreed, "I liked that we could follow a structure. I think John and I do well with structure."

I chimed in, "I noticed you were able to be creative with each other and you didn't get so stuck in blame. It was refreshing to see. How did it feel?"

"It felt much lighter!" Amy shared.

"I agree," John said as he nodded.

"What commitments could you make with each other leaving this conversation?" I asked.

"Well, the obvious commitment is to go home and organize the trip together. But I also think we should commit to using this method once a week when we have a decision to make," Amy suggested.

"I agree with that," said John, "and I also want to commit to being better at understanding what is underneath Amy's position. I think we get so caught up in the solution either person is offering that we don't understand the whole picture."

This exercise not only helped Amy and John finally get over the hurdle of planning their vacation, but it gave them a new tool for navigating disagreements in their relationship and a path toward a fair outcome. Because we practiced this on a low-intensity issue, it provided a good foundation for us to later have a conversation regarding how to relieve Amy's mental load and help John be a fair contributor in the home.

COUPLES WORKSHEET

Negotiating

How do you define the problem that is causing disagreement?
_____
_____

What is your ultimate goal for when the problem is solved?
_____
_____

Why is this important to you? If this goal is met, what will it give you a sense of? (For example: a sense of peace, security, being loved, freedom, independence, accomplishment, etc.)
_____
_____

What is your partner's goal?
_____
_____

What underlies their goal? What "sense" are they looking for?
_____
_____

Create a list of possible solutions that would benefit you both. (Be creative and stay flexible. You might have to give up some initial ideas in order to come to a solution.)
_____
_____
_____
_____

Share your lists of possible solutions with each other. Discuss where you are similar—what areas of agreement do you notice across both of your lists?

_____
_____
_____
_____

Explore the following questions together to help you narrow down your options:

What has worked well in the past?

_____
_____

What is fair to both partners?

_____
_____

What are the needs of each partner, and how can they be balanced?

_____
_____

What external standards (such as social norms, family needs, or work commitments) might help inform this decision?

_____
_____

Now, decide together which solution you will try. (You can continue to explore other mutually beneficial options if you find that you need to, but pick one for now as your temporary solution.)

_____
_____

Interventions

Interventions are techniques that the therapist utilizes during enactments to help the couple see where change is needed and learn how to do it. Without interventions, enactments are unlikely to create any change. With interventions, you'll find that intensives have the capacity to elicit profound understanding, connection, and change.

Because you've spent the first day joining with the couple, you can more easily jump into using interventions during enactments than you might in a more traditional weekly therapy model. You also do not need to be as wary of time constraints, since you have a long period of time to be with the couple to help them dig into (or dig out of) the intervention.

The following interventions are those I have found to create the most profound insight and change in intensive couples therapy.

Intervention 1: Stop the Pattern

The "Stop the Pattern" intervention is used when the therapist observes the couple entering a dysfunctional pattern (e.g., pursuit/withdrawal, the four horsemen, boundarylessness). It involves the therapist interrupting the pattern, explaining why they are stopping it, and suggesting what the couple should do instead.

First, the therapist interrupts the pattern by interjecting themselves. They then bring the client's attention to the dysfunctional pattern, asking them to pause and encouraging them to reflect on the emotions they are having. For example, if a client seems frustrated and is being critical of their partner for not completing a task, the therapist might say, "It sounds like you're feeling really frustrated with your partner right now. Can you tell me more about what's going on?"

After the client reflects on their feelings, the therapist provides psychoeducation on why the specific behavior or pattern isn't helpful for functional communication. For example, the therapist might say, "I hear you're frustrated. Sometimes, when a person has been frustrated for a long time, they become critical because they don't know what else to do to get their message heard. However, what we know is that the use of criticism does not result in effective conversations."

Next, the therapist provides quick feedback on how the client could adjust their communication to improve the outcome of the enactment. The therapist might say, "Since we know criticism isn't helpful, I want to help you say what you're trying to convey using something called a soft start-up. To say something with a soft start-up, you will say what you've noticed, how you're feeling, and what you need. For example, you might say, 'I've noticed that our house is often a mess. I feel really frustrated with it. I need help keeping up with the house.'" The therapist redirects the client to return to communication with their partner, starting where they left off, by saying something like, "How about you try it that way?"

This process gives clients real-time feedback regarding dysfunctional patterns and offers alternatives for them to utilize in the moment. The client then gets the opportunity to experience what it feels like to do things differently.

For particularly entrenched patterns, the therapist will likely have to use this technique multiple times. The process might become more truncated (by leaving out psychoeducation, for example). Often a simple reminder of the alternative behavior is enough to stop the pattern when it reemerges later.

COUPLES THERAPY SKILL

Soft Start-Up

Soft start-up is a communication technique coined by Dr. John Gottman. It provides guidance on how a person can initiate a conversation, particularly a difficult one. In their research, the Gottmans found that the first three minutes of a conversation predict the direction of the conversation (Schwartz Gottman & Gottman, 2024). Therefore, if the conversation starts harshly, it's likely that it will continue to be harsh, while if it begins softly, it has a higher chance of maintaining a gentle and respectful tone.

When the therapist notices that a partner is being critical in a conversation, the therapist can stop the pattern by intervening and then teaching the partner how to use soft start-up.

Soft start-up includes:

- **Using "I" statements:** Rather than blaming their partner or using "you" statements, a soft start-up focuses on how the person speaking feels and what they need. This reduces the likelihood of the other person becoming defensive.
    - *Example:* "I feel frustrated when I'm not heard. I need more attention when I'm speaking" instead of "You always frustrate me when I am talking because you never listen."

- **Focusing on the behavior, not the person:** Instead of criticizing or labeling their partner's character, a soft start-up focuses on specific actions that can be addressed in a nonjudgmental way.
    - *Example:* "I noticed we spent the entire weekend cleaning the house—can we work together to find a solution to keeping up with it during the week?" instead of "Our weekend was ruined because you were so lazy all week."

- **Expressing your needs or desires:** A soft start-up expresses a request or a need rather than a demand, offering the other person an opportunity to respond constructively. Even more specifically, the soft start-up encourages partners to express what is known as a *positive need*, in which the person says what they do want instead of what they don't want. This makes it easier for the other person to be "successful" with them.
    - *Example:* "I'd love it if we could spend more time this weekend having fun together" instead of "I don't want us to be cleaning all weekend."

- **Using a calm and soft tone:** Tone of voice is critical when it comes to difficult discussions. A soft start-up is delivered with a soft, calm tone, avoiding sharpness or aggression, which often triggers defensiveness.
    - *Example:* Saying "I feel really tired and disconnected when we spend the weekend cleaning instead of spending time together" in a calm tone is more likely to be well-received than shouting or using a frustrated tone.

Soft start-ups also require that the partner does not bring up multiple issues at once or bring up past grievances. Doing either of these things will be overwhelming to the listener, who is then more likely to shut down or become defensive.

Ron and Andrew: Stopping the Pattern

I had spent the second morning of Andrew and Ron's intensive helping them develop some foundational conflict tools. We discussed their major argument using the feelings wheel, which opened the door to softer and more vulnerable discussion. We also spent time talking about the importance of repair—something they both struggled with, which caused their arguments to escalate out of control and then prevented them from coming back together and fixing the rupture. We also spent time responding to flooded states. When I noticed that either partner was becoming flooded, I would intervene by pointing it out and offering a suggestion for self-soothing.

Although we had covered a lot, we had not begun the conversation regarding decision-making about staying together or ending the relationship. I had decided to delay this conversation, as I wanted to offer them an opportunity to discuss the recent hurtful event and to help them develop skills before proceeding to this highly difficult topic.

"How are you both feeling about the morning?" I asked when we resumed after our lunch break.

"I can't believe how quickly it's gone." Andrew responded. "It seemed like so many hours ahead of us when we first sat down, but now the day is half over. I feel good about what we discussed this morning. I don't think we've been able to talk to each other like that in a long time . . . maybe ever."

"And Ron, what about you? How are you feeling about the morning?"

"I feel a little drained. It's brought me to a lot of insight about myself and it's just a lot to process."

"Yes, we've discussed a lot today. Is there anything specific that feels difficult to process?"

"Maybe 'process' isn't the right word. But it's making me think about a lot and . . ." Ron started to cry as he continued, "I just feel really upset for how things have turned out. I wish we would have come to see you earlier on because I think we could have changed a lot of these patterns, so we didn't end up here."

"I hear that a lot," I told Ron. "Many couples come in here, learn something new about themselves or build new skills, and feel regret that they didn't know those things earlier to prevent problems. But you know those things now. I think the question is, what does that mean for both of you moving forward?"

"I think we need to talk about what's next for us," Andrew said. "I'm starting to feel anxious that we won't get to it, and I do want to leave here with some idea of what's next for our relationship."

[*It's common for couples to express anxiety about certain topics being addressed or not addressed. As the therapist, there will be times that you cannot get to all of the topics that feel important, so you'll need to prioritize what seems most important in terms of reaching their goals. You'll also need to remain centered in the face of their anxiety. For example, sometimes clients will want to discuss a topic that they are not prepared for. If you try to soothe their anxiety by going to the topic too quickly, you might be leading them toward frustration, as nothing will have changed when it comes to discussing the issue.*

Andrew had been wanting to discuss the topic of whether the couple should stay together all morning. He had brought it up previously, but I had intentionally delayed it. I wanted to ensure the couple had tools for communication and repair before beginning such a difficult conversation. Now, however, I felt it was important to begin the discernment discussion, as we were entering the final three hours of our intensive.]

"Yes, I know you're anxious to discuss that and I think now is a good time. Ron, are you open to having the conversation about what is next for your relationship?"

Ron nodded, looked to the ceiling, and wiped his eyes.

I asked Ron and Andrew to utilize the speaker/listener exercise to discuss where they both currently stood in the relationship, sharing specifically with each other whether they were in, out, or straddling the "door" of the relationship. I reminded them of what they had learned in the morning—how to be responsive listeners, the importance of talking about their feelings instead of blame, and, if the conversation became difficult, to work on using repair. I also reminded them to pay attention to their pattern of pursuing and withdrawing from topics. Then, I gestured to them to start talking.

Ron decided to go first. His voice was steady but emotional. "I think it's very clear how I feel. I want this relationship to work. After this morning, I understand if you don't. I hear how I've hurt you. During lunch I was reflecting on how much it hurts me to know that in many ways I was acting like my own father by being so explosive and abandoning you, and it hurts even more to know that this brought up feelings of being abandoned when you were little. I am ashamed. But I'd like to have a chance to make it right, if you'd be open to it."

Ron's words were heartfelt. He was gentle and made eye contact with Andrew. He seemed sincere. I wasn't surprised, though, when Andrew responded with a smirk and eye roll.

In an exasperated tone, Andrew said, "This is what I've been asking you for years. I've pointed all of this out. You never listened to me. But you listen to the therapist? I get that you feel bad, but it's been years."

> [*I maintained my outsider position as I observed Ron and Andrew. I expected I would need to use the "stop the pattern" interaction between them, but I wanted to give them a chance to recognize and stop their own pattern before I intervened.*]

Andrew continued, "You never listen to me until we hit rock bottom."

COUPLES THERAPIST RESOURCE

Recognizing Criticism

When a therapist notices a client becoming critical of their partner, it's important to interrupt the pattern and offer a path toward correction. This is one of the most important parts of conversational patterns to notice and intervene in. The following is a list of signs that a partner is being critical:

- **The use of absolutes:** Words like *always* or *never* signal the use of criticism. Here the partner is being painted with a broad brush, as it's unlikely that person truly *never* does something or truly *always* does something else. The therapist should encourage the partner who is speaking to discuss the issue at hand rather than generalizing on their partner's perceived shortcomings.
    - *Examples:* "You are never thoughtful when it comes to getting me birthday presents," "I always have to remind you to pay the bills."
- **Blame and personal attacks:** One partner may accuse the other of being fully responsible for an issue the couple is facing together. They are metaphorically (and sometimes literally) pointing their finger at the other person and absolving themselves of any role in the issue. This is different from sharing how an action or behavior made them feel, which can be

an effective way to discuss the impact of behavior. Here, the therapist should recognize that the language is an attack on the person as a whole and is not specific enough or rooted in emotions enough to bring the couple closer together; rather, it is likely to elicit defensiveness from the other partner.

- *Example:* "We are in this bad situation with money because of you! You are the one who spends too much."

- **Tone of voice and body language:** Criticism is often accompanied by a hostile tone and a closed-off or judgmental body posture. Sometimes the words themselves might not be harsh, but it's clear from how the message is being shared that there is an underlying criticism of their partner.

  - *Example:* "Why is it that whenever we talk about issues you act so upset?" (said with an exasperated tone and arms crossed across the body)

- **Focusing on past real or perceived transgressions instead of the current problem:** A partner might try to strengthen their point about the current problem by bringing up past grievances and piling on. Bringing up these old conflicts or "teaching" their partner about how horrible they've been only increases the conflict and does not lead to a focus on solving the issue in the here and now.

  - *Example:* "This issue with you not standing up for me has been going on for as long as I can remember. Early in our relationship, there was that time your mom was rude to me and you did nothing to fix it. Then a few months later, there was the same issue with your friends. Don't you remember any of this?"

- **Emotional intensity as a form of criticism:** When discussing an issue, a client may use emotional intensity as a way to put down their partner instead of using emotions to share more about their internal world or to connect. This can be recognized when it seems as if the person is discussing their intense emotions to make the other person feel bad rather than to move toward deeper understanding.

  - *Example:* "I am so exhausted by this issue and so sick of dealing with this stuff! You are frustrating me!"

- **Using "you" statements:** If a person uses "you statements" rather than "I statements" to describe their concern, they are approaching the issue from a critical stance.

  - *Example:* "When I was upset last night, you walked out of the room, and I know it was because you were thinking that what I had to say didn't matter. You didn't want to deal with me."

- **Failure to recognize positive efforts:** This occurs when a partner makes efforts in a positive direction for the relationship but their partner stays in negative sentiment override, refusing to acknowledge the efforts and even using the efforts to share more criticism.

  - *Example:* Partner 1 says, "I really have been trying to be a better listener for you. I think I've done a good job, especially yesterday when I spent time talking with you about everything happening with you at work." Partner 2 responds, "Yeah, you listened to me once, but you don't usually listen to me."

> With the word "never," I heard Andrew's criticism of Ron and prepared myself to stop the pattern. But before I could, Ron responded.
>
> "Okay, well, I'm not the only bad guy here. I think I'm doing a pretty good job of taking accountability, but it's like you want me to be the bad guy so you don't need to look at yourself. You always blame me and you never consider how you've played a role. This entire therapy session has been focused on my issues, not yours." Ron was being defensive in response to Andrew's criticism. Ron and Andrew would often get into a critical/defensive loop that led to physiological flooding, then activation into aggressive arguments and, finally, withdrawal and abandonment.

COUPLES THERAPIST RESOURCE

Recognizing Defensiveness

Defensiveness is a common reaction where one partner feels the need to protect themselves from real or perceived criticism or blame. Defensiveness can take many forms, and it often exacerbates conflicts rather than resolving them. Here is a list of types of defensiveness you might come across when working with couples:

- **Counterattacking:** This occurs when a partner responds to an accusation or criticism by attacking the other person rather than addressing the original issue.
    - *Example:*
        Partner 1: "You never listen to me when I talk!"
        Partner 2: "Well, you're always on your phone, so why should I listen to you?"
- **Denial:** This occurs when a partner refuses to acknowledge or admit a problem regarding the issue being discussed.
    - *Example:*
        Partner 1: "You never help with the housework."
        Partner 2: "That's not true! I do plenty around the house!" (when they actually haven't been helping much)
- **Minimization:** This occurs when a partner dismisses the significance of the issue or the other person's feelings.
    - *Example:*
        Partner 1: "I feel like you don't care about me anymore."
        Partner 2: "You're overreacting. It's not a big deal."
- **Victimization:** This occurs when a partner turns the argument around and portrays themselves as the victim in the situation rather than addressing the issue. This can be especially frustrating when one partner is trying to express their emotions and the other partner then "overtakes" by sharing "bigger" emotions.
    - *Example:*
        Partner 1: "I'm frustrated that you don't make time for me."

Partner 2: "Why do you always pick on me? I'm the one who has to work all the time! I am the one who is really having a hard time!"

- **Stonewalling:** A partner stonewalls when they physically or emotionally withdraw from the conversation, shut down, or refuse to engage. While this is a defensive response, it is often fueled by physiological flooding, so interrupting both the defensiveness and the flooding is important.
    - *Example:*
        Partner 1: "We need to talk about what's been going on."
        Partner 2: (Silent treatment, turning away, or not responding)
- **Blaming:** When one partner brings up an issue, the other might become defensive by ascribing all of the blame to their partner, making them responsible for the issue at hand.
    - *Example:*
        Partner 1: "Why don't we ever go out anymore?"
        Partner 2: "Well, it's because you're always too tired and you're constantly worried about money. You make it too difficult for us to have fun."
- **Making excuses:** This is a form of defensiveness in which one person brings up a complaint and the other offers justifications or rationalizations for their behavior instead of taking responsibility.
    - *Example:*
        Partner 1: "You said you'd fill out the kids' forms for school, but the school just called and said you didn't send them in."
        Partner 2: "I was going to, but I had so much work to do. It's not like I was just being lazy."
- **Sarcasm/irony:** Using mocking, sarcastic, or ironic remarks to deflect or avoid the topic rather than engaging in a serious conversation is a form of defensiveness. It can also be considered a form of contempt, which is when someone has a mix of feelings of superiority over their partner and disgust toward their partner. When this arises in a session, the therapist will often have to address both the defensive use of sarcasm and the contemptuous aspect of it.
    - *Example:*
        Partner 1: "You didn't even notice I did the laundry today."
        Partner 2: "Oh, wow, you did the laundry? I'm so impressed! Do you want a cookie?"
- **Global statements (overgeneralizing):** This involves making sweeping statements that exaggerate the issue or accuse the partner of doing something all the time based on one specific event. While this is a form of defensiveness, it is also often a form of criticism.
    - *Example:*
        Partner 1: "I wish you'd sit down with me and listen to how I am feeling. Last night you were scrolling on your phone when I tried to tell you my concerns—you weren't listening."
        Partner 2: "That's not true! I always listen to you!"

- **Deflecting:** A partner may become defensive by avoiding the topic or shifting the conversation to something unrelated in order to avoid addressing the original issue.
    - *Example:*
        Partner 1: "You promised you'd make dinner tonight, but you didn't."
        Partner 2: "What we really need to talk about is the fact that you didn't send me the credit card statements like I asked."
- **Playing "fair":** This occurs when a partner tries to "level the playing field" by pointing out perceived wrongs the other person has done, making the conversation feel like a battle of who's more right.
    - *Example:*
        Partner 1: "You forgot our anniversary again and that really hurts."
        Partner 2: "Okay . . . so? Last weekend you completely forgot that I had told you my parents wanted to have us over for dinner."
- **Appealing to authority or external factors:** People may become defensive by using external references or authorities to validate their own position and avoid taking personal responsibility.
    - *Example:*
        Partner 1: "You never listen to my concerns."
        Partner 2: "Well, I read an article that said when someone constantly brings up concerns, like you do, it's only natural for the other person to start tuning them out. I actually think you should read it—you'd probably recognize a lot of your own issues."
- **False reconciliation:** A partner may pretend to resolve the argument or offer a "quick fix" without addressing the underlying issue.
    - *Example:*
        Partner 1: "Is it a good time to talk about the way your mom spoke to me yesterday?"
        Partner 2: "Oh my god. I already talked to her about it. It's over. Can we move on?"
- **Deflecting with humor:** Using humor or jokes to change the tone of the conversation and deflect from the emotional depth of the argument can be a form of emotional avoidance and defensiveness. This one can be difficult to spot because at times it looks positive—and, to complicate matters further, sometimes it is positively used to de-escalate as a repair technique. The therapist should pay attention to the context of how the humor is used and whether it is helpful to the interactional process. This type of humor is not the same as the sarcastic humor; it is actually playful, not mean-spirited.
    - *Example:*
        Partner 1: "You spend all your time running your business and you never help around the house. I'm so exhausted from doing all the cleaning."
        Partner 2: "Maybe I need to start a cleaning business instead! Problem solved." (followed by a smile and a laugh)

I inhaled and put my hand up to signal to Ron and Andrew that I was going to intervene. "Okay, let's pause. Ron, how are you feeling right now?"

Ron looked up at me. "I'm overwhelmed. And so frustrated."

"I hear that you're overwhelmed and frustrated. You also seem to feel defensive. Am I getting that right?"

"Yes, I am. I know I shouldn't get defensive. But Andrew is being . . ."

Hearing this, I knew he was likely going to be critical of Andrew; I stopped it before it could happen.

"Let me pause you again," I said, putting my hand up. "You are frustrated and overwhelmed, and you feel defensive related to what you just heard from Andrew. And Andrew, what were you feeling just a few moments ago?"

"I'm just angry and frustrated and tired of how things always . . ."

As soon as I heard the word "always," I put my hand up again.

"I hear you're frustrated and mad, Andrew. And Ron, I hear you're also frustrated. This is a difficult conversation to have. I noticed, Andrew, that you were becoming critical—and Ron, you were becoming defensive. Neither of these approaches will help you have a productive conversation or get the outcome you desire. So I want to ask you both to try something new.

"Andrew, I'd like you to try something called soft start-up to express what you're feeling. You'll share what you notice, what you feel, and then what you need. It might sound something like, 'When I hear you say you understand how I've been impacted, I start to feel really angry because I'd been hoping to hear that for so long.' And then you would share what you need, if you know that.

"Ron, when you hear Andrew sharing a concern or complaint, your work is to learn how to avoid defensiveness. Instead of explaining yourself or punting back another complaint, I want you to work on letting Andrew know what makes sense about his perspective or feelings. And, if possible, I'd like you to take a little responsibility for your part in the interaction and acknowledge your partner's experience and feelings. Does that make sense?"

Ron frowned. "I guess so. I just don't think Andrew . . ."

Again, I put up my hand to stop defensiveness and potential criticism in its tracks. "I want to give you an opportunity to share your thoughts and feelings, too, but right now I'd really like you to be able to stay open to hearing Andrew. Let's try it, okay? Andrew, let's go back. Share again what you were trying to share before when you were feeling angry. This time, start by saying what you noticed, how you feel, and what you need."

Andrew turned to Ron and repeated the suggestion I gave him: "I noticed that when I hear you say you get how I've been impacted, I feel really angry." He looked at me. "What am I supposed to do next?"

I reminded him to share with Ron what he needed, if he knew.

Andrew took a deep breath. "Okay, so . . . I don't really know what I need. I think I also notice that I feel confused about what I want here. I know I feel angry when I hear you say you understand, but I also do feel hopeful. I guess what I need is to know what will be different this time if I do decide to be open to trying again."

I examined Ron's face. He seemed to have softened and no longer showed a defensive posture. Andrew sat silently as Ron took in what he said. Ron looked at me, seeming to need help with what to do next.

"Ron, I want you to keep talking with Andrew," I directed him. "Like I said before, you'll want to avoid defensiveness, so try letting Andrew know what makes sense about what he said and also talk about your own responsibility related to what he is thinking and feeling."

"That's right." He turned back to Andrew. "I hear what you're saying. I know that you've told me what you need a million times in the past and that I wasn't ever able to follow through on making changes. I get why that would be frustrating and why you don't trust me right now. I do take responsibility for how my actions have brought about that lack of trust."

I gave Ron a quick nod to let him know he was on the right track without interrupting their dialogue too much.

"I appreciate that you heard me just now. And I appreciate what you just said," Andrew responded.

I waited a moment and, when it seemed as if they didn't know where to go next, I reminded them that we were doing the speaker/listener exercise to discuss next steps for their relationship—Ron had been in the speaker role and Andrew had been listening. I asked them to return to that conversation.

They did so, with Ron continuing to talk about his hopes for the relationship and his commitment to working on himself to make it work. When he was finished, Andrew became the speaker, sharing with Ron that he was still on the fence. "However," he said, "today has opened me up a little more to the possibility we could stay together and have a good relationship."

As Andrew shared his thoughts, I noticed that Ron, while not becoming defensive or interrupting Andrew, seemed to be withdrawing. Because this was a part of their pattern, I paused the interaction and pointed it out.

"Andrew, I'm sorry to ask you to pause, but I want to check in on Ron for a moment. Ron, how are you feeling right now?"

With little emotion in his voice, Ron answered, "Shut down." He looked ahead aimlessly and held his arms across his body, indicating he was likely physiologically flooded.

"Okay, I can see that," I said. "Andrew, you've got some pretty important things to say, and I want to make sure Ron is able to hear you. Right now he is overwhelmed, so he won't be able to absorb what you're saying. Ron, how about you take a walk, grab some water, and come back in 15 to 20 minutes. Andrew, go ahead and take a break too."

With this suggestion, I not only stopped the pattern by pausing the conversation, but followed it by asking them to do something different in their cycle: attend to the physiological flooding. After they returned, I provided more psychoeducation on flooding, then asked them to return to their conversation.

As they continued discussing commitment, I moved in and out of observing and intervening in their enactment, most often intervening in criticism, defensiveness, and flooded states. Over the course of the conversation, I observed shifts in their behaviors and an increased ability for each of them to catch themselves when they were entering into dysfunctional communication patterns. This work set the stage for more effective conversations in the intensive and also gave them new skills to use with each other outside of the therapy session.

Intervention 2: Providing Psychoeducation

Providing psychoeducation to couples about the reasoning behind your requests and the underlying causes of their behavior helps them understand the scientific or psychological basis of their interactions. This approach creates a shared understanding, offers a sense of structure, and provides clear guidelines for how they can work to improve their relationship. It also depersonalizes the correction that the therapist is making. The clients can see that the therapist is not judging them for their patterns of behavior but providing a conceptualization they can use to make things better for themselves. Psychoeducation also serves as a reminder that this couple is not alone in their issue—there is an entire term for whatever they are experiencing, after all.

There are many concepts that a therapist might teach a couple based on what the couple is experiencing and the modality and training of the therapist. Therapists might provide psychoeducation about attachment, emotions, self-soothing, communication skills, trauma, and so on. In other words, psychoeducation is appropriate anytime you need to help a client understand a concept so that they can better recognize why you're asking them to do something. One important caveat, however: It's best not to provide much educational information when someone is in a flooded state.

The following paragraphs describe some of the most common topics that tend to come up during an intensive couples therapy session in which providing psychoeducation is a helpful intervention for supporting change in the relationship.

ALCOHOL AND OTHER SUBSTANCE USE

When alcohol or other substances are a part of the couple's dynamic, it can be helpful for the therapist to provide psychoeducation on these substances. This might include how alcohol influences a person, how alcohol use influences a couple, or how people can best get support for alcohol misuse or abuse.

Studies have shown that alcohol use "can operate as a chronic relationship stressor" (Leone et al., 2022). We also know that alcohol use is linked to intimate partner violence. When alcohol is involved, people are more likely to get into conflict due to lowered emotional regulation and increases in myopic thinking processes that make it difficult to nearly impossible to have effective conversations (Weiss et al., 2021). A therapist who identifies that a couple often has their worst arguments when they've been drinking can explain this to the couple and encourage them to test out sobriety to see if it reduces the frequency or intensity of their arguments.

The therapist might also provide psychoeducation and referrals related to next steps should one partner want help for alcohol use, including joining a support group like AA, considering full sobriety, or seeing a therapist who specializes in addiction and/or substance abuse. The therapist might also provide psychoeducation to the other partner on how it is important for that partner to remain sober as well, as couples tend to mimic each other's drinking behaviors, and to encourage them to get group support if appropriate with organizations like Al-Anon.

ATTACHMENT THEORY

A therapist might choose to explain how early attachment experiences influence adult romantic relationships to help a couple make sense of their patterns. They might reference the attachment styles described by John Bowlby (1973) and Mary Ainsworth (Ainsworth et al., 1978), discussing the concepts of secure, anxious, and avoidant attachment and people's ability to develop secure attachment together.

When I discuss attachment theory with couples, I talk about how, as young children, we have attachment figures. These people are supposed to be our protectors in an unpredictable world.

Based on varying factors, we either feel secure and safe with these attachment figures or feel insecure with them. If we feel insecure, we might manage that by becoming avoidant, which shows up as being more withdrawn and less likely to talk about emotions. Alternatively, we might become more activated or anxious in how we navigate the relationship by being hypervigilant and highly focused on getting connection. Some people have a mix of both avoidant and anxious attachment—also called disorganized attachment—in which they oscillate back and forth.

These attachment styles are developed based on how we are treated by those who are supposed to keep us safe, especially during moments of stress. As we grow, we create "if/then" propositions that guide how we think, feel, and behave in relation to others in moments of stress (Collins et al., 2004). For example, if a child gets upset and has emotionally neglectful parents, they might learn "If I am upset, no one will come for me," which might result in hiding their feelings from others when they are upset. In adult life, that might manifest as withdrawing rather than reaching for their romantic partner.

Although these automatic reactions might happen in a relationship without insight, the good news is the thoughts, feelings, and behavior processes can change over time, especially when there is a contradictory experience—for example, if the person who believes "If I am upset, no one will come for me" shows their partner they are upset and their partner is loving and warm in response. In therapy, we help couples do this type of work to begin to rewire these thinking processes.

BOUNDARIES

A common issue between partners is rigidity or porosity with each other or the outside world. Often, therapists need to teach couples about boundaries to help them build a more respectful and secure relationship, as "a functional couple is surrounded by a boundary sufficiently defined to demarcate the couple from its environment, yet sufficiently permeable to allow for adaptive exchange with the environment" (Gurman et al., 2015, p. 360).

Some couples have diffuse boundaries: there is not a clear demarcation of where the couple ends and "outsiders" begin. When one or both partners have diffuse boundaries, there will be a deprivation of resources—time, emotions, money, and so forth—within the relationship (Minuchin, 1974). A common example is conflict regarding in-laws; often, a partner will struggle to protect their partner from their family of origin or will feel as if the couple's resources are being unfairly squandered to the family members, leading to arguments and a sense of insecurity.

On the other hand, one or both partners might have rigid boundaries with each other or with outsiders. This means that no resources are shared, which can result in feelings of disconnect between the partners or with the outside world. For example, a partner might be very closed off toward their partner's family due to their own family of origin issues. This can cause conflict and resentment because it creates loyalty confusions for the partner whose family of origin is being pushed out.

When you notice a couple is struggling with issues regarding porous or rigid boundaries, you can let them know that this way of navigating connection tends to lead to resentment and distance over time. Support them in learning how to be adaptive with each other, considering the best ways to navigate boundaries together.

EMOTIONS

The therapist might need to provide psychoeducation on specific emotions. This can include sharing information about the function of an emotion, like explaining that anger is often a response to feeling violated. It may also involve talking about how important it can be to a relationship for the partners to share their emotions and be responsive to each other's feelings.

EMOTIONAL REGULATION

During a couples therapy intensive, there are often many opportunities to discuss emotional regulation and provide psychoeducation on what it is, why it's important, what causes dysregulation, and how to self-regulate. Therapists might talk to clients about physiological arousal and its impact on communication, the cause of triggers, the impact of utilizing breathing or mindfulness on emotions, the window of tolerance, or polyvagal theory, to name a few points of education that could be helpful for couples.

FAMILY OF ORIGIN

Psychoeducation on family of origin can help a couple understand how their families might have influenced how they behave in relationships. Therapists might provide education on family roles, intergenerational issues, and relational patterns.

THE FOUR HORSEMEN OF THE APOCALYPSE

As mentioned back in chapter 1, the Four Horsemen of the Apocalypse is one of the most popular psychoeducation concepts in couples therapy. Not only is it easy for couples to remember, thanks to its biblically derived title, but it can also significantly change the way they interact with each other.

When providing psychoeducation on the four horsemen, the therapist can talk about the decades-long research that led to Dr. John Gottman and his lab discovering four communication habits that are destructive to a relationship and will ultimately lead to its dissolution if they are not curbed. These four habits are criticism, contempt, defensiveness, and stonewalling. The therapist can also provide psychoeducation on the antidotes to the four horsemen—the replacement behaviors that improve communication.

INFIDELITY

When working with partners who have experienced infidelity, it can be important to share with them the common symptoms that result. Sharing this information with the person who participated in the affair can be a helpful way to provide context on their partner's reactions—particularly when it comes to the betrayed partner's anger, hyperfocus on the topic, or need to ask questions.

The reason this is important is because we often see the person who betrayed their partner become frustrated with their partner repeating themselves or being endlessly angry. When the therapist can remind the partner who violated the relationship that their partner's response is a common one and then provide feedback on how it can be most helpful to respond to this in turn, the experience is put into context. It feels less out of control for the betraying partner once they can follow a structure to make things better.

Providing information about responses to infidelity to the partner who has been betrayed helps to reduce any shame they might feel about having difficulty "getting over it" and, again, provides a greater context that might bring relief. It shows there is a path forward because other people have experienced similar issues.

Between 30 and 60 percent of people who have been betrayed by their partner report depression, anxiety, and PTSD after discovering the infidelity (Lonergan et al., 2021). The term "post-infidelity stress disorder" was coined by Dr. Dennis Ortman (2005) after he met with a woman who had discovered her husband's affair and was exhibiting similar symptoms to PTSD.

The response is related to the exceptionally stressful experience with components of a breach of trust, a betrayal of a relationship, a breaking of an agreement (Pittman, 1989), alongside the secrecy, dishonesty, and energy that keeps information from the betrayed partner and therefore impacts their self-esteem and their sense of safety within the relationship.

Symptoms of post-infidelity stress disorder include:

- **Rumination:** The betrayed partner might perseverate on the betrayal or have recurring thoughts about it.
- **Recall:** The betrayed partner may have flashbacks, nightmares, or memories that cause them to relive the painful experience.
- **Numbness:** The betrayed partner may seem emotionless.
- **Avoidance of the issue:** While many betrayed partners want to talk about the betrayal, some may want to pretend it never happened.
- **Avoidance of triggers:** The betrayed partner might avoid anything that could trigger recall (e.g., a previously loved location that was associated with the affair).
- **Anxiety:** The betrayed partner might feel constant worry or anxiety.
- **Depression:** The betrayed partner might feel empty, persistently sad, and hopeless.
- **Isolation and withdrawal:** The betrayed partner might withdraw from their partner, family, and friends.
- **Insomnia:** Difficulty sleeping is common.
- **Hypervigilance:** The betrayed partner might be overly watchful for any future betrayal.

THE IMPORTANCE OF PLAY

To encourage a couple to use humor and play as tools to bond or defuse tension, the therapist might teach them about the benefits of humor and fun in building connection, fostering secure attachment, and relieving stress. This information can include how humor and play release important hormones into the body that increase bonding.

INTIMACY

As we explored earlier regarding the intimacy wheel exercise (see page 179), couples often do not understand what it means to be intimate in ways other than sex. The therapist can explain what the different forms of intimacy are and how couples tend to generate intimacy and closeness.

MENTAL HEALTH

Couples therapists might also provide psychoeducation on topics regarding individual mental health. For example, it might be helpful to provide psychoeducation on a partner's diagnosis of depression or anxiety to teach both partners how to support each other while navigating this mental health challenge.

The therapist might also provide psychoeducation related to any symptoms they observe. While it is unlikely that you'd diagnose someone during the couples intensive, there might be a time when it makes sense to point out that you're noticing the possibility of a mental health condition.

For example, you might say, "It sounds like you've really been struggling since the birth of your baby. Based on what I am hearing, I wonder if it would make sense to be assessed for postpartum depression. The reason I think this is because people experiencing postpartum depression often have the following symptoms . . ."

MENTAL LOAD DISPARITIES

The *mental load* refers to the mental work required to keep households and families going. This includes identifying, remembering, delegating, researching, and reflecting on what has to happen and exactly how, when, and where it will happen. Studies show that in heterosexual relationships, most of the mental load work is performed by women, who also tend to experience the most negative consequences related to mental load, including increased stress, a negative impact on their career, and lower life and relationship satisfaction (Reich-Stiebert, 2023).

This concept will often appear undefined in couples therapy. This means that you will find yourself observing conflicts related to mental load disparities while the couple will not know how to define the cause of their argument. When you notice the role that mental load disparities might be playing in the day-to-day life and conflict cycles of a couple, providing psychoeducation can help them to label what they are struggling with, discuss it, and then begin to redistribute the mental load in a fairer way.

META-EMOTIONS

Many couples have differing beliefs about emotions, known as *meta-emotion differences*. Often, for example, one partner believes that emotions are helpful, while the other partner believes that emotions are unhelpful and stunt problem-solving. Letting the couple know that this is a common mismatch can help them feel less alone in the issue and can also provide a foundation of information for how to navigate their meta-emotion differences.

SEX

Due to social stories, many couples come in with narratives about what sex means to them. These narratives can, at times, cause dysfunction in the relationship. For example, a male partner might think his female partner is not in love with him anymore because she has been less sexually spontaneous. The therapist might have to provide sex education regarding the different reasons someone might no longer be spontaneous sexually by discussing health, desire, and connection. The therapist might want to discuss Emily Nagoski's concept of accelerators and brakes or provide more information on the different types of desire (spontaneous or responsive). The therapist might also want to provide information regarding topics such as erectile dysfunction or vaginismus and their impacts on sexual satisfaction, information on how to find a doctor for further support or discuss how trauma can influence sexual intimacy.

STRESS MANAGEMENT

Many couples come to therapy because their lives are stressful and they are struggling with stress management. In my book *'Til Stress Do Us Part* (Earnshaw, 2024b), I discuss the role stress plays in increasing conflict and distance in a relationship and provide tools for the couple to utilize to manage stress better. I often share with couples how stress impacts the body and mind and therefore impacts the relationship. Stress affects many areas of intimacy, like the ability to be intellectually intimate with each other or sexually intimate. After providing this psychoeducation, the therapist can then guide the couple toward stress management techniques.

THE TURTLE AND THE HARE

A common couple dynamic is having one partner be a slower verbal processor (a "turtle") while the other partner is a faster verbal processor (a "hare"). This can lead the hare to accuse their partner of not caring or not being invested in their conversations, and it can lead the turtle to feel as if their partner does not respect their need to think and reflect before responding. Describing this difference to couples can help each person better understand their partner's needs and reduce misunderstandings about why each person is communicating the way they are.

This is not an exhaustive list of psychoeducation that might be provided during a couples therapy intensive session; however, these are common topics that are touched on with couples in order to provide a better conceptualization of their issues.

Ebony and Karl: Psychoeducation on Betrayal Trauma

During my one-on-one with Ebony, she expressed feeling "crazy" for not being able to control her ruminations related to the affair. "I just can't stop thinking about it. I cry at the drop of a hat and then two seconds later I feel completely enraged. It's horrible. Sometimes I feel like I hate him and sometimes I love him so much and want it to work. I don't know who I am or what I think anymore."

As Ebony spoke, I looked at her, nodded, and offered words of understanding and validation. After she finished describing her frustration with her dichotomy of feelings—"I hate this man and don't want to even think about him" and "I can't stop dwelling on it and imagining what he did"—I wanted to normalize her experience by explaining how people who are betrayed in a relationship can experience symptoms like those experienced by people who have been diagnosed with PTSD.

"Ebony, I know all these feelings can be really overwhelming, and I want to share with you that you're not alone in how you're feeling. After infidelity, many people feel just like you. It's common to experience flashbacks or ruminations or bad dreams. Your brain is trying to keep you safe by keeping you hyperaware of what is going on. It's almost like your mind thinks that if you relax for a moment, something painful could happen to you again."

Ebony started to cry. "Thank you for saying that. I feel so crazy. But it does feel like this was traumatic to me, and I just can't stop thinking about it."

I listened as she talked more about how she related to what I had shared with her. Then I said, "Even though this is an incredibly painful, confusing, and frustrating process, the good news is that since many people have experienced this, there are pathways to feeling better over time." We then explored the types of support available to Ebony for these symptoms.

> [When providing psychoeducation, I often share that the reason I want the client to know that other people have experienced what they have experienced, or that there is a term for it, is it then means we have a direction to go in to improve the relationship or the client's emotional experience.]

Intervention: Cross-Tracking, Cross-Questioning, and Cross-Interpreting

Couples who find themselves in intensive couples therapy tend to have empathic failures with each other due to **misappraisal**. Throughout the intensive, a goal for the therapy is to help the partners become more attuned to each other and build a more **secure functioning** relationship.

COUPLES THERAPY DICTIONARY

Misappraisal

Misappraisal occurs when someone is not attuned to what their partner is feeling or needing and therefore responds in an unhelpful manner toward their partner. For example, say partner A thinks that partner B is quiet because they are angry with partner A. Because of this, partner A distances themselves. However, partner B is not angry with partner A—in fact, they are feeling sad and wish their partner would reach for them to offer care and concern. Because of the initial misappraisal, the couple now feels more distant than they did previously.

Secure Functioning

Secure functioning refers to a relational model where both partners operate from principles of mutuality, safety, fairness, and shared purpose (Tatkin, 2024). This looks like the following:

- The partners protect the relationship during stress.
- Conflict is collaborative, not competitive.
- Each person takes accountability and repairs quickly.
- Emotional attunement is consistent.
- There's a clear sense of "we" over "me."

Couples build secure functioning by making and keeping shared agreements (e.g., "We don't yell"), practicing co-regulation (calming not just themselves, but also each other), repairing quickly and often, creating rituals of connection and shared purpose, and prioritizing the relationship as a secure base.

Techniques such as cross-tracking, cross-questioning, and cross-commenting are interventions used in Psychobiological Approach to Couples Therapy (PACT) to help the therapist identify how collaborative the couple is, notice whether their insight into each other is accurate, and recognize their somatic responses to each other. For example, when one partner is speaking, does the other partner begin to raise their shoulders up toward their ears, indicating stress, or does their posture seem more open, indicating a willingness to listen and be vulnerable? The therapist might also notice microexpressions. For example, eyebrow raises, pursed lips, or smirks can indicate negative sentiment toward the partner, while relaxed facial muscles, genuine smiles, or gently arched eyebrows typically indicate empathy and care.

CROSS-TRACKING

Cross-tracking is when the therapist shifts their gaze to the non-talking partner during an enactment to observe any shifts in emotional or physiological arousal. The belief here is that the non-talking partner is using fewer resources and therefore their body will show more related to how they are feeling (Tatkin, 2020b). Thus, the therapist moves their gaze to whichever partner is not speaking at the moment and observes their face, body, breathing, and movement. The therapist also tracks their own emotional states, noticing any shifts and countertransference, using the information to consider whether there are any denied or repressed emotional experiences the couple is not mentioning.

> ### Ron and Andrew: Cross-Tracking
>
> As Andrew and Ron discussed the future of their relationship, I sat back, quietly watching them as they engaged with each other. While Ron spoke, I moved my eyes to Andrew. Andrew was sitting politely, with his hands across his lap. But as Ron spent more time talking, Andrew's eyes began to wander and look heavy, and he began to have a blank stare.
>
> When Ron stopped talking, I turned my gaze back to him, noticing that as he became quiet, he began to puff up his chest and open his shoulders wider. He looked up at the ceiling and did not make eye contact with Andrew.

CROSS-QUESTIONING

During cross-questioning, the therapist is interviewing one partner about the other partner. For example, the therapist might ask one partner, "What do you think your partner is feeling right now?" to see if they can accurately appraise their partner's experience. The other person gets to act as a "fly on the wall" listening to how their partner perceives them. Then the therapist asks if the appraisal was correct. For example, when asked "What do you think your partner is feeling right now?" the questioned partner might say, "I don't know; they look mad." The therapist would turn and ask the other partner, "Are they right—are you mad?"

During this time, the therapist might allow their own feelings to emerge as a way to express something that might be "denied or repressed within the couple system" (Arduman, 2020). For example, if the therapist is noticing themselves feeling irritated with a partner, perhaps they ask the other partner, "Are you feeling irritated with anything that has been said?"

The goal of this intervention is to help the couple recognize the ways in which they accurately or inaccurately read each other and to help them become more attuned with each other by seeking out accurate information about each person's state.

> ## Ron and Andrew: Cross-Questioning
>
> I was curious what Andrew made of Ron's body language. I had the sense that he often saw Ron's "puffing up" to indicate that Ron was taking a one-up or aggressive position. "Andrew," I asked, "what do you think Ron is feeling right now?"
>
> Andrew, who hadn't been looking at Ron, turned his head and observed Ron's body language. "I never know what to make of this. He will talk and talk about how much he loves me and wants our relationship to work, and then he will just end the conversation by looking like he's not involved at all and could not care less."
>
> As Andrew was saying this, I watched Ron to see any reactions. His brow furrowed; he looked confused and perhaps disappointed.
>
> "Ron, is that true? Are you disconnected and feeling as if you don't care right now?"
>
> I shifted my gaze back to Andrew, who was starting to seem more interested. His eyes were curious and his body leaned slightly toward Ron.
>
> Ron said, "It's not true at all. I care so much!"
>
> As Ron spoke, I looked at Andrew. His eyes were now looking off to another corner, and his body had begun to turn away.
>
> "Ron, what is Andrew feeling?"
>
> I continued to watch Andrew as Ron answered, "He's mad. I don't know why."
>
> "Is that right, Andrew?" I asked. "Are you mad?"
>
> I looked at Ron as Andrew answered, "No, I'm not mad. I'm taken aback. I've been wanting to hear something like that for a long time. It always feels like he doesn't care, so to hear him say that he does . . . I just don't know how to respond."
>
> I looked back at Andrew, curious to see if there had been any more shifts in his state. He certainly didn't look tuned out anymore. He was leaning forward and thinking. Ron, meanwhile, had slouched forward and was rubbing his face, something I'd noticed he did when he was feeling upset or disappointed in himself. "When I'm talking about my feelings, I tend to look away," he admitted. "It's uncomfortable for me to look at the other person."
>
> I looked back at Andrew and noticed he was tuned into what Ron was saying. "Andrew," I asked, "do you know that Ron doesn't feel comfortable looking at you when he's having a difficult conversation with you? That it's really overwhelming to him?"
>
> Andrew shook his head. "I don't believe it. It's been this way for so long. I think he just doesn't want to connect and have intimate conversations."

CROSS-INTERPRETATION

In cross-interpretation, the therapist interprets something about one partner to the other partner. This strategy reduces the defenses that might otherwise come up if you directly interpret someone to themselves. Dr. Tatkin (2020b) has found that the approach is especially effective with those who exhibit insecure attachment styles and those who exhibit personality disorders. It is also effective when dealing with feelings of shame, exposure, criticism, and disapproval.

During interpretation, the therapist can utilize the concepts of pain, soothing, and defense to talk about the interpretation (Masterson, 1981). For example, I might say of Ron: "When Ron is overwhelmed emotionally (pain), he soothes (soothing) and protects (defense) himself by taking a deep breath and disengaging."

Whenever the therapist makes an interpretation, they are taking a risk that they might be wrong. If they are wrong, they must then work to repair. The therapist should continually check for the nod factor and other signs that their interpretation is correct by moving their gaze back and forth between the partners.

Ron and Andrew: Cross-Interpretation

Both Andrew and Ron had insecure attachment styles. Historically Andrew had been more anxious, although at this point he seemed withdrawn. Ron, on the other hand, seemed disorganized—sometimes pursuing Andrew and at other times remaining distant. This was confusing for Andrew, who had only been able to make sense of it by concluding Ron didn't care for him. When Andrew stated that he didn't believe Ron's distancing was related to being emotionally overwhelmed, I glanced at Ron and noticed that he was feeling overwhelmed.

"Ron, I want to help you out here. Please correct me if I am wrong." I turned to Andrew and interpreted what was happening for Ron during intimate conversations.

"I understand, Andrew, why you would think that Ron is withdrawn and perhaps disinterested in intimate conversations. I think there's something you don't understand about Ron, though. I think that if you looked very closely, you would see that when Ron is talking with you, he feels nervous, exposed, and vulnerable. I get the sense that Ron is very sensitive to sharing his feelings and then potentially being dismissed or getting 'in trouble,' so when he's talking, he doesn't really connect. He keeps himself at a distance. And when he's done talking, it's almost like he emotionally runs away to avoid getting in trouble or to avoid being rejected or dismissed. Ron, please correct me if I am wrong."

I looked at Ron, who was nodding in agreement. "I wouldn't have been able to articulate it, but that's exactly it. I just kind of word vomit and then try to be done with it because I really don't know how to handle it if the other person is upset with me."

I turned back to Andrew. "I imagine that it's all heightened for Ron because there is a very real likelihood that you will dismiss him—because right now you aren't so sure if you can take in what he has to say. So, this is a very vulnerable conversation for him to have because he's feeling exposed and at risk for rejection or criticism."

I glanced over to Ron to see if he was giving me any signals that I was getting it wrong. He was nodding, so I continued.

"Ron is worried about rejection, so he soothes that discomfort by puffing up and protects himself by withdrawing. Can you think of anyone who might have been rejecting or critical to Ron in his early years?"

Andrew nodded. "He experienced both. His family was very critical and withdrawn. They would say awful things to each other and to Ron, and then they'd just abandon him."

I turned to Ron and used cross-questioning: "Is Andrew right?"

Ron nodded. "I don't want to make excuses for myself, but I was never able to talk to someone about my feelings without being berated or just abandoned. And I'm so nervous right now to talk about how I feel because you could do either of those things, Andrew—and you'd have every right to."

I empathized, "It must have been so hard for you to go through that. It was so hot and cold and confusing. I can understand why this would be so hard for you to do and how it would feel scary to really try to connect with Andrew."

After this, I asked Ron and Andrew to continue their conversation, encouraging them to show engagement with each other. Earlier in the intensive, Andrew had often responded to Ron's emotional bids with sarcasm or disengagement. But as their attunement increased, Andrew seemed increasingly capable of remaining present. Even so, at one point I noticed that Andrew started to "drift off" again. Although Ron was showing engagement—he was turned toward Andrew and even touching him from time to time—Andrew was still moving in and out of focus. I decided to cross-question again by asking Ron, "What do you think Andrew is feeling?"

From here, the same pattern followed. I used cross-questioning to understand their appraisals of each other more thoroughly and to help them develop more accuracy, and I offered an interpretation to Ron for Andrew's behavior. I shared that I believed Ron didn't understand that for Andrew, it was hard to hear this all again. That he was opening himself up to being disappointed by Ron, and so anytime he began to engage, he might get overwhelmed and shut down so as not to get too excited.

Then I asked Ron, "Do you know if there was ever anyone who made false promises to Andrew when he was growing up? That he might have learned to not get too excited?"

Ron took Andrew's hand and said to him, "Yes, your dad made promises he didn't keep and that was awful for you. I want to be different for you—and I will be if you give me the chance."

I asked Andrew, "Is that right? Did you have to protect yourself from any sort of hope that your dad would come back?"

Andrew nodded and squeezed Ron's hand. "It's hard for me to lean into this because I don't want to be stupid and have false hope."

Using cross-interpretation with Andrew and Ron began to address some of their issues regarding insecure attachment: They often misread the situations between each other due to their personal histories. Ron often felt disorganized—wanting to be close and then wanting to get out of Dodge—while Andrew didn't want to be too hopeful because he'd experienced that all before. As Andrew and Ron developed an accurate read on each other during this exercise, I watched both adjust their nonverbal states, showing more relaxed and open states. They felt safer with each other and were less defensive.

Thanks to this and the previous exercises, Ron and Andrew now had the ability to discuss feelings, repair with each other, and respond to each other in a more attuned and curious manner. All of this made it easier for us to enter into more effective conversations about the future of their relationship—a topic that usually was much too emotionally complex for either of them to touch.

While Andrew and Ron had the capacity to attune with each other during the exercise, there are times when you will meet with a couple that struggles to get to that point. Sometimes a partner might become upset with their partner's interpretation of their thoughts or feelings and conflict could escalate. This does not mean cross-interpretation is not a useful exercise, as uncovering how much they are misreading each other is an important part of beginning to help them change that. It might simply require more work on the therapist's part to recognize any dysregulation and to utilize soothing exercises and breaks if necessary

John and Amy: Cross-Tracking, Cross-Questioning, and Taking a Break

Eventually, it was time for Amy and John to begin to discuss the elephant in the room: Amy's unhappiness regarding mental load disparities. Up until this point, we had been setting the stage by building some more effective communication tools—learning to listen to each other and negotiate. Now, it was time to test the waters on how they could utilize those skills when talking about a heavier issue for the two of them.

I asked them if they were willing to discuss the conflict around fairness of housework, and they agreed. First, I defined what I was hearing of the conflict: "It sounds like the two of you are struggling with housework not feeling fair. From what I've heard, I think you're struggling with not only the physical labor but also the mental load, which is what Amy feels frustrated with."

I provided some psychoeducation on the mental load—what it is, how it tends to show up in families—and then normalized that it's an issue that causes conflict for a lot of couples.

Finally, it was time to set Amy and John up in an enactment. I used the speaker/listener exercise and reminded them of the rules. I let them know that I would be observing their interactions but that I wanted them to try to talk to each other about their thoughts and feelings on how this issue is impacting them as individuals and their relationship.

As they spoke to each other, I cross-tracked, moving my eyes to John when Amy spoke and my eyes to Amy when John spoke. I paid close attention to changes in their physiological and emotional states.

At one point, John shared, "I think this is all overblown. You make things harder on yourself." As Amy heard this statement from John, her face moved into a grimace and she took a deep inhale.

I turned to John, who had stopped talking, and observed him briefly, noticing that he hadn't quite taken in Amy's response. "John, what do you think Amy is feeling?" I asked.

"I think she's feeling mad."

"Oh, you're so smart!" Amy remarked sarcastically.

"Amy, is John, right? Are you mad?"

Amy looked at me, her eyes narrowed. "What are you trying to get at here? We all know I'm mad! It's why we're here!"

As Amy was talking, I watched John, who was staring ahead so as not to make any eye contact with Amy.

"Amy, what do you think John is feeling?"

"I really don't care what he's feeling. We've spent hours here today and he still isn't getting how serious the issue is. He just said that he thinks I'm overblowing the issue. John, if this wasn't a big issue, would I have threatened divorce? You must think I'm crazy and that I just start fights over nothing."

As Amy spoke, I noticed that John continued to stare ahead, his eyebrows raised as if to say "whatever"; his body language seemed to indicate both defeat and a sense of dismissiveness toward Amy. I noticed my own frustration toward John and recognized it as countertransference.

"John, Amy is frustrated with you." I shared this to see if the way I was feeling mirrored Amy's feelings. "Am I right, Amy?"

"More than frustrated! I can't sit here and have this conversation if he's just going to dismiss me like this."

> I noticed that Amy was becoming flooded—her arms crossed akimbo, her legs bouncing, her eyes looking toward the ceiling, her face red. She needed a break.
>
> I looked over at John. I sensed he was also flooded and his "dismissive" stance was more likely stonewalling, caused by his sense of internal overwhelm. Instead of continuing to question either of them or offering interpretations they wouldn't hear, I suggested a break. "Let's come back in 20 minutes."
>
> Amy grabbed her jacket and stomped out of the room. John sat for a minute, tapping his fingers, before he slowly looked up at me to make brief eye contact, nodded, grabbed his coat, and wandered out.
>
> *[John and Amy were feeling activated and insecure with each other. When Amy heard John's opinion that the issue was overblown, she felt criticized, something she already feared regarding the issue because she was a high performer and did not want to be judged as someone who couldn't do it all or who complained too easily.*
>
> *While there were interpretations I could have made to help them attune to each other more powerfully, it wasn't the right time. They were flooded and they needed time to soothe and come back.]*

Intervention 3: Joining Through the Truth

Historically, therapists have been encouraged to err on the side of neutrality when it comes to difficult truths about a person. However, in my experience with couples therapy, a complete dedication to neutrality only slows down the process, causes confusion, and ultimately leaves the couple with an unclear view of their issues. When the therapist finally attempts to address the difficult truths, such as a partner's behavior habits being the cause of conflict in the relationship, this can cause a rupture in trust. Realizing that you were waiting so long to finally say something makes the couple wonder what you were thinking all along.

Joining Through the Truth, an intervention developed by Terry Real (2012), involves the therapist being very honest about what they are seeing in the relationship, presenting the clients with a clear reflection of their individual roles and behaviors within the relationship. This helps the couple address their issues and build trust with the therapist. The goal is for the therapist to help the clients see their own contributions to dysfunctions while maintaining a supportive stance.

Therapists can join through the truth by:

- **Using directness over caution:** It is important to confront clients with direct—and yes, sometimes uncomfortable—feedback about their behaviors and relationship dynamics. This is why they are investing in an intensive. They know something is wrong and they want help with changing it.

- **Pointing out maladaptive behavior:** Being honest with couples means that we don't only focus on emotional experiences (although this is a huge focus, of course). We also focus on each client's responsibility to recognize that their behaviors related to their emotional experiences and history might be maladaptive. We do so by pointing out the maladaptive behaviors and encouraging change.

- **"Taking sides":** Responsibility in relationships is often uneven. Therapists are encouraged to recognize and address imbalances in responsibility, rather than treating all issues as equally shared; otherwise the therapist is enabling the imbalances and is entering into dishonesty when discussing the issues.
- **Handling grandiosity:** Clients who exhibit grandiosity or entitlement need a therapist who can address issues directly and maintain boundaries.
- **Being authentic:** When the therapist is transparent, in a clinically appropriate way, about their own struggles and personhood, their feedback feels more truthful to the client.

Therapists should only join through the truth in a loving, warm, and kind way. Doing it with harshness, criticism, contempt, or aggression only serves to break the therapeutic alliance and cause harm.

Ebony and Karl: Joining Through the Truth

Joining Through the Truth became necessary during the middle of my second day with Karl and Ebony. Even after our enactment and a couple of exercises, I was still not sure that Karl was being completely honest. There were moments when he was able to extend empathy, but they were few and far between. Although I had provided Karl psychoeducation on the importance of him showing Ebony empathy and patience while working to rebuild her trust, he seemed to quickly withdraw from any opportunity to do so. It happened again when, after I directed Ebony to ask Karl questions she had about the affair, Karl shut Ebony down by telling her she needed to get over it. To me, it was clearly time for more direct communication.

"Let's pause," I said. "Karl, what's going on?"

Karl huffed, "I don't know how many times I have to answer these questions. It's getting ridiculous."

I gave him a direct gaze. "I need to be honest with you, Karl. If your goal is to rebuild trust and fix this, you're not doing what needs to be done to get there."

Karl met my gaze with narrowed eyes. "I *said* I want things to work out."

"I hear the words," I told him, "But I don't see the actions. Right now, Ebony is in distress due to your actions. The reality is that you violated the contract of your relationship, and those actions have major consequences on Ebony's emotional state. For things to improve, you'll need to take accountability for that, and that's going to take time."

I paused, letting him take in what I'd said.

"Karl, I am thinking back to our time together, just you and I talking about your childhood. And I'm wondering if you can think back to a time in your own life when something really shocking happened to you and it felt like the people around you didn't take accountability for how much it hurt you." I maintained a calm and kind voice, not showing any frustration with him.

Karl looked down at his hands and nodded. "Yes. My entire childhood was full of secrecy—and like I shared with you, it wasn't a great way to live. Right now, I'm thinking specifically about when my dad lost his job and then my mom gambled our money away. We were getting evicted, and they never even told me. I came home one day to find a chain on the door. If I would have known, I could have gotten some of my things out of the house before I went to school. I still haven't forgotten the fact that I never got the last photo I had of my grandma back."

I could feel Karl's pain. I allowed my face to show it. I looked over at Ebony, who was watching Karl quietly, then turned back to Karl. "And did they ever take accountability for doing that to you?"

"No, they always did what they wanted and made me suffer the consequences."

"When did you decide to be in cahoots with them?" I chose a neutral and direct term.

Karl looked at me. "Yeah, I see that."

"Tell me more."

"I see that my dishonesty and then refusal to take accountability is exactly like what my parents did to me. And it felt awful. I don't know what happened to me because when I was young, I promised I would never be like them."

"You probably did what you had to do to survive emotionally. It sounds like when you were growing up it wasn't a great environment to take accountability. It sounds like if you did, you'd get eaten alive. But now is different. You're not that small child anymore. You're an adult and you can handle accountability now. But you get to decide."

It was Karl's life. He got to decide whether he wanted to take accountability or continue the cycle.

I continued, "If you want to end the cycle here, you can, and I can show you how. You can be different from all of that. You can tell your parents, 'Thank you for everything you've given me that was good, but no thank you to all of this crap about secrecy and lack of accountability. I am letting go of that legacy.'"

As I approached Karl in this way, I began to see something shift. His shoulders slouched and he let out an exasperated sigh. He looked around the room, rubbed his palms to his eyes, and then said, "I need a break."

Karl left the room for a moment. Ebony sat quietly, unsure of what to do or say next. "Do you need a break too, Ebony?" I asked.

"I think that might help," she responded.

Ebony left the room and Karl returned. "Do you think I could spend some time with you one-on-one?" he asked.

"Sure," I replied. Not wanting to leave Ebony feeling confused when she returned from her break to a closed door, I went into the hallway to find her and let her know the plan. She decided to go for a walk while I had my one-on-one time with Karl.

I walked back into the office to find Karl sitting on the couch, slouched over with his head in his hands.

"The affair isn't over," he admitted.

"Tell me more," I said calmly. I was cautious not to have any tone in my voice that would express judgment or frustration with Karl. I was glad that he was sharing the truth with me.

It seemed like a sign that he was ready to take real accountability, at the risk the relationship might not be able to recover.

Using this intervention at this part of the intensive was important because I'd had a deep sense that something wasn't measuring up that I could not shake. It would have been dishonest for me to continue in the intensive as if I did not have that feeling. Of course, I am no psychic, so there was a possibility that I was wrong and that Karl was not hiding a continued affair. However, letting Karl know that something wasn't adding up was still pivotal. It opened the door to him either correcting me or being honest in some capacity.

Joining through the truth isn't always related to uncovering some deep betrayal that the client is intentionally hiding. Sometimes this intervention is utilized to bring a person awake to their own character, and this can be challenging.

> ## Kimmie and Selah: Joining Through the Truth
>
> When Kimmie and Selah were discussing new agreements related to how they would deal with Selah's dad, Selah began to defend her reasoning for going over to her dad's so frequently. Although she had initially seemed on board for improving boundaries with her time, she started to backpedal.
>
> "I thought we were on the same page hours ago!" Kimmie sounded exasperated. "What changed?"
>
> "It just feels wrong. My parents have given me everything, so for you to ask me to stop supporting my dad . . . it feels wrong."
>
> I brought in cross-questioning: "Kimmie, what do you think Selah is feeling right now?"
>
> "I think she's anxious," said Kimmie.
>
> "Is she right, Selah?" I asked.
>
> Selah rubbed her temples. "I don't know."
>
> "Kimmie," I asked, "when Selah gets anxious, does she usually guilt you?"
>
> Kimmie frowned. "I haven't thought of it that way, but yes. When she's upset, she tends to tell me why I should feel bad or why I am doing something wrong."
>
> I looked at Selah to see how she was receiving this. Her lips were pursed, but overall, she seemed calm.
>
> "Selah, when you guilt Kimmie for her needs, it's not respecting her boundaries," I advised gently. It was important for me not to sugarcoat my observation. However, my honesty caused Selah to react.
>
> "How so?" she demanded. "She isn't respecting *my* boundaries by making me do something against my values."
>
> "Kimmie isn't *making* you do anything," I told her. "Kimmie is saying, 'My boundary is that I can't overextend myself anymore. My desire is that you do the same with your family to preserve resources for us. You can either agree to that or say no.'"
>
> I continued, "Selah, I think you often agree to things you don't actually agree to. On one hand, you agree to give a lot of your time and money to your family even though deep inside you know you need to keep some of that time for you, for Maisie, and for Kimmie. On the other hand, you agree with Kimmie that you'll set a boundary with your family only to express later you don't really agree with it. I have to say—and I am saying this with love—it must be hard to know where you stand. There is something confusing about the way in which you agree with things."
>
> Kimmie's nonverbal communication indicated that I had expressed something she had struggled to articulate herself. Selah's face tightened, but she took a breath and slowly nodded, as if still processing the feedback.
>
> "Selah, how are you feeling hearing this from me?" I asked.
>
> She took a deep inhale and exhale. "It's hard to hear that, but it's why we are here. I appreciate the honesty, but it's hard." She lifted her hands and let them drop. "I think you're right. I agree to a lot of things verbally, but then I get resentful later because it isn't totally what I want to do."
>
> "I could help you to be more honest about what you're willing to do and not do," I offered. "It's hard work, so you'd really have to be willing to tolerate how uncomfortable it can be to say no to

someone. I think it would improve your relationship with Kimmie and probably with others too. But it's up to you."

Selah looked at me with moist eyes. "I need to be able to do that. I'd like to be able to do that. And I want to be clear that I do want to give more resources to Kimmie and have more boundaries. I think I was starting to feel anxious about having to set the boundaries with my dad, so I was taking it out on you, Kimmie. I'm sorry for that."

From here, Kimmie and Selah had a conversation regarding how Kimmie could support Selah in navigating her difficulties saying no. This helped Kimmie and Selah better understand an underlying, unsaid motivator to some of Selah's behaviors that were resulting in conflict, and it gave the couple a path to discuss this motivator and come up with ways to reduce the likelihood it would continue to cause problems.

When talking about the joining through the truth intervention with new therapists, the most common response I get is something like "I could never do that! What if the client gets mad?" I encourage therapists to remember that the client is paying you to share your observations and to help them change. It's your job to avoid colluding with the parts of them that are stuck in a dysfunctional homeostasis, even if it's uncomfortable.

Intervention 4: Doubling

Doubling is a technique developed by Dr. Dan Wile (2013), the creator of Collaborative Couples Therapy. It consists of the therapist speaking as if they were one of the partners speaking to the other. While it seems like the cross-interpretation exercise, in which you interpret to one partner something about the other partner, this is different—it's more theatrical because you actually "speak as" the client, attempting to show more of their underlying emotions and helping their partner to be moved by those emotions. When I notice that a client is having a difficult time expressing themselves in a way that their partner can listen and understand, I use doubling to speak on their behalf.

Doing this serves several purposes:

- The person you're speaking for feels seen by you, even if not yet by their partner. This experience of having someone on their "side" can build a sense of confidence and trust.
- You provide the person you're speaking for space to regulate and consider their own words. You give them an opportunity to hear back what you've heard.

Because you're not a part of the relationship, you are able to say what the client is feeling using a tone of voice and words that are calm and more vulnerable. You are less likely to elicit defensiveness from the partner you're speaking to, and they may feel "moved" where they have felt "unmoved" in the past.

Doubling can be very effective when a couple continues to argue over the same issue or when a partner has been incredibly hurt and feels as if their partner doesn't understand them on a deep enough level. I use it most when I can see a vulnerable part underneath what is coming out—such as vitriol toward me or toward the other partner, or perhaps a frozen affect where the person is unable to express what they need to say.

One noteworthy aspect of doubling is that the therapist must feel for themselves what the client is saying. According to Dan Wile, "When you double, you don't just repeat what the person says. And you don't simply say the same thing in different words. You show what the person might say were they to speak with an increased generosity of spirit, from a place of greater vulnerability, or from a perspective above the fray" (Wile, 2013). In other words, the therapist is not only helping one partner express themselves, but also modeling what true empathy looks like—that it requires one person to step into the shoes of another.

Because this process involves the partners letting each other into their internal worlds and being vulnerable, therapists should consider whether it is an appropriate intervention. For example, if there is a client who is abusive and uses vulnerable information against their partner, you might not want to leave the partner's feelings exposed to further abuse.

Doubling requires vulnerability and differentiation on the part of the therapist. The therapist must be open enough to work toward "feeling" as the client might feel in order to express those feelings in the way the client would if their defenses weren't present. However, the therapist also needs to remain differentiated, keeping their own emotions separate from the emotions of the client, so as not to be overtaken by the client's feelings.

John and Amy: Doubling

When Amy and John returned from their break, I had a sense that I would need to help them get to a more vulnerable place with fewer defenses present before having them hop back into a conversation about how they'd like to navigate their mental load disparities. Rather than continuing with cross-questioning, I decided I would act as a proxy for Amy, who had struggled to share her more vulnerable feelings with John, instead protecting herself by attacking him with sarcasm and contempt. And then, I would do the same for John, who wasn't able to share anything about his internal world and instead sounded dismissive and uncaring, followed by looking withdrawn.

"Welcome back. How are you both feeling?" I asked them as they sat back down.

"I'm okay," said Amy. "Sorry that I went crazy."

"What about you?" I asked John.

"I'm fine."

"That was a difficult interaction," I noted. "I think you're both feeling and thinking really important things and you're having a hard time expressing those things to each other in a way where your partner can actually understand you and take in what you're saying. Amy, if it's okay with you, I'd like to try to share with John what you're trying to express."

Amy nodded.

"Okay, I'm just going to come here beside you and kneel down next to you." I knelt beside Amy and looked toward John.

"John, as Amy, I want to share with you how it feels when I hear you say that my concern is overblown. When I hear that, I start to feel totally dismissed and so angry. I don't want to be angry with you. I want to relate to you because I love you. But when I hear you dismiss my concern like that, I start to wonder if you'll ever get it. I start to wonder if you care for me, because this is something that is causing me so much stress and pain and difficulty every day of my life. And you're supposed to be my best friend. So, I know all you said just now was one small thing, but it really made me feel so alone. If my best friend in the whole world doesn't get how much the burden I am under is killing me, then who will get it? And how will I ever get any help? So, I am mad, but I'm also so sad and disappointed and I feel alone."

I said all of this while expressing those feelings in my voice. I used eye contact, facial expressions, and my tone of voice to express what I believed Amy was feeling but in a softer and deeper manner.

Once I'd finished, I looked up at Amy. "Is there anything you'd like to fix?"

A tear ran down Amy's face. She shook her head, took a deep breath, and said, "That's exactly it. John, you're supposed to be my best friend and I am suffering. I'm trying to tell you that, and when you don't understand I feel alone."

I asked Amy if I could add a little more and she agreed. I turned back to John from my kneeling position and said, "Sometimes it feels like if I am going to be lonely anyway, maybe it will be less painful to be alone by myself. And that thought scares me."

Amy nodded again and added, "I never want that, John. But it is how I start to feel."

"Okay, Amy, is there anything else you'd like to add?"

She shook her head.

I stood up and explained, "John, I'm going to come over to you and I want to try to express to Amy how you are feeling as you. Is that okay?"

John agreed and I moved to kneel beside him, looking toward Amy.

"Amy," I began, "sometimes when you bring up how overwhelmed you are with the mental load, I do start to feel frustrated. I think it's a few things: One, I don't fully know the whole picture. To me, from what I am seeing, it looks like we should be able to figure this out. So maybe my frustration is based on what I know about what needs to be done and that isn't the whole picture. Two, I start to feel frustrated but also disappointed in myself that I haven't been what you need. It's hard for me to see us in any other light than happy. When you're unhappy, I start to feel overwhelmed and anxious, and then I try to pretend everything is okay so that I don't have to imagine us as unhappy. I'm afraid that if you stay unhappy our relationship will end. That thought breaks my heart and I get so overwhelmed that I end up being frozen. So, I either try to avoid talking about it or I freeze up. I just can't stand the idea of losing you and failing you, and I don't know how to make it right."

Amy softened as she heard the more vulnerable positioning. I looked to John and asked if he needed to fix anything I said.

"You got it right, except I would add there's a part of me who does think we could take it easier."

"Okay," I said as I "became" John again. "Amy, there's a part of me that worries we do too much. That we could take it easier. I worry that if I tell you I think some of our stress is somewhat self-induced, you'll think I'm dismissing you. I don't want to dismiss you, but I also want to be honest with you. Sometimes, I'm afraid of the conflict with you, so I just don't say it. It's painful for me to be in conflict with you because I just want us to be happy."

John took Amy's hand and nodded. "That's how I feel," he shared with her.

The doubling intervention had softened their defenses. Amy was no longer in the mode of aggressor—criticizing and showing contempt to protect herself—and John was no longer withdrawing and shutting down. They were both present and connected with each other. This intervention helped to redirect the couple back toward a conversation that offered them a chance to effectively discuss their primary concern.

Intervention 5: Externalizing

Externalizing is an intervention within narrative therapy developed by Michael White and David Epston (Carey, 2019). It is the practice of separating the problem story from the identity of the couple and to see it as something not intrinsic to their relationship. In other words, it "locates problems not within individuals, but as products of culture and history" (Carey & Russel, 2021). Externalizing is a powerful intervention you can utilize when you notice that the couple has turned toward blaming individual failures for issues that you, as the outside observer, can see as being caused by a greater system. This intervention can help when one or both partners are overwhelmed by anxiety, when there is a deep-seated pattern of blame, within intercultural relationships, and with couples who are gridlocked on specific problems and have not been able to move toward finding a solution.

THE DOMINANT STORY

The underlying belief in narrative therapy is that a family (in this case, a couple) has a dominant story about the problems they face together. These dominant stories are inflexible and related to cultural messages we receive throughout our lifetime from our family, community, and institutions (White & Epston, 1990). In this theory, the therapist's job is to help people consider the alternative stories to the problem they are facing by externalizing the problem, looking at it as separate from the identity of the family or the relationship.

The dominant story might be something like "Whenever partner A is anxious, our lives are completely controlled by her anxiety" or "We are always fighting when life is stressful; we don't know how to manage it" or "We have terrible communication and are always in conflict."

The use of absolutes (such as "always" or "never") or the word "should" can be a sign that externalizing might work. For example, if a couple says, "We really should be able to navigate parenthood better; we are failing at it when things get stressful," the therapist will want to look at what happens when "Stress" shows up or explore the "Should," as in, "What happens when 'Should' tells you what to do?" The external problems are almost anthropomorphized; they are revealed to be the villains of the couple's story, which helps the partners to stop unfairly blaming themselves or each other.

EXTERNALIZING QUESTIONS

When the therapist notices that the couple is stuck within a dominant narrative they've connected to their identity, the therapist can help the couple to name the problem as a way of beginning to separate it from the partners' individual and relational identities.

The following are examples of externalizing questions:

- "You say you often feel anxious. Would you say that when Anxiety shows up, it contributes to the problem you're both facing at home?"

- "You express yourself as always being so stressed and it's why you get irritable. Would it be a good idea to call the problem you're facing together 'Stress?'"

- "You say you are always in conflict. Would you say this is a good example of when Conflict took over?"

Once the therapist has named the problem, they ask more questions to better understand the development of the problem and how it influences each partner's life. Some questions that help to get to this are:

- "What is the earliest you remember Anxiety infiltrating your relationship?"
- "When Stress has visited your home in the past, how has it influenced you both?"
- "What rules does Conflict try to make you follow when you're in disagreement?"

The therapist can then invite the couple to use this externalization to explore how they would like to respond to the problem differently. The therapist can help the couple identify different stances by asking questions like:

- "Is Anxiety useful to managing the uncertainties in your relationship?"
- "Do you think it's acceptable that Stress had overtaken your relationship in this way?"
- "Do you like what Conflict has you thinking of each other?"

UNIQUE OUTCOMES

As the therapist continues to help the couple look at the issue separate from blame, they can begin to identify unique outcomes. These are moments when a couple was able to respond to the problem differently than they had in the past. Identifying unique outcomes brings awareness to the couple that their dominant story is not the only way of being. For example, if their dominant story is "We can't handle stress" and yet they have a story of a time they handled stress well, the couple is awakened to the reality that they can and have lived differently with Stress in their lives.

The therapist might ask questions like:

- "I know that right now Anxiety is calling the shots for how you raise the children. Was there ever a time when Anxiety did not call the shots with the children? What was different?"
- "Right now, Stress has overtaken your relationship and your ability to connect. It has a lot of power. Can you remember a time when even though Stress wanted to make it difficult for you to connect, you still did? Tell me the story."
- "Tell me about a recent time Conflict didn't make the rules during a disagreement. How did you get the upper hand together? What did you do differently?"

ALTERNATIVE STORIES

Lastly, the therapist can help the couple use externalizing to move away from blame and rigid stories and perspectives by helping them consider alternatives to their dominant story.

For example, the couple who talks about getting the upper hand over Conflict might say that they were able to collaborate during their unique outcome. Now, the therapist will talk about Collaboration—for example, "When Collaboration shows up, what is different for the two of you?"

The therapist will continue to ask questions about this alternate story, keeping it externalized. They might ask things like, "If Conflict saw the way Collaboration worked with you, what would surprise

Conflict?" or "When you're in your most difficult moment together with Conflict, what do you think you would need from Collaboration to get out of it?"

> **COUPLES THERAPIST RESOURCE**
>
> ### Narrative Therapy with Intercultural Couples
>
> Most couples will struggle with some differences in culture that influence their values and ideas about power, gender, and family. However, some couples have particularly great cultural divides between them, which can at times account for their conflict. The therapist must be comfortable helping the couple navigate these differences. Studies have shown that intercultural couples struggle to define shared visions for their relationships due to different cultural lenses (Gaines & Ickes, 1997; McGoldrick et al., 2005).
>
> Relationship expert Esther Perel (2000) believes that there are three basic goals for intercultural couples therapy:
>
> - The therapist should normalize different beliefs and behaviors.
> - The therapist should help couples recognize that their differences can be complementary.
> - The therapist should work with couples to create a third reality so that couples are not stuck within a gridlock of each partner trying to get their partner to fully adopt their own culture—rather, the partners work together to integrate the parts that make the most sense for them.
>
> Therapists can help partners navigate the externalized "Difference" between them by following these three steps:
>
> 1. Normalize that couples have Differences and that those Differences show up.
> 2. Help the couple recognize the ways in which their Differences can collaborate.
> 3. Help the couple come up with an alternative story for how their Differences impact them.

John and Amy: Externalization

After the doubling intervention, Amy and John were more open toward each other. They spent some time discussing their differing perceptions regarding conflict in their relationship: Amy believed she was carrying too much of the mental load, while John felt as if they just took on too much in general—if they could only let some of it go, then perhaps their relationship would improve.

"I don't want Amy to have to take on so much," John said, "but I recognize she does. I think we just aren't great at handling stress in general. We should be able to handle it all better at this point."

> [*Hearing the word "should," I knew that John was internalizing the issue; his belief was that they were facing the problem because of some personal or relational failing on how stress was handled between the two of them. Likely, John had a story of what it looks like for adults to manage stress, and he thought he and Amy were not meeting the mark.*]

I looked at Amy to see her reaction.

"Tell me about it," she agreed. "I know we should handle stress better, but we don't. I know I shouldn't be so frazzled by all of this and that we should just handle it. It's stuff people have always handled. But we don't do it well, and I think it's because you don't see it like you should."

> [*It appeared that Amy had internalized how she managed stress as well. She described a belief that she "shouldn't" be so frazzled, which implied a social story she carried about how people "should" manage adulthood or stress. She also had a story about their relationship: "We don't handle stress well." This was a rigid and stuck belief. Further, she began to point blame toward John related to a belief that he wasn't doing what he should. All of these came back to a story about what she* should *be like, what John* should do, *and how their relationship* should *manage stress.*]

I wanted to support John and Amy in better understanding their stories and removing themselves from the rigid beliefs underlying those stories. Their ability to navigate stress would begin with learning to look at stress management not as an issue within them, which resulted in either feeling shame about themselves as individuals or feeling frustrated with each other, but as a problem they could solve together.

"What I am hearing," I said, "is that Stress is something that can cause problems for the two of you and your relationship."

"I would agree," Amy confirmed. "Stress causes us a lot of problems."

"If we were to name the problem, do you think naming it Stress is helpful? Or is there something else we should call it?"

"The Burdens of Life," Amy suggested with an animated tone.

John, smirking, repeated the phrase in a deep voice: "The Burdens of Life. It sounds like a supervillain team."

"Okay, let's call it that, then," I said. "So the Burdens of Life show up for you, Amy—what do they think you should do?"

"They think I should be like my mom," she replied.

"What does that mean?"

"My mom did everything for us. Her house was clean, we had everything we needed, we participated in everything. And she just did it and she didn't complain. She never said, 'We're too busy so I can't do that.'"

"Okay, so the Burdens of Life tell you that your role is to do everything with a smile," I repeated, "and to take on as much as possible—no limits."

"That's right." Amy sighed. "So I get myself into a pickle sometimes because I can't really do it all, but I take on more and more and then I feel really frustrated. I also think that society has made me believe I should be responsible for it all. And somehow made John think he's not responsible for it all—or maybe society has made it so he doesn't even know what he is responsible for."

"So, the Burdens of Life have given you some rules. Amy, you are supposed to take it all on, take all the responsibility, and if you don't you're failing. And Society has blinded John to seeing all of this."

Amy nodded in agreement.

"Tell me," I said, "about a time when the Burdens of Life and Society didn't have so much control. Was there a time when something needed to get done, Amy, and you decided not to do it? Or when John was able to see what needed to be done and did it, and Society wasn't able to blind him?"

John looked at Amy and said tentatively, "I think so . . . I think there have been times when I've been better at this. When I've been able to see what needed to be done and do it. I'm worried that you don't see those times, though."

I asked him, "How were you able to do something different from what Amy thinks Society prevents you from doing?"

"I took Amy's concerns seriously and really spent time looking around to see what needed to be done. I think that growing up, I did learn to be blind to a lot of what needed to be done. I just didn't see it. My mom did it all and my dad didn't. But from time to time I see it, and I think I am getting better."

"Amy, what about you?" I asked. "Were you ever able to take the upper hand over the Burdens of Life and not allow them to make the rules for you?"

"Yes—last year I got really sick, and I was overwhelmed at work, and I just couldn't do it all. I said no to a lot of things, and I checked out and told John he was in control and he needed to take care of it all."

"What was that like for both of you?"

As I continued to ask them more about these concepts, they were able to deconstruct how they both had been influenced by their families and society. Amy had internalized a sense of responsibility and had become an overfunctioner. She believed that a "good mom" and a "good wife" did it all and did it all invisibly. While she had that internalized belief, it was causing her a great deal of resentment and stress, which resulted in conflict. Over the course of the conversation, Amy expressed that she didn't want the Burdens and Society to call the shots anymore. She wanted to feel comfortable letting some things go, asking for help, and saying no.

John believed he had been raised to be blind to how much his mom was doing and, therefore, did not notice how much his wife was doing either. Society and his family had created a world in which he was not able to see or identify what needed to be done. He had also been socialized by his dad (and his dad by others) to think that his wife was only nagging or creating her own problems if she was stressed. He was now beginning to see that these narratives were creating a rigid set of beliefs that were limiting the relationship's ability to move forward.

When Amy would bring up the Stress, John would respond with his rigid belief of "you brought this on yourself" or "you are just nagging me" instead of listening to Amy or looking around and noticing the extent of the work to be done. Amy, due to her internalized narratives, waited too long to ask for help and had trouble letting anyone down.

By the end of the conversation, Amy agreed that she would work on saying no, asking for help, and letting John take more on. John agreed to become more aware of the tasks that needed to be done and to acknowledge his wife as a lifelong expert in this arena and be willing to believe her when she pointed out something that needed to be done.

The couple had removed the blame from each other and had begun to see the issue in the larger context of gender roles and stories. Out from under the blame, they could imagine a new way of managing life together and could start to take responsibility rather than fighting or feeling shame.

After they finished this conversation, I took out Eve Rodsky's *Fair Play* card deck (2020). I asked John and Amy to look over the cards—each of which represents a different task or responsibility—and discuss who was responsible for each. This helped them come up with agreements for navigating household tasks, creating positive change in their relationship.

Intervention 6: Mapping the Dance

"Mapping the dance" is a couples therapy intervention commonly used in Emotionally Focused Couples Therapy (EFCT) (Johnson, 2004) that helps partners visualize and understand the recurring patterns in their interactions, often referred to as their relational "dance." In this approach, the therapist observes and highlights the cyclical behaviors, emotional reactions, and communication styles that both partners contribute to their conflicts. By mapping out this dynamic, couples can see how their actions and reactions influence each other, gaining insight into how negative cycles are sustained. The goal is to break these maladaptive cycles and replace them with healthier, more attuned ways of relating. The partners come to better understand their own roles in perpetuating conflict, allowing them to step back, reflect, and begin to change their interactions.

When the therapist observes the "dance" of interactions during a session, they first pause the conversation and draw the couple's attention to this interactional cycle. The therapist then encourages the couple to either explore the predicted upcoming steps of the dance or reflect on a previous exchange. They may ask questions such as, "What happened first?" "What did you think?" "What did you feel?" and "What did you do?"

To facilitate understanding, the therapist can use a whiteboard or paper to visually map out the different stages of the dance. This visual representation aids in deep reflection and promotes further discussion on the necessary changes for the couple to improve their interactions. Helping a couple map their dance brings the rigid conflict patterns they've developed into conscious awareness and offers them pathways for doing it differently.

Kimmie and Selah: Mapping the Dance

Halfway through their second day, Kimmie and Selah continued to get stuck on the idea of boundaries. During one conversation, Selah started to get quiet. She stopped offering her thoughts or suggestions and became short with Kimmie. Having noticed this pattern the day before, I decided it was worth bringing it to their attention through the Mapping the Dance intervention. I interrupted their enactment to discuss what I was seeing.

"Selah and Kimmie, I've noticed a pattern that is coming up again, and I was wondering if we could pause this conversation for a moment to flesh it out a little bit. I've noticed that when you're talking about an issue that's connected to emotions, Selah tends to become quiet and stop sharing. Does that sound right?"

"Yes," Selah admitted, "I just stop talking once I notice the conflict."

"What are you feeling in those moments?" I asked.

Selah bit her lip. "Probably afraid of conflict."

"Okay, so you feel afraid of a conflict and then you stop talking and contributing to the conversation," I repeated. "What happens next between the two of you?"

"Then I get frustrated," Kimmie broke in, "and I ask her to talk and tell her she is being unfair by not being involved in our conversation."

"So, the cycle so far is that there is a difficult topic, Selah feels fearful of conflict and she withdraws, then Kimmie feels frustrated and starts to criticize. Then what happens?"

"I try to get her to talk to me for a little while longer," Kimmie said, "then I just give up too."

"So," I said, "if we drew this pattern out, it would be a pattern where an issue is discussed, Selah withdraws, Kimmie pursues, Selah continues to withdraw, so Kimmie also withdraws. And this results in the loneliness you mentioned at the beginning of our session yesterday."

Kimmie nodded sadly. "Exactly."

"What we want to do with this knowledge is to choose new moves that you'll make at any point in this 'dance' that you're doing. For example, Selah, when you notice you are feeling afraid of conflict, instead of pulling back, it might be helpful to practice leaning in. Kimmie, when you see Selah withdrawing, instead of criticizing, you could change the pattern by giving her space or saying something gentle and kind. You could choose to do anything other than what you're doing right now, and it will create change. What do you both think about how you could change your dance?"

Kimmie shared first. "I think I could practice saying something loving when I notice Selah leaning out. I understand now that she mostly shuts down to avoid the conflict. Like we talked about earlier, she doesn't set boundaries with her family because she doesn't want to let them down. And I think she doesn't have conflict with me because she's worried it'll upset me. Instead of showing her the opposite is true and being loving, I prove her point when I get critical."

"So, you're saying that when you notice Selah withdrawing, you want to work on leaning toward her and saying something loving."

Kimmie nodded.

"What would be an example of that?" I encouraged Kimmie to think through how this would look so she could preplan and so Selah could hear it and recognize it during a moment of conflict.

"I think just saying something like 'Hey, even though we disagree, I love you' would help."

"And what about you, Selah? How could you interrupt this pattern?" I asked.

Selah responded that she would like to try to recognize when she is getting overwhelmed and at least say something about it rather than just shutting down. "I think it would make a difference if I could at least say, 'I'm feeling overwhelmed and I need a second.' Then Kimmie wouldn't feel so disrespected."

"Great, so your idea is to shift this pattern a bit by at least naming what is happening. Is that right?"

Selah nodded.

"I want the two of you to keep tracking this pattern as you continue your conversation and after you leave here. When you notice you're getting stuck in it, try to do something different. Changing one dance move can change the entire dance. Now, go ahead and keep having the conversation you were having. I will be here observing, but keep in mind what we just discussed."

Kimmie and Selah returned to their conversation. They were able to stay engaged longer than they had previously had because Selah now let Kimmie know when she was feeling as if she wanted to withdraw and Kimmie offered affection and warmth when she saw the possibility for conflict.

Intervention 6: Physiological Soothing

During an intensive couples therapy session, it is likely that one or both partners will become flooded at some point, and often more than once. As the therapist, it's important to notice the signs that someone is becoming flooded so that you can intervene quickly and then teach them to self-soothe. When intervening in flooding, you want to make sure that you do not immediately provide psychoeducation; when someone is flooded, they cannot take in information. Instead, you'll want to intervene by responding to the physiological state in one of the following ways:

- Ask if the couple would like a break (long or short).
- Ask the couple to close their eyes and take some deep breaths.
- Ask the couple to engage in a guided imagery or some other guided meditation with you.
- Instruct one or both people to do some movement (e.g., "Cyra, why don't you just take a quick break and walk down the hall to get some water").

Therapists should note that sometimes breathing exercises, muscle relaxation, or guided imagery might not work for a client for varying reasons that include physical injuries or in the case that these exercises trigger more physiological distress because they serve as a trigger.

In these cases, the therapist can use other modes of physiological soothing, such as distraction or taking a break (asking the client to draw, respond to their emails, go for a walk, grab some food, etc.).

Soothing interventions are often utilized several times during an intensive session as the couple is learning how to navigate their physiological responses to conflict. Sometimes, if a client struggles to self-soothe and cannot move out of a physiologically flooded state or seems to flood repeatedly without improvement, it might indicate that the client needs further individual support. The therapist might ask to have individual time with the client to help them to self-soothe in the one-on-one environment, to explore what it has been like for them to flood multiple times during the session, and then to support them in finding resources for after the intensive.

Ron and Andrew: Taking a Break

When asking a couple to take a break, it's important to direct them to the break without too much lecturing or explaining. When someone is flooded, they cannot take in information the way they can when they are in a calm state.

For example, at one point I asked Ron and Andrew to take a break by saying, "I can see you are having a hard time. Let's take a break. Andrew, I know you've needed to get back to an email. How about you stay here and do that, and I'll bring you some water to drink. Ron, how about you either go sit in the office next door and take some breaths and drink some water or walk down the street and grab something to drink at the deli. Come back in 30 minutes."

My instructions were clear, and Ron and Andrew didn't ask any questions. Andrew inhaled deeply and took out his phone. Ron said he'd grab himself a coffee and left the room.

I brought Andrew some water and went into the office next door to give him space.

When we reconvened after the 30 minutes, I asked them, "How are you both feeling?"

Ron responded that he was feeling better. "I was able to clear my head. The cold air helped."

"Yeah, I feel better," Andrew agreed. "I distracted myself for a little bit with work emails and took some deep breaths. Ron, when you were out, Sammi sent me this adorable picture of her new puppy." Andrew reached into his pocket to show Ron the text message.

I could see that Ron and Andrew were no longer flooded—they were in a physiologically calm state, able to connect and smile. I gave them psychoeducation on flooding, letting them know that it's something that happens to our bodies when we feel threatened and that in some ways it incapacitates our ability to be relational. I encouraged them to take breaks whenever they noticed they were getting to that point. Overall, this was important for our in-session work (it would increase the likelihood they could get through conversations effectively) and also for their lives at home, where physiological flooding often sent them into a tailspin of destructive conflict.

Kimmie and Selah: Deep Breaths

When a couple isn't completely flooded but the therapist can see that they are getting there, the therapist can intervene by asking the couple to close their eyes and take some deep breaths. At one point during our second day, I could see that Selah was beginning to feel flooded. Her arms were folded across her chest and she was biting her lip, all signs that she was trying to self-soothe because of internal overwhelm. As this happened, I noticed that Kimmie was becoming irritated. Her knee started to bounce and her brows furrowed. She was also becoming flooded.

My clinical opinion was that if I could intervene at this point, before they became "full-blown" flooded, we would not need to take a long break.

"Let me pause you for a moment," I intervened. "I want to ask you to do me a favor and close your eyes. I'll close my eyes, too, so you don't think I'm staring at you." Selah and Kimmie smiled and closed their eyes.

I closed my own eyes and took a deep inhale, then directed them to do the same. "As you have your eyes closed, take a moment to inhale through your nose all the way into your belly . . . and hold it there for 4, 3, 2, 1. Good. Now, I want you to slowly allow the air to exhale through your mouth, allowing the air to take with it any tension or stress, for 1, 2, 3, 4, 5. Beautiful."

I continued to guide them through a few more deep breaths. I watched as their shoulders began to drop and as tension released.

"Good job. Let's start coming back by hearing what's around you in the room. Now notice the temperature of the room. Notice how it feels on your skin. Maybe notice how the couch feels on your body. Finally, start to open your eyes gently, allowing yourself to come back and look around the room."

After giving them a few moments to come back to our space, I asked how they felt. "Much better," Selah said. Kimmie agreed.

"When you start to notice yourselves becoming overwhelmed—Selah, when you become shutdown, and Kimmie, when you feel irritated—I want you to try to focus on your breathing, just allowing yourself to inhale and exhale and letting that help to reduce some tension in your bodies so you can be present with each other."

I directed them back into the conversation and I removed myself from the dynamic, returning to my role as observer.

John and Amy: Movement

As Amy and John used the *Fair Play* cards to navigate the distribution of household tasks, they hit a snag. They disagreed on who should be responsible for a certain task and this resulted in minor physiological flooding. Neither Amy nor John was threatening to leave the room, fully shutting down, or yelling, but the signs of internal discomfort were clear.

In order to stop the flooding before it got worse, I asked them to use movement to reset.

"Let's take a moment before we finish this conversation. How about we all just stretch for a moment? Follow me. First, I want you to reach across the room as if you're trying to grab the wall. Reach, reach, reach. Good job. Now, allow your arms to relax. Do it again. Reach across the room as if you're trying to grab the wall, noticing the tension in your arms. Then allow your arms to drop by your sides as if they are spaghetti."

"Continue on by pushing your legs together as tight as you can. Squeeze your legs together, feeling the tension. Now, release. Let's do it again. Squeeze, squeeze, squeeze. Now release. Very good.

"Now, push your feet into the ground as hard as you can, as if you're stomping them into the floor. Then allow your legs to relax. Do it again—pushing into the floor, feeling the tension in your legs and feet . . . and then release.

"Now, arch your back, pushing your front forward toward the opposite wall. Notice the stretch in your back. Now relax. Again, arch your back, drawing your shoulders back and feeling the stretch in your back. Then release.

"Good job. Lastly, let's bring those shoulders all the way up to your ears. Hold them there, noticing all the stress and tension in your shoulders. Now, release. Again. Hold it there . . . and now release. Beautiful."

Once Amy and John did some movement, they seemed more energized and reconnected to themselves. I let them know that sometimes when a conversation is becoming difficult it can be helpful to release the stress in our bodies through movement. Then I asked them to return to their conversation, which they were able to do.

COUPLES THERAPIST RESOURCE

Breathing Exercise

Read the following script to the client to guide them through a breathing exercise. Please note that generous pauses and a slow voice tend to bring about safety, calm, and relaxation.

All right, let's begin by finding a comfortable position. You can sit back in your chair or lie down if that feels better for you. Close your eyes if you feel comfortable doing so.

Take a moment to notice how your body feels. Are there areas of tension or discomfort? Just notice it; no need to change anything right now.

Now, I want you to focus on your breathing. Let's begin by taking a slow, deep breath in through your nose . . . and as you breathe in, allow your stomach to expand. Don't worry about your chest, just let your belly rise as you fill your lungs with air.

Hold that breath for a moment . . .

Now, slowly exhale through your mouth, letting the air flow out gently and completely. As you exhale, feel your body begin to relax. You can even imagine the tension leaving your body with the breath.

Let's do that again. Take a slow, deep breath in through your nose . . . feel your belly rise as you inhale.

Hold for a moment . . .

And slowly exhale through your mouth. Feel your shoulders drop, your muscles soften, and your mind begin to clear with each breath.

Keep breathing like this for a moment. In through your nose . . . hold . . . and exhale slowly through your mouth.

Now, as you continue to breathe, I want you to notice if any thoughts are coming up. That's okay. Just notice them, but don't follow them. Instead, bring your focus back to the sensation of your breath. Feel the air entering your body and feel the calm that comes with each exhale.

Let's do a few more breaths together. Take a deep, slow breath in . . . hold it for just a moment . . . and gently release it . . .

One more time. Breathe in deeply . . . and exhale slowly, letting go of any tension you might still be holding on to.

When you're ready, gently bring your awareness back to the room. Start to notice the sounds around you, the feeling of the chair beneath you, the space you're in. And when you're ready, open your eyes, taking this sense of calm with you.

COUPLES THERAPIST RESOURCE

Muscle Relaxation

Use the following script to encourage muscle relaxation. Please note that generous pauses and a slow voice tend to bring about safety, calm, and relaxation.

Let's begin by finding a comfortable position. You can sit back in your chair or lie down if that feels better for you. Close your eyes if that feels comfortable. Now, take a moment to check in with your body.

Notice how your body feels right now. Are there any areas of tension, tightness, or discomfort? Just acknowledge them without judgment. We'll be working to release some of that tension during this exercise.

Let's begin with your feet. Gently curl your toes, squeezing them tight. Hold the tension . . . for just a few moments. Feel the tightness in your feet. And now, slowly, let go of the tension and let your feet relax completely. Feel the difference as your feet soften and release.

Next, bring your attention to your calves. Lift your toes up and back to tense the muscles in your calves, squeezing them as tightly as you can. Hold the tension for a few seconds . . . and now, release. Let your calves relax, allowing the muscles to soften. Feel the heaviness and relaxation there.

Now, focus on your thighs. Tighten your thigh muscles by squeezing them, bringing your thighs and knees closer together. Hold that tension . . . and then let go. Release the tension and notice how your thighs feel as they relax and loosen up.

> *Move your attention up to your hands and arms. Clench your fists, tightening your forearms as well. Hold the tension in your hands and arms for a few seconds... and then, release. Let your arms soften, feeling the relaxation in your hands and forearms as the muscles unwind.*
>
> *Now, focus on your shoulders. Raise your shoulders up toward your ears, as if you're shrugging them. Squeeze the muscles tight... and hold for a moment. Now, let them drop. Release the tension and allow your shoulders to feel heavy and relaxed.*
>
> *Next, bring your attention to your face. Tighten your face by clenching your jaw, furrowing your brow, and closing your eyes tight. Hold the tension... and now, slowly release. Let your face soften. Feel your jaw relax and your forehead smooth out.*
>
> *Finally, take a moment to scan through your entire body. Check in with each muscle group you've just relaxed. Notice how your body feels now—calmer, more at ease.*
>
> *Take a few deep breaths. Let each inhale bring in more relaxation, and each exhale release any remaining tension.*
>
> *When you feel ready, slowly bring your awareness back to the room. Gently wiggle your fingers and toes, and when you're ready, open your eyes, carrying this sense of relaxation with you.*

Concluding the Intensive

Although 12 hours sounds like a long time, the days speed by and before the therapist knows it they will find themselves nearly at the end of the intensive session. The following sections will provide an overview of each part of the final hour (or so) of an intensive. This format works well with various couple outcomes, although I recommend modifications for specific scenarios, as I will illustrate within the overview and the client vignettes that follow.

The Final Hour

As the therapist becomes aware that they are about two hours out from the end of the intensive, they should begin to plan for transitioning into the farewell conversation by changing the cadence of the session, wrapping up the ongoing conversation, and being aware of whether they are opening anything up that would require more time than is left.

As the final hour draws near, the therapist starts to close the final enactment and then segues by saying something like "It's hard to believe we are already in our final hour together. I want us to spend some time now reflecting on our time together, then discussing recommendations and takeaways, and, of course, planning for next steps. Let's start by reflecting."

> **COUPLES THERAPIST RESOURCE**
>
> ## The Parts of the Farewell Conversation
>
> The last hour of the intensive should focus on the farewell conversation, which includes:
>
> - Reflection from the couple and the therapist on goals, the experience, and progress
> - Recommendations and takeaways
> - Planning for next steps
> - Gratitude
>
> After the intensive, the therapist will send a follow-up email that summarizes the work that was done together and includes any recommendations or referrals.

REFLECTION

I start the final hour of an intensive by reflecting with the couple on their goals, the experience overall, and the progress they've made. Prior to offering my own reflections, I ask each partner to share their own. I use questions like the following:

- "When you think about your goals coming in yesterday and where you are today, what comes up for you?"
- "Tell me what you noticed today."
- "What were some things you learned about each other?"
- "Did anything surprise you about our time together?"
- "What was this experience like for you today?"

As is the case throughout the intensive, I direct the couple to talk about these things with each other. Although I've asked the questions, I don't need the answers provided to me. I want them to hear the answers from each other.

After they've reflected, I share my own reflections, which often include what I observed early in the intensive, the goals we set, what I've learned about them as individuals and as a couple throughout our time together, and how I've seen them grow.

An important caveat: If, at the end of the intensive, there is a reason why it would not be helpful for the couple to reflect (there is emotional dysregulation, the couple has decided to split and asking them to reflect while still integrating information would be unsettling, etc.), I will skip that part and proceed to my own reflections. During this time, I will observe whether it seems like the clients will be able to offer each other reflections or if they seem to still be in a dysregulated state.

RECOMMENDATIONS AND TAKEAWAYS

After we share our reflections, I ask the couple to share their biggest "takeaways" with me. These might include new insights about themselves, action steps they need to take, and commitments they've made to each other. I follow their takeaways by providing my recommendations for next steps. Throughout the intensive, I've been recommending activities to do at home, tools to use, patterns to pay attention to, and skills to practice; however, at this time I synthesize everything I've recommended and add anything I haven't yet mentioned but would like to encourage them to do.

I try to thread their own takeaways into my recommendations to connect my suggestions with the insights that meant the most to the couple.

PLANNING THE NEXT STEPS

Next, I discuss next steps with the couple. During this part of the session, we look together at whether it would be beneficial for the clients to continue couples therapy, and if so, whether they would like to see me or another therapist and whether it would be a third intensive day or traditional weekly therapy.

I also check in on any next professional steps the clients should take apart from couples therapy. For example, if a client indicated they were interested in individual therapy or a support group during the intensive, I will revisit that interest by asking how the client will take next steps toward that and by providing referrals or recommendations as requested.

GRATITUDE

Lastly, I ask the couple to share their gratitude with each other. There might be times when it is best to skip this stage—for example, perhaps the couple has decided to end the relationship and are antagonistic toward each other at the end of the session, so sharing gratitude would not be easily accessible to them. However, in most cases, the clients can share what they appreciated about each other by the end of the session.

Then, I share my own gratitude toward the couple, letting them know what I appreciated about our work together. I may share that it has been an honor to support them and express how grateful I am to have been given their trust.

At this, the session ends. I create a follow-up report to send the couple that includes the goals, takeaways, and next steps we discussed so the clients are able to remember and follow through on their plans.

The following stories of the couples we've followed throughout this book provide a more detailed picture of the farewell process and offer a few different examples of how intensives can end. Let's begin our farewells with Karl and Ebony, whose final hour required a slightly different approach from my usual format.

Ebony and Karl: The Final Hour

After Karl admitted that his affair was ongoing, couples therapy was no longer possible for him and Ebony. I would not have been able to help the couple, at that point, rebuild trust or reach their initial goals. Once she heard Karl's disclosure, Ebony stated that she would like a divorce and that she would not be able to move forward in the relationship.

Because of that, the second day of the intensive changed course. No longer would we be doing enactments, practicing speaking and listening exercises, or having Ebony ask questions to get the answers she needed. Instead, we all agreed it would be best to not meet as a unit for the rest of the session. I would work with each of them one-on-one for equal amounts of time to explore their individual next steps, provide them with resources, and discuss how they could best manage coparenting and welcoming a new baby into the world.

First I met with Karl, providing him psychoeducation on how to best navigate Ebony's decision to separate in a way that would be healthy for the children. I listened to Karl's anxiety and worries that were a result of the decision. I gave him resources on navigating a separation and coparenting effectively. We also discussed plans for leaving the intensive, which included Karl taking the car back to the house and then going to stay with his parents, allowing Ebony to have some space.

As the final hour with Karl approached, I provided him with a similar farewell to what we would have done if we were all meeting together. I asked Karl to reflect on our time together. He shared that while the intensive did bring up a new host of issues for him and Ebony to solve, he was grateful that it had happened. He recognized that his family legacy of secret-keeping had been standing in his way of being truthful and that if I had not challenged him, he likely would have maintained the lie. He said he felt relief knowing that the truth was out there and that he no longer had to keep up the facade. He explained that he wasn't sure why he had been kicking the can down the lane, but that the intensive made him realize he ultimately did not want to be in the marriage anymore and that it was unfair to Ebony to mislead her into believing he did.

I then reflected to Karl my own observations and thoughts regarding our time together. "I think you did a lot of work over the past day to respond differently to a family pattern. When you came into the intensive, you were willing to maintain the legacy of secret-keeping. But today, you decided to do things differently. That won't save your marriage, but it has the capacity to change things for your children."

I let Karl know my recommendations, keeping my voice calm and compassionate. "Karl, I highly recommend you continue therapy with a therapist who can help keep you accountable when it comes to this pattern of secrecy. If you don't change the pattern, I believe you'll continue to face hardship and cause pain."

I went on, "It's going to take time to navigate a divorce. It's a long and arduous path. Your goal with the divorce is reducing the negative impact on the children. It will be important for you to work on navigating the divorce in a way that honors their emotional needs and pays attention to the ways in which they might be impacted. When you and Ebony are ready, after some of the pain here has settled, it will likely be good for you to attend some family counseling or coparenting counseling. The goal will no longer be your marriage but to build good enough communication skills between the two of you so you can coparent."

I gave him a few moments to take in what I'd said before asking, "What do you think are your own takeaways from our time together?"

"I think my biggest takeaway is that I really need to work on this destructive secret-keeping. I'm so upset with my behavior. Shocked by it. I hated what my parents did to our family, yet I've caused so much destruction to my own family. I didn't want to be in this marriage, so why didn't I just say that? This really opened my eyes to what I need to change. I don't want my kids to have to deal with this. I hate that I've blown up their childhood like this."

I nodded encouragingly. "I know it must be very painful to reflect on how you've impacted your family. This is the first step toward making things right. So perhaps we add that a next step or goal for you is to consider how you will take care of yourself and get the therapy and support you need to change this pattern. And then second, to consider how to manage the guilt I can hear that you feel."

"Yeah." Karl looked down at his hands. "I don't know how I'll deal with this guilt."

"It's painful," I validated. After a few moments of silence, I added, "It sounds like you recognize you'll need support to manage the pain."

"Yes, and then I'll need to make it right with my kids," Karl responded.

"You can be different from your parents. You can take accountability. You will be different."

I segued into planning by asking Karl what his most immediate next steps were. He shared that, as agreed upon earlier, he would drive the car back to the house and then go to his mother's. He said that he would also look up some therapists when he get home as to not delay getting support.

"Should I get a lawyer?" he asked.

"I can't make those decision for you, but what I can say is that past clients have gotten attorneys with varying outcomes. What I would say is that for the sake of your children, if you do seek out counsel, look for someone that will want to work collaboratively and create as much of a low-conflict divorce as possible."

"I'll do that," he murmured.

When it became clear we had discussed goals and next steps thoroughly, I let Karl know our time together was coming to an end. Usually, I ask the couple to extend gratitude to each other at this point and then I also give gratitude toward them. This time, however, I just gave Karl my own gratitude.

"Karl, I know today was not easy. I'm grateful that you trusted me in this process, and I have a lot of gratitude for your honesty today. Thank you for coming clean. It allowed our work together to be honest."

Karl responded, "Thank you for helping me get there. It's a relief to be honest and I do think we will all be okay in the long run."

I let him know that I would send him some referrals and I wished him a safe drive home. At this, we said goodbye and Karl left the office.

I then got Ebony from the waiting room and spent the remaining time with her. When our final hour was approaching, I explained, "Our time is almost up, so there are some important things I'd like to discuss, if that's okay with you."

First, I asked Ebony, "When you think about the time we just spent together, what comes up for you?"

"So much." She looked at me with wide eyes. "This is certainly not what I expected."

"I know," I responded gently.

"I have to say that in a weird way, I am . . . relieved?" She smiled ruefully. "Living with him every day was painful. I had so much hate in my heart and it's not who I am. I don't want to be that way around my kids. I just knew deep inside that he wasn't being honest and so I couldn't let the rage go. I am devastated with what was shared today, but also I knew it—and so now I don't feel crazy and I don't have to be around him for the time being." At this, Ebony started to cry. "How am I going to have this baby alone? How could he do this to me?"

"It's terrible, Ebony," I validated. "It is terrible you have to go through this."

I let her cry for a moment. I didn't want to spend too long sharing my own reflections—there wasn't much else for me to say when Ebony and I had just spent the last hour or so discussing what had happened. But I did reflect that I had seen her pain, that I understood how the lies and uncertainty were impacting her, and that I had witnessed her make a very difficult and brave decision for herself.

Then, I asked her to talk to me about her own takeaways and plans. Ebony shared that the biggest takeaway for her was the compassion she feels for herself now that she understands her symptoms and responses are like PTSD. "That really helped me not feel so crazy," she said. "Now I understand why I'm having such a hard time."

She shared that, as we'd discussed earlier, she was going to get into therapy for herself. She had decided eye movement desensitization and reprocessing (EMDR) would be helpful. She identified her support people and repeated that she was going to lean on her mom, who was coming to get her from the appointment and would be staying with her for the week. We discussed her next steps for the divorce—she had decided she would contact a lawyer after she sat with her decision for a week and that she would only talk to the children about the separation after she took a little time to reflect. She hoped that for the sake of the children she and Karl could find a way of parenting together over time, but for now, she was interested in parallel parenting.

I gave her some referrals, then let her know how grateful I was for the opportunity to get to know her. I told her that I wished her the best and encouraged her to reach out for support from a therapist as soon as she could. I walked her down the hallway to where he mother was waiting to take her home. I watched her mom give her a big hug and Ebony cry into her shoulder. And with that, I walked back down the hallway to my office to write their note.

Months later, I received an email from Ebony. She expressed gratitude for our time together, saying how helpful it was to have enough time to process the painful news she received. She also thanked me for intervening with Karl regarding secrecy. She believed that had they not gone to the intensive, it would have taken much longer for her to uncover the affair and that she wouldn't have had the immediate support she received in the intensive. She reported that she and Karl were parallel parenting, as it was too hard for her to work directly with him, but that she was hopeful over time that would change. She was in EMDR therapy and finding it helpful. Lastly, she'd had the baby, her mother had moved in with her permanently, and she was finding her "new normal."

Karl referred another couple to me a few years later, leading me to assume the intensive ultimately made a positive mark on him, too.

If Karl and Ebony had attempted weekly therapy, it is my opinion he would have withheld the information for quite some time until it was discovered by Ebony. Likely the couple would have gone to a few sessions with a couples therapist in which Karl could maintain the facade. Then, the couple likely would have dropped out after the birth of the baby and not had time to come back. At some point, Ebony would have uncovered the affair, and this would have resulted in more pain.

Instead, not only did the intensive provide Karl time to build trust and courage to share the truth, but it also gave Ebony enough time to process with me and come up with a plan for next steps.

Kimmie and Selah: The Final Hour

Selah and Kimmie's session was naturally wrapping up as we reached the final hour. They finished the enactment they were in and then I directed them to notice the time: "We're about an hour out from being finished for the day. If it's okay with you, I'd like to transition into wrapping up our time together by reflecting on what you've done over the past two days, exploring recommendations, and then talking about next steps."

"Wow, I can't believe we're already at the final hour!" Kimmie responded.

"Same," Selah agreed. "You weren't lying when you said it flies by. I didn't believe you at first, but it really does go by fast."

"It wasn't nearly as painful as you expected?" I smiled at them.

"Not at all! This weekend has been great. It's been so helpful," Kimmie enthused, while Selah nodded in agreement.

I segued into reflection. "Tell me more. What has been helpful?"

"First of all, the time together has been helpful on its own. I don't know the last time we spent one hour talking together, let alone . . . what was it? Twelve hours?" Selah expressed.

Kimmie agreed, "Having time to talk was huge for us. As you know, we just don't get it."

"Share this with each other," I redirected them. Eagerly, they shifted in their seats to face each other.

"Selah, I loved talking to you," Kimmie said, sounding almost shy. "I think it was so helpful to have the time. I also think being forced by Liz"—she flashed me a smile—"to just sit and listen to you, and not interrupt or get into an argument, helped me to finally hear what you struggle with. I think I was too focused on myself before. It was good to hear that you aren't seeing me as unimportant but that you're struggling with your own stuff too. I guess I already knew that, but the way we talked here was more intimate and gentler."

Selah took Kimmie's hand. "I agree. I've been so focused on what I need to get done, I haven't really heard the real impact on you. I have heard your complaints . . . it's hard not to," she added in a playful tone. They both laughed. "But I just heard them through a lens of you being pushy instead of really caring about your feelings. So it was helpful to hear how things have impacted you. I'm sorry. I love you."

"I love you too," said Kimmie.

"Talk to each other about anything new you've learned about yourselves over our time together," I suggested.

"Well, I learned I am afraid of people." Selah laughed. "Just kidding . . . but it's kind of true. I try to avoid disappointing anyone, but then I disappoint everyone, including myself. It was important for me to hear how trying to make everyone happy is making you unhappy, Kimmie. Honestly, it makes me unhappy. So that was good insight to learn about myself. I want to work on that."

I waited for a moment to see if they'd naturally continue their conversation. When it seemed clear they needed further direction, I prompted Kimmie to share insights about herself.

"Well, I learned that when I feel shut out, I get critical," said Kimmie, "and that's not something I like about myself. That was a powerful insight for me. And it's something I want to change."

"Is there anything else you want to talk about regarding the experience? Anything you've learned or experienced that feels important to discuss?" I asked.

"I think we are a great couple," Kimmie said. "I'm sure you have people come in here who are mean to each other and are in awful positions with each other. As we talked, I realized in the grand scheme of things we have such a wonderful relationship, and we're just experiencing a stressor. Life is out to get us right now, but we'll be okay."

Selah squeezed Kimmie's hand in agreement.

"If you're open to it," I said, "I'd like to share with you my own reflections of our time together."

"Absolutely," they agreed almost in unison.

"When you came in," I began, "you shared that you'd been distant with each other and that you felt disconnected and withdrawn. You shared that this didn't really fit with the rest of your experience of the relationship and that you were worried about what it could mean. I noticed quickly how strong of a relationship you have. I remember in the first hour or so, there was a moment when you started to get into an argument and you both did a beautiful job of using humor and warmth to repair. I also really enjoyed hearing how you talked about your early days.

"So, early on, I could see you had a strong relationship and that it seemed like there was a lot going on with boundaries, stress, and your pattern of conflict. We talked about all of that, and your ultimate goal was to be more connected. In order to do that, we wanted to improve the conflict patterns, figure out what was going on with boundaries and priorities, and also work on how to navigate your current stressors.

"There were a few things that really stuck out to me," I continued. "First, your ability as a couple to take feedback from each other is remarkable. Second, I thought it was profound when we mapped your conflict pattern—it seemed like something clicked for both of you regarding that cycle and you were each able to take away some ideas for how to change the pattern. Lastly, I saw you both take personal accountability for the ways in which you've contributed to this period being more difficult between the two of you.

"Do you have any thoughts about what I've said?" I asked.

"No, that all sounds right on. I think those are the things that stick out to me too. What about you, Kimmie?" Selah asked.

"I agree," said Kimmie.

"How about takeaways?" I prompted. "What would you like to do with these new insights? What are you committed to doing at home?"

"Well, I want to work on using soft start-up," Kimmie shared. "That was helpful to learn about. I need to print out the steps and put them on my desk so I don't forget."

"I need to have a conversation with my dad and brother and start working with them to come up with other forms of support. I feel really motivated to start working on that tomorrow," Selah said.

Kimmie added, "I also think it's a takeaway for both of us that we need to make the time for each other. It won't just happen on its own, and when we let time get away from us, we end up in a bad spot. So, I want us to pick times we commit to protecting for each other."

"These are really good takeaways." I paused to let their reflections settle. "I've given you some recommendations while we've talked together, and I want to touch on them again. I am going to write this down for you, but here's a quick overview. First, I recommended that you do a State of the Union Meeting every week. This will help you stay in tune with each other's worlds. I encourage you to pick the same time every week and come up with a nice way to sit down and talk. During your talk, you'll check in with each other about what you appreciate, what went well over the week, and any concerns or plans that need to be made."

COUPLES THERAPIST RESOURCE

The State of The Union Meeting

The State of the Union Meeting, a common homework assignment in Gottman Method Couples Therapy, is a structured conversation designed to help partners check in with each other and discuss the health of their relationship. The meeting is inspired by regular "State of the Union" addresses in politics, where leaders assess and communicate what is occurring within a country or other geopolitical entity. Similarly, in relationships, this meeting provides couples a chance to assess and improve the state of their partnership.

The meeting involves the following steps, which can be changed to suit the couple's needs (Panganiban, 2023):

- **Set aside time:** Schedule the meeting when both partners are relaxed and have the time to engage fully. This ensures that the conversation isn't rushed and both partners can give their full attention.
- **Create a safe space and design a ritual:** The meeting should take place in a nonjudgmental, respectful environment where both partners feel heard and valued. The goal is not to criticize but to communicate openly. Creating a safe and enjoyable space can be done by ritualizing the event (for example, always having the meeting with Sunday morning coffee).
- **Follow a structured format:** The meeting is typically divided into four key sections:
  - *Five appreciations:* The partners begin by sharing positive aspects of the relationship. This helps set a tone of appreciation.
  - *What went right:* The partners share what has gone right in the relationship recently.
  - *An issue to discuss:* The partners take turns sharing any current issues or concerns in the relationship.
  - *Action plan:* The partners discuss what can be done over the next week to support each other, maintain connection, and improve any issues between them.
- **Active listening and validation:** Each partner should practice active listening, offering empathy and validating each other's feelings. The goal is mutual understanding, not solving everything in one sitting.
- **End on a positive note:** The partners wrap up the meeting by reinforcing their positive intentions and emphasizing their love and commitment in the relationship.

"The next thing I recommend," I continued, "is that you hang this picture of your pattern somewhere, as a reminder of your current conflict cycle, and make a commitment to just change one dance move. Kimmie, yours is to be softer when you notice Selah is withdrawing. Selah, yours is to work on engaging, even if it means just engaging to let Kimmie know you need space.

"I also want you to work on the antidotes to the four horsemen—thinking about how to avoid criticism, defensiveness, stonewalling, and contempt.

"And lastly, use the speaker/listener exercise a few times a week to check in on each other and commit to just following that process. Even if it feels rigid, it will help you build the listening muscle, which will improve emotional intimacy."

"How does that all sound?" I asked.

"It sounds great. I'm really looking forward to trying these things and continuing to see everything improve," Selah responded. Kimmie agreed.

"Let's spend a little bit of time talking about next steps," I said. "Based on the progress you've made, I don't think you need regular therapy; however, I do think having little check-ins time and again might be helpful to you. This means meeting with a couples therapist in your area who can check in on how you're both doing with all the stress and give you ideas and support for staying connected. What do you think about that recommendation?"

"I agree—I don't think we need weekly therapy," Kimmie answered, "nor do I think we have time for it. But there is something nice about having time carved out with a third party who can help guide the conversation and provide suggestions and feedback. I'd like to do something like that."

"I like that idea too," Selah said. "I agree with both of you—I don't think we need anything weekly. I'd like us to test out what we've learned here and see how things go for a month or so, and then maybe meet with someone once a month."

"Would you like me to provide some referrals?" I offered.

"That would be really helpful," Kimmie replied.

"Great, I'll do that. And, if you'd like to sign a release, I would be happy to provide all the information from our intensive session with the therapist so you're not starting completely from scratch."

Selah and Kimmie both agreed that they'd like to sign a release. From there, I moved toward closing out the session with gratitude.

"Now, Selah and Kimmie, I'd like you to look at each other and share why you're grateful toward each other right now. It could be feelings of gratitude related to the work here in the intensive or other feelings of gratitude that arise."

Kimmie and Selah held each other's hands and smiled.

"I'm so grateful to you, Kimmie," Selah shared. "You've been so supportive of me over the past year, and I know you are always there for me even if we are distant. I'm glad we decided to do this together. I know you've been hurt, and so I'm grateful you opened your heart to talk to me about everything that's going on."

Kimmie gave Selah a hug and expressed her gratitude as well. She shared that she knew how hard it had been for Selah to make everyone happy and how much stress Selah had been under. "I know making time for this wasn't easy," she acknowledged. "I'm so thankful you did it for us."

I expressed my thanks to them, letting them know it was an honor getting to know them and that I appreciated their openness and willingness to engage in the therapy process. I reminded them that I would be sending my recommendations to them later. We said our goodbyes, and Selah and Kimmie left the session to travel back home.

Later in the afternoon, I sent them an email as promised with my recommendations, attachments for exercises I would like for them to do at home, and referrals for couples therapists in their area. Finally, I thanked them again and wished them well.

For Selah and Kimmie, the intensive provided time that was otherwise hard to find for the type of intimate conversations they wanted. If the couple had tried weekly therapy, they likely still would have had success, as their relationship had a strong foundation; however, the intensive helped them more quickly identify their issue and begin to develop the skills they needed to become closer with each other.

> ## Ron and Andrew: The Final Hour
>
> Andrew and Ron had come to therapy because their relationship was hanging on by a thread. After a series of terrible arguments and feelings of abandonment throughout their relationship, Andrew seemed certain the relationship was over—both feet out the door. I didn't have much hope that he would change his mind; I believed that the work done in the intensive would result in supporting Andrew and Ron as they parted ways.
>
> However, as therapists, we know that the couples we work with can surprise us, and that is why it's important for us to be open to being surprised. As their intensive progressed, Andrew began to move a foot back inside the door. He learned more about himself and Ron, they practiced new communication and soothing skills, and Andrew seemed more open to the idea that the relationship could continue.
>
> When we had about three hours left in the session, we moved into discussing what Andrew and Ron would like to do regarding the relationship moving forward.
>
> "There is a type of counseling called discernment counseling," I explained, "where the counselor helps a couple who has uncertainty about the future discern between three paths for their relationship."

COUPLES THERAPIST RESOURCE

Discernment Counseling

Discernment counseling was developed by William Doherty (Doherty et al., 2015) to help mixed-agenda couples decide whether they would like to end their relationship or work toward reconciliation. He developed this process after recognizing that mixed-agenda couples were not well served by couples therapy—which is focused on improving the relationship—before determining whether they'd even like to remain in the relationship.

Discernment counseling is not couples therapy; rather, it is used to help the couple decide whether they'd like to do couples therapy. In discernment counseling, the couple is developing clarity on the relationship and their individual contributions to the relationship issues. The emphasis is placed on differentiation and self-responsibility, which help the clients to make the clearest decision about their relationship.

In discernment counseling, there are three paths described to the couple:

- **Path 1: Stay the course**—The couple neither separates nor does couples therapy. They choose to maintain the status quo.

- **Path 2: Separation or divorce**—The couple decides to end the relationship.

- **Path 3: Six months of couples therapy**—Divorce is temporarily taken off the table and the couple commits to making a good-faith effort to improve their relationship through six months of couples therapy. After the six months, they check in with each other and decide to either fully commit to or end the relationship.

A study of couples who went through discernment counseling showed that 47 percent decided on couples therapy to work toward reconciling, 41 percent choose to separate, and the remainder chose to maintain the status quo (Doherty et al., 2015).

I paused to ensure that Ron and Andrew were still with me. They looked engaged and curious, so I continued, explaining how discernment counseling works and the three paths it presents to the couple. After a pause to let them process the information, I asked, "What are your reactions to those three paths?"

"I know I'm all in," Ron responded. "My hope would be that we could commit to six months of couples therapy with everything we've learned today as the foundation and really give ourselves an opportunity to improve with the support of a professional."

I nodded, letting Ron knew I heard him, then turned to Andrew. "How about you, Andrew?"

Andrew let out a sigh. He looked at me and then at Ron. "I really want to give it a shot, Ron, but I'm nervous. I can't go through what I've already been through."

Ron took a deep breath and centered himself. This was new for Ron, and I could see it had been developed over the work he had done during the intensive. He said, "Andrew, I want you to do what's best for you. I can commit to taking couples therapy really seriously and I also want to do individual therapy, but I understand you might not trust me."

Andrew's expression softened. "I'm still worried," he shared, "but I think our conversations today really opened my eyes to the fact that we could have a good relationship. I regret that we didn't do this sooner. I know a lot of the focus today has been on how I am upset with you, but I also have grown to recognize today that it isn't all you. I have avoided our conflicts and not been honest about my feelings, and that hasn't helped us."

I let Andrew and Ron continue to talk back and forth. Unlike earlier conversations, they were able to engage and dialogue with each other rather than become flooded and reactive. It was very different from what they had experienced with each other in the past. Ron was able to hear Andrew without reacting and then withdrawing, and Andrew was able to speak up and express himself without becoming passive or completely cutting off from Ron. This was growth.

As we reached the final hour, I redirected them to our farewell conversation. "We are nearing the end of our time together," I smiled. "How are you both feeling about that?"

"I wish we had more time," Andrew lamented.

"I know," I said, "It's so many hours, but sometimes it doesn't feel like enough."

"I could do another day of this," Ron agreed. "I'm exhausted and would need a break of about a week, but I think we need more time."

"Well, it sounds like you've decided that you do want more couples therapy," I said.

"Yes," Andrew responded. "I really like the idea of taking separation off the table for six months and giving our best effort to improve our relationship during that time. I think that I was having a hard time making a decision because I really wasn't ready to end the relationship, but I also felt like I wasn't willing to continue as it was. This gives me an option that doesn't feel forced. It feels right."

> [Here, I allowed the flow of the farewell to be different from usual. Instead of forcing us to start with reflections, I followed Andrew and Ron's lead. They opened up a conversation regarding the plan for next steps, so I wanted to go there with them. I would then transition from this conversation into reflections and come back to the plans they've made at the end again.]

"That makes sense," I affirmed. "Ron, do you agree with this?"

"Absolutely," Ron answered. "I will do whatever it takes."

"So, it sounds like your next steps after our intensive will be for you to commit to six months of couples therapy with each other. I would be happy to meet with you for those sessions, or I can provide referrals if you'd like to go somewhere closer to home. It's up to you."

With a look at Ron to confirm, Andrew said, "I think we'd like to continue to meet with you. Would it be possible for us to do some of the sessions in person and some virtually?"

"Yes, we could work that out," I agreed. "After our meeting today, we can look at our calendars and figure out what works for everyone. I do ask that if we are meeting weekly, we commit to the same time each week, as I believe that creates the best path toward success."

"We can agree to that," Ron said.

"I know you also both mentioned wanting individual therapy—do you need any referrals for that?"

"I had a therapist I used to go to that I really liked," Andrew expressed. "I think I'll go back to him."

Ron requested some referrals and I made a note to send those to him after our session.

"This sounds like a plan," I said. "Now, I'd like to hear your reflections from the work you did these past two days. What have you learned? Or understood differently about each other?"

Ron shared that he better understood how his behavior was not only hurtful in the moment, but also had brought up feelings in Andrew related to his painful childhood abandonment. Ron also expressed that it was an aha moment for him to understand what happens to him physiologically when he feels threatened. "I am much more aware now of how important it is for me to find a way to calm myself down before continuing the conversation."

Andrew shared next. "I understand a lot more about Ron," he began.

"Tell Ron," I urged.

Andrew turned to address his partner. "It makes sense that when you feel upset, you do the things you do based on your childhood. And I can understand that the way I avoid sharing my feelings might trigger some of that for you. I've also realized we just didn't have the skills. Today already felt better just because we learned some new things. I really liked the idea of repairs."

Once Andrew and Ron finished sharing their reflections with each other, I shared mine. I reflected on how they had entered the intensive—a mixed-agenda couple unsure about the future—and how they managed conflict during the earlier hours of the intensive. Then, I shared with them the growth I saw: that already they were beginning to speak on their feelings, regulate their emotions, and show openness toward each other.

At this point, I asked Ron and Andrew to share with me their takeaways.

Andrew responded that he was committed to accepting more repairs from Ron—that instead of becoming rigid, he would be open. Ron expressed a commitment toward taking breaks when he becomes flooded. They both wanted to work on expressing their emotions. "Maybe we should print out the feelings wheel," Andrew proposed.

Then it was my turn to share my recommendations. "First, as we've already discussed, I recommend consistent, weekly couples therapy. With that, I want to urge you both to remove divorce talk from your language. When you're angry it becomes easier to threaten that, so you have to make a strong commitment not to do it. In order for couples therapy to be effective, there has to be a sense that you can rely on the other person to be committed to it just as much as you are."

Ron and Andrew nodded.

"Second, I want you to try to abstain from alcohol through the course of couples therapy. This can be something you talk more with your individual therapists about and we can discuss it more in our future sessions. A pattern throughout many of your worst arguments is that there was drinking involved. When people drink, they are more impulsive, and so you're more likely to say or do things you don't actually mean. Let's not muddy the waters further."

They both agreed that alcohol seemed to be a contributing factor and that they'd like to continue to get support on how to have fun together without alcohol being involved.

"Next, I'd like you to find 20 minutes a day to check in with each other. Let's pick a time now."

Andrew and Ron decided they'd do it around 8 p.m., before winding down for bed.

"This check-in can be quick," I added, "but I think it will help you build in more security with each other, as it's a time you can rely on. Check in on how each other's days went. Offer affection.

"Other than that, I don't need you to do much at home other than to focus on what we discussed—making repairs, de-escalating by taking breaks if needed, talking about your emotions. But I will continue to support you in those areas while we continue to meet. Do you have any thoughts about anything I shared?"

"Is there a way you could write this down for us?" Andrew asked.

"Oh yes! I forgot to tell you—I'll send you an email after this with all my recommendations so you have it to look at."

"Great!" Andrew smiled. "That helps."

"Now, I'd like for the two of you to look at each other and offer some gratitude toward each other for the past two days. What do you appreciate?"

Ron turned toward Andrew. "I appreciate that you were willing to give this a shot. I recognize that I've been a difficult partner and I've hurt you, and it means so much to me that you still showed up yesterday and were willing to hear me. I appreciate that you're willing to give couples therapy and our relationship a chance."

Andrew nodded. "I appreciate that you were open to the feedback you got this weekend and that you let Liz guide us. Even when you got upset, you tried to do something differently. I really do appreciate that. It's given me a lot of hope."

Andrew and Ron gave each other a hug.

Then, I shared my appreciations with them. "I want to let you know I really appreciate both of you and the work we've done together. It's truly been an honor to sit with you and to learn more about you. I also am grateful to have the opportunity to continue to work with you."

After this, we looked at our calendars together to pick a consistent time for our future meetings. Finally, I let them know our time was done, reminded them to expect an email from me with the recommendations, and said goodbye until the next week.

Ron and Andrew's intensive was effective because they were able to spend a sustained amount of time with each other, which allowed them to move past reactivity and begin to consider options from a more differentiated and grounded place. In my opinion, had Ron and Andrew tried weekly therapy, they likely would have struggled to move past their status quo. In between the weekly sessions, they would have had more arguments, which would have hurt the relationship further and made the therapy convoluted. Instead, they were given a long period of time to discuss their issues, process their feelings, and learn new skills—all of which helped them to maintain some of the growth they had made between the intensive and their next therapy session. The intensive served as an opportunity to "clean things up" and kick-start the rest of the process.

John and Amy: The Final Hour

Amy and John were able to go through the *Fair Play* cards together, assigning and reassigning tasks to create a more equitable distribution of mental and physical labor in their home. They both agreed that this exercise helped them to better conceptualize all of the tasks that needed to get done in their house. For John, it was a physical reminder of how much Amy was carrying—"Seeing it as a stack of cards makes me realize how much she was doing."

After this, Amy and John were on better terms. I let them know that in our final hour, I wanted us to reflect on the process, discuss recommendations and takeaways, and explore a plan for next steps. I started by asking them to reflect on our time together.

Amy shared, "I didn't know what to expect at all when we came in here, but I knew I was so miserable that I had to take the risk of trying this. Otherwise, we wouldn't have any time to work on things."

Amy was turned toward me, so I gestured toward John.

"Oh, right. Sorry. John, I think I learned a lot more about you and also a lot more about myself. It was helpful for me to spend so much time talking about our relationship—both listening to you and being able to talk to you."

"What about for you, John?" I asked.

John looked toward Amy and shared, "Yeah, I agree. I think I knew even less about what to expect than you did—not surprising, since you were the one to plan it. And I think that's what I learned: I really was not aware of how much you do or how stressed you were. I also was really dismissive. I see now that there was a lot that I could have been helping with that I didn't. It was helpful to hear how you believe you have to take on all of this to be a good wife . . . I need to do more to make sure you know you're amazing, so you don't feel the need to always have to work hard to prove it."

Amy started crying, which meant John had hit the mark—he understood something about her she wanted to be understood.

I then began to share my reflections. I noted that at first, Amy was so upset that she was considering ending the relationship. Early on, it became clear that Amy didn't really want to end the relationship but she felt unsure of how else to express how overwhelmed and upset she was. "I think that moment made it really clear how serious this was for Amy. She felt so much pain that she didn't know what else to say other than to say she needed to end the relationship."

I went on, "I noticed during the session that you both seemed to have a continued willingness to understand each other more and more. I saw you both really grow in your ability to hear each other out and work toward negotiating your differences. I also think we were able to identify some bigger issues that are making it difficult for the two of you to navigate your lives: how much stress you have and how chaotic it feels, which you called 'the Burdens of Life,' and also these stories you have about who you 'should' be in this relationship—what it means to be a good mom and wife, what it means to be a good dad and husband. These stories are fogging your view of other ways you could be together. They have too much power in your relationship."

"Yeah, I really want to think about how much of what I do is driven by stories I have," Amy agreed.

"Based on the new skills you've learned and agreements you've made, what are some takeaways? How do you want to use our work together in your lives moving forward?"

"Well," Amy began. "The most tangible is that we have an agreement for the vacation and some agreements on redistributing the household tasks. That feels huge. I'm excited to go home and just plan the trip instead of arguing about it. And to have John take on some of the tasks that were overwhelming me."

"I agree," said John. "I think the way we learned to do negotiation was a big takeaway for me. I'd like to keep using that process when we disagree from now on. It made it much easier to come up with something. Otherwise we just go back and forth, and someone tries to win."

"Those would be my recommendations too," I shared. "What do you think about plans for therapy? Do you think you need continued support?"

"I do think we would benefit from continued therapy, but there's no way we can do it weekly," Amy replied. "I was wondering if we could do a third day of this in like a month or so? I think this format works better for our schedules."

"We could do that. I agree that continued therapy would be good for you both to support you as you try this new distribution of the household labor and to help you navigate all the Burdens of Life by building new skills together. I think we could meet in four to six weeks to check in for four hours. How does that sound?"

Amy and John agreed, and we picked a date and time to meet.

Lastly, I guided them to share their gratitude toward each other.

John started by sharing, "Amy, I am so grateful to you and everything you do for us. I know you do a lot. I'm sorry I was dismissive, and I appreciate that you brought us here for this. I love you." He gave her a wink. She smiled, leaned in, and kissed him.

"I'm grateful you came even though you didn't understand why it was a big deal," Amy said to John. "I appreciate your taking my feedback and being open to hearing how things were for me. And I appreciate how we were able to come to some agreements together today and not get so stuck. I do hope that we can continue it—I worry with how busy things are . . ."

I interrupted gently, "Amy, let's just stick with gratitude right now." Amy was getting close to becoming critical, and I didn't want them to get back into an argument.

Amy laughed. "Oh gosh, sometimes I can't stop myself. John, I am just grateful. Thank you." She hugged him. Then they both looked at me.

"Well, that is the end of our session today. What are you both going to do after you leave here today?" They spend a few moments telling me their plans, then I let them know I would be sending them a recommendation email, we said goodbye, and they left.

I met with them several weeks later as a check-in. At that point, they shared that the redistribution of chores had been helpful but that they wanted to rework some more things, they'd had a nice vacation, and they'd continued to use their new negotiation skills.

The intensive format was helpful for Amy and John for two main reasons: First, they didn't have much time in their schedules to commit to weekly therapy. If they had started weekly therapy, they would likely have been inconsistent and had difficulty even getting through the assessment process. Second, the couple had several disagreements that required longer, guided conversations toward agreements. The intensive format provided them enough time to practice negotiating with each other.

The Follow-Up Email

Following the intensive, the therapist should provide a follow-up note to close the loop. This email includes brief reflections, recommendations, referrals, and any attachments the couple might need for exercises to do at home. You can use the following sheet to keep track of these items during the session.

Special Considerations for the Final Hour

Most intensives end as they did with the examples I've described. Occasionally, however, the couple might choose not to come back for the second day of their intensive or you might uncover information that leads you to choose not to continue working with the couple. Please refer to the policies section of this book (beginning on page 26) for more information on planning for and navigating those situations.

Sometimes, if you choose to offer this option, the couple will schedule three days of intensive therapy up front. In this case, the third day will look the same as the second regarding enactments, exercises, and interventions, and the farewell conversation will occur in the final hour of the third day.

COUPLES THERAPIST WORKSHEET

Intensive Session Follow-Up Notes

Below, write down the reflections, takeaways, recommendations, referral information, and any other notes you'd like to keep track of for the follow-up email.

Couple's Reflections

Write what the couple shared as reflections.

_____
_____
_____
_____

Therapist Reflections

Write the couple's initial goal for therapy and your reflections on their work together.

_____
_____
_____
_____

Recommendations and Takeaways

Write down any commitments the couple has made and practices they want to continue, as well as your recommendations for homework.

_____
_____
_____
_____

Referrals/Plans

Write down any referral information or plans for further work (e.g., continued couples therapy, individual therapy, support groups).

_____
_____
_____
_____

Attachments

Note any links or files you'd like to attach to your follow-up email (e.g., instructions for exercises).

_____
_____
_____
_____

Other

Write any other notes you'd like to send the couple in the follow-up email.

_____
_____
_____
_____

Conclusion

Intensives are a powerful model of couples therapy, and they provide a unique opportunity to dive deep into the heart of relational issues—issues that often take far too long to address in the typical weekly model. This format allows therapists to take the time that is so often missing from traditional therapy to assess and intervene in patterns that have been ingrained for months, years, or a lifetime. The intensive model also helps couples stabilize and regulate in ways that lead to lasting change because the therapist has the time to support them as they build the skills needed to improve, repair, or separate.

Reflecting back on my first intensive experience with Harry and Leona, whose relationship had been deeply impacted by infidelity, I recall their pain and their urgency. It would have been incredibly difficult for them to repair their relationship when meeting for only one hour a week. Leona was raising the possibility of divorce, while Harry was emotionally frozen and unable to respond in a way that could heal the rift. They were in crisis, and I knew I couldn't ask them to wait weeks for help. That moment marked a turning point for me. I offered them an all-day session on a Saturday, an instinctual decision that turned out to be transformative. It was in that long-format session that I began to understand and feel committed to the unique power of intensive therapy. Not only did Leona and Harry leave with a sense of hope, but I felt energized and inspired in a way that traditional 50-minute sessions had never allowed me to experience.

As I continue to explore and refine this model, I am continually reminded of how powerful it can be for both the therapists conducting intensives and the couples whose lives are transformed through their participation. The extended time allows us to dive deeper into the issues that often can't be resolved in shorter sessions. As I've shared throughout this book, intensives provide the time to help couples process emotions, communicate effectively, and regulate their responses. We can go beyond surface-level problems and begin to address the root causes of dysfunction—whether it is patterns from childhood, unresolved trauma, or deeply embedded relational habits.

The stories in this book—Andrew and Ron, Ebony and Karl, Kimmie and Selah, and Amy and John—demonstrate the diverse presenting issues and outcomes of this intensive approach. Each couple faced unique challenges, but all benefited from the structure, length, and depth that intensives allow. These examples also show how some cases are straightforward while others take a more winding path as the therapist helps the couple to clarify their goals, delve into their presenting issues, and create positive change over the course of the weekend.

Intensives don't just push couples toward new insights, change, and decision-making; they also push the therapist. Working with couples in this way forces us to grow in our professional journeys by becoming more skilled at navigating complex emotional terrain, recognizing patterns, offering interventions in real time, and building a deepened level of self-awareness so that our own projections don't interfere in the work. In short, therapists who offer intensives must have a deep knowledge of the field and themselves and be able to think on their feet. All of this can be gained through practice, continual openness to learning, and supervision.

I encourage you to set aside some time in the near future to continue exploring this model. Because couples therapy intensives will introduce the therapist to a variety of topics beyond the scope of this book, I encourage anyone offering intensives to be in continued supervision and training. As you gain experience in this format and tailor it to your own modality and specializations, my hope is that you will find it as fulfilling and invigorating for your couples as I have with mine.

References

For your convenience, worksheets from this book are available for download at www.pesipubs.com/intensivecouples

Ainsworth, M. D. S., Blehar, M. C., Waters, E., & Wall, S. (1978). *Strange Situation Procedure (SSP)* [Database record]. APA PsycTests. https://doi.org/10.1037/t28248-000

Aponte, H. J., & Kissil, K. (Eds.). (2016). *The person of the therapist training model: Mastering the use of self*. Routledge.

Arduman, E. (2020, August 24). *Getting to the truth through cross-tracking*. The PACT Institute. https://www.thepactinstitute.com/blog/getting-to-the-truth-through-cross-tracking

Bowen Center for the Study of the Family. (n.d.). *Differentiation of self*. Retrieved March 6, 2025, from https://www.thebowencenter.org/differentiation-of-self

Bowen, M. (1978). *Family therapy in clinical practice*. Jason Aronson.

Bowlby, J. (1973). *Attachment and loss: Vol. 2. Separation: Anxiety and anger*. Basic Books.

Brown, R. L., & Rounds, L. A. (1995). Conjoint screening questionnaires for alcohol and other drug abuse: Criterion validity in a primary care practice. *Wisconsin Medical Journal, 94*(3), 135–140.

Butler, M. H., & Gardner, B. C. (2003). Adapting enactments to couple reactivity: Five developmental stages. *Journal of Marital and Family Therapy, 29*(3), 311–328. https://doi.org/10.1111/j.1752-0606.2003.tb01209.x

Butler, M. H., Harper, J. M., & Mitchell, C. B. (2011). A comparison of attachment outcomes in enactment-based versus therapist-centered therapy process modalities in couple therapy. *Family Process, 50*(2), 203–220. https://doi.org/10.1111/j.1545-5300.2011.01355.x

Bütz, M. R. (1991). Negotiation as a therapeutic technique in brief couples therapy. *Mediation Quarterly, 8*(3), 211–223. https://doi.org/10.1002/crq.3900080306

Carey, M. (2019). Externalizing in narrative therapy with couples and families. In J. L. Lebow, A. L. Chambers, & D. C. Breunlin (Eds.), *Encyclopedia of couple and family therapy* (pp. 990–994). Springer. https://doi.org/10.1007/978-3-319-49425-8_822

Carey, M., & Russel, S. (2021, October 4). *Externalising – Commonly-asked questions*. The Dulwich Centre. https://dulwichcentre.com.au/articles-about-narrative-therapy/externalising/

Christensen, A., & Heavey, C. L. (1990). Gender and social structure in the demand/withdraw pattern of marital conflict. *Journal of Personality and Social Psychology, 59*(1), 73–81. https://doi.org/10.1037/0022-3514.59.1.73

Collins, N. L., Guichard, A. C., Ford, M. B., & Feeney, B. C. (2004). Working models of attachment: New developments and emerging themes. In W. S. Rholes & J. A. Simpson (Eds.), *Adult attachment: Theory, research, and clinical implications* (pp. 196–239). Guilford Press.

Combs, G., & Freedman, J. (2004). A poststructuralist approach to narrative work. In L. E. Angus & J. McLeod (Eds.), *The Handbook of Narrative and Psychotherapy* (pp. 137–155). SAGE Publications. https://doi.org/10.4135/9781412973496.d11

The Couples Institute. (n.d.). *Couples intensives training*. https://www.couplesinstitute.com/couples-intensives-training-workshop

Danna, J. (2011). *Therapist and client experience of collaborative assessment: A qualitative study* [Doctoral dissertation, Duquesne University]. Duquesne University. https://dsc.duq.edu/etd/456

Davis, S. D., & Butler, M. H. (2004). Enacting relationships in marriage and family therapy: A conceptual and operational definition of an enactment. *Journal of Marital and Family Therapy, 30*(3), 319–333. https://doi.org/10.1111/j.1752-0606.2004.tb01243.x

Dehnavi, T. G., Yousefi, Z., & Farhadi, H. (2023). The effectiveness of Imago therapy on marital satisfaction and emotional experience towards the spouse among the men with marital conflicts. *Journal of Education and Health Promotion, 12*(1), Article 418. https://doi.org/10.4103/jehp.jehp_520_22

Dennett, D. C. (2013). *Intuition pumps and other tools for thinking.* W. W. Norton & Company.

Derogatis, L., Lipman, R., & Covi, L. (1973). SCL-90: An outpatient psychiatric rating scale—Preliminary report. *Psychopharmacology Bulletin, 9*(1), 13–28.

Doherty, W. J., Harris, S. M., & Mussa, K. (2024). Relationship undermining in couple therapy. *Contemporary Family Therapy, 46,* 243–248. https://doi.org/10.1007/s10591-024-09702-2

Doherty, W. J., Harris, S. M., & Wilde, J. L. (2015). Discernment counseling for "mixed-agenda" couples. *Journal of Marital and Family Therapy, 42*(2), 246–255. https://doi.org/10.1111/jmft.12132

Earnshaw, E. (2024a). *The couples therapy flip chart: A psychoeducational tool to help couples identify patterns of disconnection, manage relationship conflict, and create a thriving partnership.* PESI.

Earnshaw, E. (2024b). *'Til stress do us part: How to heal the #1 issue in our relationships.* Sounds True.

Erskine, R. G., & Zalcman, M. J. (1979). The racket system: A model for racket analysis. *Transactional Analysis Journal, 9*(1), 51–59. https://doi.org/10.1177/036215377900900112

Fisher, R., & Ury, W. (2012). *Getting to yes: Negotiating agreement without giving in* (3rd ed.). Random House Business.

Foster, D. A., Caplan, R. D., & Howe, G. W. (1997). Representativeness of observed couple interaction: Couples can tell, and it does make a difference. *Psychological Assessment, 9*(3), 285–294. https://doi.org/10.1037/1040-3590.9.3.285

Frank, J. D. (1974). Common features of psychotherapies and their patients. *Psychotherapy and Psychosomatics, 24*(4/6), 368–371. http://www.jstor.org/stable/45114354

Gaines, S. O., Jr., & Ickes, W. (1997). Perspectives on interracial relationships. In S. Duck (Ed.), *Handbook of personal relationships: Theory, research, and interventions* (pp. 197–220). Wiley.

Gladding, S. T. (2014). *Family therapy: History, theory, and practice* (6th ed.). Pearson.

Goicoechea, J., Rickard, K., Hallinan, T., & Sampson, K. (2009, March 4–8). *Clients' experiences of collaborative assessment at the Duquesne University Psychology Clinic* [Paper presentation]. Annual Conference for the Society for Personality Assessment, Chicago, IL, United States.

Gottman, J. M. (1993). A theory of marital dissolution and stability. *Journal of Family Psychology, 7*(1), 57–75. https://doi.org/10.1037/0893-3200.7.1.57

Gottman, J. M. (1994). *Why marriages succeed or fail.* Simon & Schuster.

Gottman, J. M. (1999). *The marriage clinic: A scientifically based marital therapy.* W. W. Norton & Company.

Gottman, J. M. (2011). *The science of trust: Emotional attunement for couples.* W. W. Norton & Company.

Greenberg, L. S. (2017). Introduction. In L. S. Greenberg, *Emotion-focused therapy* (Rev. ed., pp. 3–11). American Psychological Association. https://doi.org/10.1037/15971-001

Gurman, A. S., & Fraenkel, P. (2002). The history of couple therapy: A millennial review. *Family Process, 41*(2), 199–260. https://doi.org/10.1111/j.1545-5300.2002.41204.x

Gurman, A. S., Lebow, J., & Snyder, D. K. (Eds.). (2015). *Clinical handbook of couples therapy* (5th ed.). The Guilford Press.

Hare-Mustin, R. T. (1978). A feminist approach to family therapy. *Family Process, 17*(2), 181–194. https://doi.org/10.1111/j.1545-5300.1978.00181.x

Hawkins, M. W., Carrère, S., & Gottman, J. M. (2002). Marital sentiment override: Does it influence couples' perceptions? *Journal of Marriage and Family, 64*(1), 193–201. https://doi.org/10.1111/j.1741-3737.2002.00193.x

Heaven, P. C. L., Smith, L., Prabhakar, S. M., Abraham, J., & Mete, M. E. (2006). Personality and conflict communication patterns in cohabiting couples. *Journal of Research in Personality, 40*(5), 829–840. https://doi.org/10.1016/j.jrp.2005.09.012

Hendrix, H. (2007). *Getting the love you want: A guide for couples* (20th anniversary ed.). Henry Holt and Company.

Hendrix, H., & Hunt, H. L. (2021). *Doing Imago relationship therapy in the space-between: A clinician's guide*. W. W. Norton & Company.

Holtzworth-Munroe, A. (2001). Standards for batterer treatment programs: How can research inform our decisions? *Journal of Aggression, Maltreatment & Trauma, 5*(2), 165–180. https://doi.org/10.1300/J146v05n02_10

Huston, T. L., Caughlin, J. P., Houts, R. M., Smith, S. E., & George, L. J. (2001). The connubial crucible: Newlywed years as predictors of marital delight, distress, and divorce. *Journal of Personality and Social Psychology, 80*(2), 237–252. https://doi.org/10.1037/0022-3514.80.2.237

Jacobson, N. S., & Christensen, A. (1996). *Integrative couple therapy: Promoting acceptance and change*. W. W. Norton & Company.

Jacobson, N. S., & Gottman, J. M. (1998). *When men batter women: New insights into ending abusive relationships*. Simon & Schuster.

Johnson, S. M. (2004). *The practice of emotionally focused couple therapy* (2nd ed.). Brunner-Routledge.

Kerr, M. E., & Bowen, M. (1988). *Family evaluation: An approach based on Bowen theory*. W. W. Norton & Company.

Kim, H., & Rose, K. M. (2014). Concept analysis of family homeostasis. *Journal of Advanced Nursing, 70*(11), 2450–2468. https://doi.org/10.1111/jan.12496

Hill, C., Knapp-Loker, S. E., & Real, T. (2025, January). *Conceptualizing the couple dance with the relationship grid: A practical approach for assessment and intervention*. Relational Life Foundation. https://www.relationallifefoundation.org/relationship-grid-survey.html

Lassiter, L. (2017). Undifferentiated family ego mass in Bowen therapy. In J. Lebow, A. Chambers, and D. Breunlin (Eds.), *Encyclopedia of Couple and Family Therapy* (pp. 3089–3090). Springer. https://doi.org/10.1007/978-3-319-15877-8_357-1

Leone, R. M., Jarnecke, A. M., Gilmore, A. K., & Flanagan, J. C. (2022). Alcohol use problems and conflict among couples: A preliminary investigation of the moderating effects of maladaptive cognitive emotion regulation strategies. *Couple and Family Psychology: Research and Practice, 11*(4), 290–299. https://doi.org/10.1037/cfp0000160

Locke, H. J., & Wallace, K. M. (1959). Short marital-adjustment and prediction tests: Their reliability and validity. *Marriage and Family Living, 21*(3), 251–255. https://doi.org/10.2307/348022

Lonergan, M., Brunet, A., Rivest-Beauregard, M., & Groleau, D. (2021). Is romantic partner betrayal a form of traumatic experience? A qualitative study. *Stress and Health, 37*(1), 19–31. https://doi.org/10.1002/smi.2968

Mallory, A. B., Spencer, C. M., Kimmes, J. G., & Pollitt, A. M. (2018). Remembering the good times: The influence of relationship nostalgia on relationship satisfaction across time. *Journal of Marital and Family Therapy, 44*(4), 561–574. https://doi.org/10.1111/jmft.12311

Mardani, F., Navabinejad, S., & Yousefi, E. (2023). The effectiveness of Gottman approach intervention on marital burnout, emotional divorce, and emotional regulation of conflicted couples. *Journal of Assessment and Research in Applied Counseling, 5*(3), 16–22. https://doi.org/10.61838/kman.jarac.5.3.3

Masterson, J. F. (1981). *The narcissistic and borderline disorders: An integrated developmental approach*. Brunner/Mazel.

McGoldrick, M., Giordano, J., & Garcia-Preto, N. (2005). Overview: Ethnicity and family therapy. In M. McGoldrick, J. Giordano, & N. Garcia-Preto (Eds.), *Ethnicity and family therapy* (3rd ed., pp. 1–40). Guilford Press.

Meissner, M. N. (1978). The conceptualization of marriage and family dynamics from a psychoanalytic perspective. In T. J. Paolino Jr. & B. S. McCrady (Eds.), *Marriage and marital therapy: Psychoanalytic, behavioral, and systems theory perspectives* (pp. 25–88). Brunner/Mazel.

Minuchin, S. (1974). *Families and family therapy*. Harvard University Press.

Mittelmann, B. (1948). The concurrent analysis of married couples. *Psychoanalytic Quarterly, 17*, 182–197.

National Council on Family Relationships. (2024). Ernest Groves. *NCFR History Book*. https://history.ncfr.org/people/ernestgroves

Notarius, C. I., & Markman, H. J. (1989). Coding marital interaction: A sampling and discussion of current issues. *Behavioral Assessment, 11*(1), 1–11.

Ortman, D. C. (2005). Post infidelity stress disorder. *Journal of Psychosocial Nursing and Mental Health Services, 43*(10), 46–54. https://doi.org/10.3928/02793695-20051001-06

Panganiban, K. (2023, September 6). *How to have a state of the union meeting*. The Gottman Institute. https://www.gottman.com/blog/how-to-have-a-state-of-the-union-meeting/

Panichelli, C. (2013). Humor, joining, and reframing in psychotherapy: Resolving the auto-double-bind. *American Journal of Family Therapy, 41*(5), 437–451. https://doi.org/10.1080/01926187.2012.755393

Papp, L. M., Goeke-Morey, M. C., & Cummings, E. M. (2013). Let's talk about sex: A diary investigation of couples' intimacy conflicts in the home. *Couple and Family Psychology: Research and Practice, 2*(1), 60–72. https://doi.org/10.1037/a0031465

Pence, E., & Paymar, M. (1993). *Education group for men who batter: The Duluth model*. Springer Publishing. https://doi.org/10.1891/9780826179913

Perel, E. (2000). A tourist's view of marriage: Cross-cultural couples—Challenges, choices, and implications for therapy. In P. Papp (Ed.), *Couples on the fault line: New directions for therapists* (pp. 178–204). Guilford Press.

Pittman, F. (1989). *Private lies: Infidelity and the betrayal of intimacy*. W. W. Norton & Company.

Plutchik, R. (1980). A general psychoevolutionary theory of emotion. In R. Plutchik & H. Kellerman (Eds.), *Emotion: Theory, research, and experience: Vol. 1. Theories of emotion* (pp. 3–33). Academic Press.

Rapoport, A. (1960). *Fights, games, and debates*. University of Michigan Press.

Ray, W. A. (2000). Don D. Jackson—A re-introduction. *Journal of Systemic Therapies, 19*(2), 1–6. http://dx.doi.org/10.1521/jsyt.2000.19.2.1

Real, T. (n.d.). *The Relationship Grid Assessment*. Retrieved January 24, 2025, from https://quiz.terryreal.com/quiz

Real, T. (2012, November/December). Joining through the truth. *Psychotherapy Networker*. https://www.psychotherapynetworker.org/article/joining-through-truth

Reich-Stiebert, N., Froehlich, L., & Voltmer, J.-B. (2023). Gendered mental labor: A systematic literature review on the cognitive dimension of unpaid work within the household and childcare. *Sex Roles, 88*, 475–494. https://doi.org/10.1007/s11199-023-01362-0

Relational Life Institute. (n.d.). *How does RLT work?* Retrieved January 24, 2025, from https://relationallife.com/how-does-rlt-work/#

Rodsky, E. (2020). *Fair play card deck: A game-changing solution for couples and families*. Penguin Random House.

Rubin, R. H., & Settles, B. H. (2012). The Groves Conference on Marriage and Family: History and impact on family science. *Groves Monographs on Marriage and Family, 2*(1). https://doi.org/10.3998/groves.9453087.0002.001

Sabatelli, R. M., & Bartle-Haring, S. (2003). Family-of-origin experiences and adjustment in married couples. *Journal of Marriage and Family, 65*(1), 159-169. https://doi.org/10.1111/j.1741-3737.2003.00159.x

Schaefer, M. T., & Olson, D. H. (1981). Assessing intimacy: The PAIR Inventory. *Journal of Marital and Family Therapy, 7*(1), 47–60. https://doi.org/10.1111/j.1752-0606.1981.tb01351.x

Schwartz Gottman, J., & Gottman, J. (2024). *Fight right: How successful couples turn conflict into connection*. Harmony.

Selzer, M. L. (1971). The Michigan Alcoholism Screening Test: The quest for a new diagnostic instrument. *The American Journal of Psychiatry, 127*(12), 1653–1658. https://doi.org/10.1176/ajp.127.12.1653

Siegel, D. J. (1999). *The developing mind: How relationships and the brain interact to shape who we are*. Guilford Press.

Simpson, L. E., Atkins, D. C., Gattis, K. S., & Christensen, A. (2008). Low-level relationship aggression and couple therapy outcomes. *Journal of Family Psychology, 22*(1), 102–111. https://doi.org/10.1037/0893-3200.22.1.102

Snyder, C. R. (1994). *The psychology of hope: You can get there from here*. The Free Press.

Snyder, C. R., Rand, K. L., & Sigmon, D. R. (2002). Hope theory: A member of the positive psychology family. In C. R. Snyder & S. J. Lopez (Eds.), *Handbook of positive psychology* (pp. 257–276). Oxford University Press.

Spanier, G. B. (1976). Measuring dyadic adjustment: New scales for assessing the quality of marriage and similar dyads. *Journal of Marriage and Family, 38*(1), 15–28. https://doi.org/10.2307/350547

Speer, M. E., & Delgado, M. R. (2017). Reminiscing about positive memories buffers acute stress responses. *Nature Human Behavior, 1*(5), Article 0093. https://doi.org/10.1038/s41562-017-0093

Stanley, B., & Brown, G. K. (2012). Safety planning intervention: A brief intervention to mitigate suicide risk. *Cognitive and Behavioral Practice, 19*(2), 256–264. https://doi.org/10.1016/j.cbpra.2011.01.001

Stith, S. M., McCollum, E. E., Amanor-Boadu, Y., & Smith, D. (2012). Systemic perspectives on intimate partner violence treatment. *Journal of Marital and Family Therapy, 38*(1), 220–240. https://doi.org/10.1111/j.1752-0606.2011.00245.x

Stith, S. M., Rosen, K. H., McCollum, E. E., & Thomsen, C. J. (2004). Treating intimate partner violence within intact couple relationships: Outcomes of multi-couple versus individual couple therapy. *Journal of Marital and Family Therapy, 30*(3), 305–318. https://doi.org/10.1111/j.1752-0606.2004.tb01242.x

Straus, M. A., & Gelles, R. J. (1986). Societal change and change in family violence from 1975 to 1985 as revealed by two national surveys. *Journal of Marriage and Family, 48*(3), 465–479. https://doi.org/10.2307/352033

Tatkin, S. (2020a, September). PACT: Psychobiological Approach to Couples Therapy—Part 1. *The Science of Psychotherapy, 78,* 4–20.

Tatkin, S. (2020b, October). PACT: Psychobiological Approach to Couples Therapy—Part 2. *The Science of Psychotherapy, 79,* 4–15.

Tatkin, S. (2024). *Wired for love: How understanding your partner's brain and attachment style can help you defuse conflict and build a secure relationship* (rev. 2nd ed.). New Harbinger Publications.

Vincent, J. P., Friedman, L. C., Nugent, J., & Messerly, L. (1979). Demand characteristics in observations of marital interaction. *Journal of Consulting and Clinical Psychology, 47*(3), 557–566. https://doi.org/10.1037/0022-006X.47.3.557

Weiss, R. L., & Cerreto, M. C. (1980). The Marital Status Inventory: Development of a measure of dissolution potential. *The American Journal of Family Therapy, 8*(2), 80–85. https://doi.org/10.1080/01926188008250358

Weiss, N. H., Hogan, J., Brem, M., Massa, A. A., Kirby, C. M., & Flanagan, J. C. (2021). Advancing our understanding of the intersection between emotion regulation and alcohol and drug use problems: Dyadic analysis in couples with intimate partner violence and alcohol use disorder. *Drug and Alcohol Dependence, 228,* Article 109066. https://doi.org/10.1016/j.drugalcdep.2021.109066

White, M., & Epston, D. (1990). *Narrative means to therapeutic ends.* W. W. Norton & Company.

Wile, D. B. (2013, June 29). Doubling in collaborative couple therapy. *Collaborative Couple Therapy.* https://danwile.com/2013/06/doubling-in-collaborative-couple-therapy/

Willcox, G. (1982). The feeling wheel: A tool for expanding awareness of emotions and increasing spontaneity and intimacy. *Transactional Analysis Journal, 12*(4), 274–276. https://doi.org/10.1177/036215378201200411

Woods, S. B. (2019). Goal setting in couple and family therapy. In J. L. Lebow, A. L. Chambers, & D. C. Breunlin (Eds.), *Encyclopedia of couple and family therapy* (pp. 1303–1307). Springer. https://doi.org/10.1007/978-3-319-49425-8_562

Yalom, I. D. (1995). *The theory and practice of group psychotherapy* (4th ed.). Basic Books.

Acknowledgments

To the clinicians who show up every day in the therapy room with courage, curiosity, and care—this book is for you. Your willingness to hold space for complexity, to navigate conflict with empathy, and to keep learning even when the work is hard is what makes this field not only meaningful, but transformative.

To those I've had the honor to train, supervise, or consult with over the years—your questions, insights, and integrity have shaped my thinking and strengthened this work. Thank you for trusting me to walk alongside you.

To my colleagues, especially those at A Better Life Therapy—you model what it means to do relational work with both clinical excellence and deep humanity. I am constantly inspired by you.

To the couples I've worked with—thank you for letting me into the most sacred corners of your lives. Your openness, resilience, and honesty are what make this work possible.

To my family—thank you for your patience, support, and humor as I wrote this book around the edges of our life.

And to you, the reader—thank you for caring about this work. I hope this book offers you clarity, validation, and a framework for helping couples create something better together.

About the Author

ELIZABETH EARNSHAW, MA, LMFT, CGT, is a licensed marriage and family therapist, certified Gottman Method couples therapist, certified clinical trauma professional, and AAMFT approved supervisor. She is a clinical fellow of the American Association for Marriage and Family Therapy (AAMFT) and the founder of a national therapy practice, A Better Life Therapy, which provides systemic therapy to individuals, couples, and families.

Elizabeth is known for her work as a couples therapist specializing in intensive couples therapy and for training other therapists in this modality. She has provided continuing education to thousands of clinicians and regularly speaks at conferences, offers workshops, and consults with companies on relationships and mental health.

She is the author of *I Want This to Work*, *'Til Stress Do Us Part*, and *The Couples Therapy Flip Chart*, and her expertise has been featured in publications such as *The New York Times*, *The Washington Post*, *Psychology Today*, and *MindBodyGreen*. Elizabeth lives in West Chester, Pennsylvania, with her husband, children, and dog. You can read more about her at ElizabethEarnshaw.com or www.abetterlifetherapy.com.